SHAMANS, QUEENS, AND FIGURINES

Routledge
Taylor & Francis Group
LONDON AND NEW YORK

Shamans, Queens, and Figurines

The Development of Gender Archaeology

Sarah Milledge Nelson

Routledge
Taylor & Francis Group
LONDON AND NEW YORK

First published 2015 by Left Coast Press, Inc.

Published 2016 by Routledge
2 Park Square, Milton Park, Abingdon, Oxon OX14 4RN
711 Third Avenue, New York, NY 10017, USA

Routledge is an imprint of the Taylor & Francis Group, an informa business

Library of Congress Cataloging-in-Publication Data
Nelson, Sarah M., 1931-
Shamans, queens, and figurines : the development of gender archaeology / Sarah Milledge Nelson.
pages cm
Includes bibliographical references and index.
ISBN 978-1-61132-946-9 (hardback) -- ISBN 978-1-61132-947-6 (paperback) -- ISBN 978-1-61132-948-3 (institutional eBook) -- ISBN 978-1-61132-764-9 (consumer eBook)
1. Feminist archaeology. 2. Social archaeology. 3. Women--History--To 500. 4. Sex role--History--To 1500. 5. Queens--History--To 1500. 6. Women shamans--History--To 1500. 7. East Asia--Antiquities. 8. Women archaeologists. 9. Archaeology --Social aspects. 10. Archaeology--Fiction. I. Title.
CC72.4.N457 2014
930.1082--dc23

2014026769

ISBN 978-1-61132-946-9 hardback
ISBN 978-1-61132-947-6 paperback

Contents

Preface

Selecting, compiling, and commenting on papers written throughout one's career ought to be easy, but the task for me seemed more difficult than writing an entirely new book. Some of my articles overlap but make significantly different points; some of them were part of symposia in which the papers needed one another for maximum effect. Some papers were written in earlier eras, with different expectations and even different technology. Some earlier papers are lost.

The choices of papers I ultimately made boiled down to relevance to the trajectory of gender archaeology, why it was important, and whether my writings were in or out of the mainstream of archaeology. Where was archaeology going? Was I forging new directions for gender archaeology or picking through the crumbs?

I was always interested in the distant past. As a teenager, I read every word of the Will and Ariel Durant books on the ancient world. In college, I majored in Biblical History. When we lived in Europe, before I began a graduate program in archaeology, I visited archaeological sites from Scandinavia to Egypt. I was thirsty for more.

Women's career tracks are often different from those of men. Mine was especially deviant, because I began to study archaeology in graduate school when my youngest child was in first grade. Who would expect a mother of three to have any kind of career at all, especially in archaeology, where one was expected to spend time "in the field" in some faraway place? And which of the professors would waste his time on a student who never had a single undergraduate course in anthropology and whose knowledge of archaeology was based on reading about and visiting sites, not working on them?

Worse still, archaeology was seen as a male profession, both by the public and by professionals. Everybody loved Indiana Jones. Would there be a place for me? In my graduate school years, women had issues about inequities, but I acknowledge here that the professors in the Archaeology Museum at the University of Michigan when I was a student, at that time all men, were helpful to me with suggestions and letters of introduction and recommendations, even though I sometimes felt like an orphan student. The leading-edge archaeology I learned from the Michigan archaeologists has stood me in good stead for my entire career.

Some of my career choices depended on circumstances over which I had little control. While I was doing fieldwork and teaching and writing, I was also raising our three sons (and my husband Hal gets credit for them as well). I was sometimes a den mother and sometimes a cheering fan of Little League teams. Later I met girlfriends of the boys and still later organized rehearsal dinners for their weddings. I traveled with Hal, especially when he was invited to some exotic locale, and put on parties and dinners for his fellows and his peers. A bit of my personal life creeps in here and there in this account of scholarship, because the personal is not only political, it was sometimes relevant to my career in archaeology, if only through the limitations it imposed.

It is important to acknowledge Mitch Allen as a major player in my career, publisher of several of my books and believer in the power of a gender perspective to change archaeology. Heather Myers helped put the book together with patience over my indecisiveness about which papers to include, and Ryan Harris finished the compilation and shepherded it into print. Orla McInerny, University of Denver Anthropology Department Assistant to the Chair, walked me through the mysteries of new technology for copying old manuscripts and sending them through impossible Internet programs with skill and good cheer. Jeremy Haas, University of Denver graduate student, helped with the bibliography and index, and Carol Leyba contributed her precise editing.

Finally, I thank all four of the males in my family for helping me pursue a satisfying career. My husband, Hal, was always supportive, and the boys pitched in with housework more or less without griping. Once my son Stan overheard me say to a friend that women shouldn't become liberated by oppressing other women. "No," said Stan. "Just oppress your children." He said it with a smile. But I think none of the boys suffered, and all have wives with careers who have expected them to help with the household and children, which they have (more or less) cheerfully done.

Denver, June 2014

PART I

Introduction: Learning the Field and Breaking Taboos

THIS BOOK IS A CAREER memoir using some of my published papers to demonstrate one way to do feminist archaeology. It might be used as an extended response to Sheryl Sandberg's popular book, *Lean In* (2013), in which women are encouraged to be more aggressive in business situations. While I haven't worked in a large business setting, and can't speak to Sandberg's advice in that environment, I have spent my career in a university, applying for grants, publishing my work, competing for resources for my department, and generally leaning out as often as I leaned in (if I understand Sandberg's vocabulary) in order to achieve desired results. In the academic world, in the museum world, in the world that includes both government and public archaeology, the rules are different. Just leaning in will not necessarily produce good results and sometimes could produce unwanted results.

Archaeology is an immensely satisfying way to spend a career, but it has had high barriers for women that often could not be leapt in a single bound. When I began studying archaeology, the practitioners were not all male, but the field was dominated by male practices and male metaphors (Nelson 1997a: 42–46). A friend recently described her place of work as "a cowboy atmosphere," and the very existence of trowel holsters (Woodall and Perricone 1981: 507) puts the cowboy mentality in context for many women archaeologists.

In spite of the "cowboys," archaeology is a satisfying profession. Discovery stimulates new ideas, solving puzzles posed by artifacts and sites is intellectually rewarding, and imagining the past through artifacts can lead to writing novels. Being part of the gender-in-archaeology movement has added even more spice for me, because it brings fresh insights into archaeological theory, encourages new methods of excavation, and suggests new means of interpretation. In addition, friends and colleagues who pursue gender in archaeology make interesting and lively comrades. But archaeological success isn't just a matter of leaning in. The field of archaeology is more subtle than that.

Some events in my career were not at all fun, and they belong to the gender story as well. Events along my career path will find echoes in the experiences of others, women who have had to learn their field and then break taboos or at least twist the rules a bit to make them fit.

Insisting on becoming an archaeologist was the first rule I broke, since I had already accepted the societal role of wife and mother. Aiming for accessible writing was another no-no, but it didn't inflict much punishment, except that one member of my dissertation committee complained (and that is the correct word) about my "graceful writing." Apparently graceful writing meant unscholarly writing to him. Those were minor breaks, really only cracks in the rules. Taboo subjects, however, were well guarded by the gatekeepers. My infringements included taking women seriously in the present as well as in the past, followed by writing about ideology, shamanism, and even archaeoastronomy. It took a long time for any of these topics to be acceptable in the promised land of publication.

Archaeology is both practice and theory. The way archaeology is practiced may make as much difference to understanding gender in the past as articulating any kind of theory (Gero 1985). Because the personal is political, as early feminists noted cogently and insistently, the circumstances of a life are also relevant to the pursuit of a career in archaeology. Thus in this book, I use my own career track in archaeology to illustrate both the importance of equity issues for archaeologists in the present and the reverberations in archaeology resulting from putting women in the center of research into the past. To reach the point of being allowed to play in the field of archaeology, I had to learn the rules, and then I had to break some, and once in a while I helped to create new rules. Feminist archaeology, according to my definition, seeks equity for women in the past, present, and future.

I believe that gender in archaeology is important precisely because it isn't merely theoretical. Each of us is constrained to live a life according to our gender, as well as other ways in which we are "situated" in the world. For example, when I did my first archaeology in Korea, I was a short and skinny, shy and non-threatening, dark-haired female who was invisible in a Korean crowd. People spoke to me in Korean on the subway if they didn't see my face. It was a good place for me. Never before had I been grateful for not being tall and blonde.

On the other hand, I didn't choose Korea because I would fit in. I wouldn't have been in Korea at all had I not been wife and mother as well as archaeologist. My husband's job took him to Korea, and I followed with our three sons. This was the beginning of my understanding that scholars do not interpret archaeology as disembodied minds but as part of a social system with a particular place in it. Our minds may embrace particular intellectual traditions, but our culture can provide stumbling blocks. Daily life can trump long-term plans.

My archaeological career has spanned more than four decades so far, during which changes in the anglophone world of archaeology have been extensive and profound. These events are reflected in my endeavors, as I abandoned my first love of Near Eastern archaeology and then ditched my alternate plan to work in Europe. Not only did I change the place of my research, I switched from researching the ungendered notion of subsistence and settlement in favor of pursuing gendered questions about leadership, power, and ideology. I created a niche in Chinese archaeology for myself after pioneering in Korean archaeology, and eventually tried other pursuits, especially writing novels about archaeological sites in Korea and China.

The attempt by a large contingent of archaeologists to shift the topic of gender into the center of archaeological discourse was an endeavor that I joined enthusiastically. While it has been only partially successful, for me the most important outcome of the gender in archaeology movement has been to make gender a respectable topic in archaeology. Some evidence of success of the gender in archaeology movement is an e-mail I recently received from a student in England, asking if gender is still an important topic. I thought, "Would you be writing to me from 6,000 miles and seven time zones away if it were not an important topic? And would you still be asking about a book I wrote twenty years ago if the topic didn't have legs?" I declined to do the student's research for her—instead, I directed her to the index of *Gender in Archaeology*—but I was pleased that there are still questions to consider. While inquiries from students can range from stimulating to amusing, their interest is a boon to the topic. I hope students will keep writing to me.

One of the best things about gender in archaeology is the friends I have made around the world. In addition to my American colleagues, I have been inspired by women who live far away—Miriam Rosen-Ayalon in Israel, Vivian Scheinsohn in Argentina, Rasmi Shoocongdej in Thailand, to name a scattered few (I'm afraid to start listing friends, for fear of leaving someone out).

I have chosen my friends on three criteria—those who were bold enough to break the rules, those who were smart enough to know which rules to break, and those who were willing to put up with me. These friendships make a network that provides both energy and ideas, even if I don't tap into it often enough.

Claire Smith, before she became president of the World Archaeological Congress, was a champion at intercontinental connections. From Australia, she would round up some of us to speak to her students at odd hours in an electronic chat room. Her students made dolls to represent archaeologists whose work they read, showing how they imagined them. I hope Claire will put on an exhibit of those dolls some day. I'd like to see what a Sarah Nelson doll looks like (or maybe I wouldn't!).

Some other positive results of the gendering effort are that discussions of gender in archaeological site reports appear more often than they did three decades ago, and there is hardly an encyclopedia or handbook of archaeology that fails to include articles on gender. The field has been improved by greater awareness of the possibilities of adding gendered perspectives to our interpretations.

Gender in archaeology has been approached in many productive and interesting ways, and I have learned and borrowed from many others. This volume is not a history of research on gender, but it is offered as a record of one archaeologist's responses to the changes in archaeology since the late 1960s, and the ways my own interpretations of the past have been both broadened and challenged by developments in the field.

Let me briefly recount the context of my classes as a graduate student in archaeology at the University of Michigan as a reminder of archaeology before gender. In the spring term of 1968, cultural evolution was the hot issue. "Man the Hunter" (Lee and Devore 1968) provided an all-encompassing explanation of early prehistory, based on extensive observations of current hunters and laced with a strong androcentric bias (Zihlman and Tanner 1978). The "Neolithic Revolution" (Childe 1951), with its perspective that the Mesopotamian region and Egypt were the cradle of everything, from the earliest plant and animal domestication to the beginnings of cities and civilizations, was still a viable topic. Archaeology was beginning to be interpreted according to Elman Service's (1962) division of human social groups into bands, tribes, chiefdoms, and states (Sanders and Price 1968) and aspired to be a real branch of anthropology (Binford 1962).

In that era, new archaeological methods included both the broad and the detailed: for example, surveying wide areas, on the one hand, and flotation of soils from sites to detect evidence of plant use, on the other. Archaeologists were challenged to discover the causes of changes from hunter-gatherers to farmers, and from chiefdoms to states.

But there were many ways that women were left out: they simply didn't appear in the evolutionary schemes. Focusing on gender in archaeology is important because discrimination against women is frequently based on stereotypes about women's abilities, bodies, or brains. When archaeology can falsify such stereotypes, women gain in the here and now. Equity for women in the past has always seemed necessary to gain equity for women in the present. When I wrote *Gender in Archaeology, Analyzing Power and Prestige* (1997a), it was intended to be a counterpart to my co-edited book *Equity Issues for Women in Archaeology* (1994). Awareness of gender in the past and in the present is necessary to restore a balance in our understanding of the human past.

CONTENTS OF THIS BOOK

Part II, "Social Archaeology Gives Birth to Gender Archaeology," is in part a retrospective of the era of processualism and social archaeology, with a few inklings even then of the ferment for change in archaeology, moving beyond process to people. I understood it as social archaeology, which became a platform for researching gender. In hindsight, I've been surprised by the fact that the Binfordian paradigm led me into social archaeology and then to gender. Perhaps it is even ironic.

The Korean work discussed in Part II describes my attempts to conform, but sometimes I had to invent new rules to get the job done as I perceived it should be. When I did my first independent work on subsistence and settlement in Korea, it fit into the then-current paradigm, becoming the title of my dissertation. In the Han River Survey, our intention was to locate Neolithic sites, but besides surveying we also dug test pits hoping to find evidence of plant use in the flotation samples.

I describe my life in Korea because when I wrote a version of this episode for a memoir class, the women all wrote in the margins versions of "me too." Friends have been pleased to read how other women helped with the project. It may also be useful to current students to realize how much of any project involves studying beyond the immediate problem. Finally, my trials in creating a project have found echoes in other situations. For a woman to succeed in archaeology meant extra effort.

Part III, "Figurines and Equity Issues: Measuring Gender," is situated in the early days of feminism in academe. As a result of a new emphasis on women in cultural anthropology, I became interested in female figurines, which seemed to offer possibilities for archaeologists to join anthropological discussions about women. I planned a session on worldwide female figurines that never came to fruition, but with extensive pictures it would have made a great coffee-table book. Someone could make a mint on such a book. I offer the idea freely.

Because these figurines are so varied, I thought representations of female bodies could be an important way to understand women of the past. For my first sabbatical, I created a project to photograph and measure Upper Paleolithic figurines of Europe. My research showed that the few figurines that were both truly obese and realistically carved demanded an explanation that included at least partial sedentism of the Paleolithic peoples of Europe. Both my hypothesis and my conclusions were unpalatable to the archaeological gatekeepers at the time, so I broke a big taboo and published the results myself (Chapter 1).

Equity for women in archaeology was also measurable. Bringing attention to the ways in which women archaeologists were silenced or prevented from contributing fully to the discipline resulted in an edited book. I've included the conclusion to *Equity Issues for Women in Archaeology*, co-authored with Peggy Nelson (with her permission) (Chapter 2), to remind readers of the uphill journeys many women had to endure in order to become archaeologists.

Part IV, "Queens: Women Wielding Power," begins with a queen of the kingdom of Silla, one of the Three Kingdoms of Early Korea, which was sometimes ruled by queens at the dawn of statehood. Three Silla queens were recorded as "female kings" in ancient histories. After my foray into Late Pleistocene female bodies, I turned to a particular Korean burial—that of an unknown queen of Silla in the fourth/fifth century AD. The presence of a female ruler drew me to Silla's magnificent burials lavishly outfitted with gold. The more I studied the queens of Silla, the more I perceived that their activities and status might illuminate women rulers in general, especially in that magical time known as "the origin of the state." Chapter 3 describes Tomb 98 in Kyongju and discusses what a reigning queen might imply about gender in the Silla Kingdom. Another way to think about queens is as people who perform power as shamans do, the topic of Chapter 4. My interest in ancient queens culminated in an edited book, *Ancient Queens: Archaeological Explorations* (Nelson, ed. 2003).

Part V, "Gender in Archaeology Spreads," discusses some of the many conferences on archaeology and gender and shows how the feminist endeavor grew and sprouted many branches. Chapter 5 is my first published paper about gender in archaeology, based on an unusual site I had visited in China. Chinese archaeologists considered this site highly important, demonstrating an early complex polity in Inner Mongolia and Liaoning Province, far to the north of the Yellow River. The *nüshen miao* (goddess temple) was the Chinese name for a lobed building with fragments of life-sized statues and interior wall decorations. The fragments included an intact smiling face with inset jade eyes. The Chacmool Conference of 1989 on The Archaeology of Gender was the venue of my first attempt to apply gender to a particular archaeological site.

My "goddess" paper leads into a discussion of the goddess movement, a parallel use of goddesses in the past because many archaeologists felt that studying ancient goddesses was not entirely scholarly, although the topic was embraced with enthusiasm in other circles.

That first gathering of women archaeologists in the Americas also explored grant-getting for women archaeologists, still a matter of concern, which was addressed at a special meeting of the Society for American Archaeology in 2014. Networking was important at Chacmool, and new projects, meetings, and friendships arose from the interactions here.

The question of feminist theory is approached in Chapter 6. Not everyone who writes about women in the past or gender in the past would agree that their work is feminist. This paper demonstrates the reasons I believe feminism and theory are necessary for considering women and gender in the past.

Part VI, "Perspectives from China," shows that not only a gender perspective but that of an unfamiliar ancient culture can throw new light on the ways that archaeological sites can be interpreted. "Ideology and the Formation of an Early State," Chapter 7, offers new ways to consider state origins in the light of a complex culture with artifacts that reflect female associations.

"Shamans and Ideology," Part VII, continues my thinking about the state and shamanism, revealing my growing sense that shamanism, leadership, and women belong together in order to understand the origin of states in East Asia. Several threads of my previous research led me in this direction.

Chapter 8, "Feasting the Ancestors," demonstrates another way that an unfamiliar culture can add depth to an ongoing archaeological discussion. Feasting in China, as seen from archaeological sites, takes place at gravesides for the purpose of turning the deceased into a helpful ancestral spirit. This is in sharp contrast to the usual aggrandizement perspective on feasting.

I had been interested in the women shamans of Korea since my first visit there. Not only were current women shamans active, but also the rulers of the Silla polity of the first half of the fifth century wore crowns similar to those of shamans in Manchuria and Central Asia. The site of Niuheliang in northeastern China was called "Nüshen Miao," the goddess temple, but the statue could have been a representation of a shaman rather than a goddess. Large mounded tombs and other features of the site implied a high degree of complexity. What were the implications for the social and political systems? Did the face with green jade eyes at Niuheliang represent a shaman or a leader—or both? In the meantime, as I wrote archaeological fiction about the sites I had studied, I realized that I was portraying all the leaders as shamans, based on the archaeology of the sites. Discussing ancient religion, or any form of ideology, had been a subject almost as unthinkable as gender in the archaeology of my graduate school days. Influential archaeologists derogated an interest in anything not tangible as "paleo-psychology." But post-processualism was creating space for interpretation, and my interest in shamanism could be pursued.

Chapter 9, "What Is a Shaman?" is a short excerpt from *Shamanism and the Origin of the State* (Nelson 2008a), a book in which I tied these ideas together. The basic question is whether ancient shamans were like the reverential model of early Chinese writing or the contemptuous picture largely derived from Russian ethnographers recording a suppressed people.

I have tried my hand at writing archaeological novels, the topic of Part VIII: "Archaeological Stories." I challenged myself to think about archaeological sites in Korea and China as scenes of action and wondered what a woman's entire life would have been like in each place. Excerpts from my novels (Chapters 10, 11, and 12) demonstrate my thought processes when turning artifacts into events. The novels are examples of thinking about archaeological sites as peopled locations, but they are also tests of the possibilities of women as leaders of different-sized polities.

The Afterword is a short conclusion, with a paper that summarizes some of what I have learned from pursuing gender in archaeology in the context of

East Asian archaeology. Chapter 13 wraps several ideas together, suggesting new ways to approach archaeological data when women are included and, in this case, from an East Asian perspective.

The overall theme of this book is that attention to gender enhances any archaeological topic or perspective. Gender creates a wider impact on whatever issue is addressed. Many feminist archaeologists labored on another front as well, trying to make the places archaeologists work better places for women. In my view, and in my life, the two belong together—equity issues and gender in archaeology.

It has been a fascinating journey for me, doing archaeology in the midst of a time of ferment of ideas and actions. Without the women's movement, who knows what would have become of me? But to whatever extent there were struggles in academe and archaeology, I was able to do the work I wanted to do, and I am grateful to have been in the thick of the creation of a subdiscipline of archaeology.

PART II

SOCIAL ARCHAEOLOGY GIVES BIRTH TO GENDER ARCHAEOLOGY

THE "NEW" ARCHAEOLOGY I LEARNED as a graduate student in 1968–69 had many variations. I privately thought that there were as many ways to do processual archaeology as there were professors who professed it. Lewis Binford and his students had announced a brave new archaeology, shaking up the way archaeology was done, especially changing what questions could be asked of the data.

I found asking anthropological questions of archaeological sites appealing. Several papers in *New Perspectives in Archaeology* (Binford and Binford, eds. 1968) were based on details of pottery assemblages (Hill 1968; Longacre 1968; Whallon 1968), asking, for example, if matrilineality could be inferred from the variations of the pottery styles in archaeological sites or between sites. While gender archaeology would have to wait a while longer, these studies were groundbreaking, because social questions had rarely been asked of archaeological data. Unintentionally, perhaps, they opened a space for gender studies. One assumption of the papers was that women were the potters. Although that aspect became contentious, it was the beginning of archaeologists noticing that there were women in the past and that their activities and products were important, not only to their social group but to interpretations of cultures.

As a relative newcomer to archaeology, what I took away from the intellectual ferment of the times was the sense that we should all be doing social archaeology, analogous to social anthropology. Lewis Binford's battle cry was that archaeology is anthropology or it is nothing. I responded to the call, but I didn't yet have a feminist awareness, in spite of the fact that reading Betty Friedan's *The Feminine Mystique* was one of the events that propelled me to graduate school. I didn't ask, even timidly, if the Study of Man (anthropology) included women, although Prof. Jimmy Griffin chuckled at a definition of anthropology as "the study of man, embracing woman." When I heard this joke

Shamans, Queens, and Figurines: The Development of Gender Archaeology, by Sarah Nelson, 19–32.

I think I managed a weak smile. It was the only possible response to sexist remarks at the time.

In retrospect, I can see that one problem with using anthropological categories to describe archaeological sites is that the original categories were flawed, but arriving at that insight required much trial and error. I eventually understood that by considering only what men do, or what men are presumed to do (embracing women or not), other members of the society are treated as if they didn't really exist. For some cultural anthropologists, only the men were important; Levi-Strauss, for example, described all the men departing in a canoe as "the entire village," leaving him behind with "the women and children" (Wylie 1991:38).

Another exciting new approach that fell under the rubric of processual archaeology was borrowing anthropological categories to describe and interpret archaeological sites, especially the categories of political organization that had been arranged in evolutionary order. I used the band, tribe, chiefdom, and state approach in my Korean work without questioning the basic idea, although I did use Korean data to consider whether tribes had boundaries or not. I argued that that tribes in Korea wouldn't have needed boundaries, because there was plenty of room between communities, but that pottery styles nevertheless could be grouped, implying closer connections between some villages (Nelson 1990b). I also became disillusioned with the notion that "tribes" had certain characteristics in common that could be assumed when describing archaeological "tribes." In a festschrift for Professor Kim Won-yong, I suggested that "if we already know all about tribes, or all about matriarchies, why don't we let the artifacts lie in the ground? What is the point of finding another example of what we already know?"

While productive at first, eventually the evolutionary paradigm became a pigeonholing exercise. When I reexamined my Korean data, I began to realize that to speak of bands, tribes, chiefdoms, and states is to obscure women's roles, women's work, women's spirituality, and, in short, to erase women from cultural evolution altogether. I was particularly interested in women's leadership roles and wondered what a matrilineage would look like archaeologically. I dared to address the lineage question at a meeting of the Indo-Pacific Prehistory Association:

> If we must posit lineages, then matrilineages seem more likely than patrilineages [in Korean Neolithic sites]. Women's place seems to have been equal to men's. But the only argument in favor of lineages is the need to inherit

> land. Since there are no signs of crowding of sites, we might suppose that when a given village outgrew its space, a group from that village would strike out and find a free stretch of coast or river bank. [In this way] the interior of Korea might have become populated. . . . It seems likely that the village itself was the social unit, with subunits composed of nuclear families. Although there are no direct clues about the division of labor, it seems likely that men and women were equally valued and mutually dependent. The evidence does not favor lineages at all. (Nelson 1990b)

The mind-set with which I approached Korean archaeology was that of social archaeology, which to me meant understanding social categories in the past, but that concept was difficult to apply. The archaeology of Korea could hardly have been recommended as a perfect set of data with which to attempt social archaeology. In 1970 Korea, the basic time/space systematics were just being sorted out, and the problems addressed by Korean archaeologists were related to migrations of peoples into the Korean peninsula. Much attention was given to discussing which groups, named in ancient Chinese documents, arrived at what time and in what order (Nelson 2006). Waves of "invasions" was the model used to understand archaeological sites (Pai 2012).

Furthermore, archaeology in Korea was struggling to create itself, with no trained archaeologists and only a few PhDs in related fields. The first archaeology in Korea had been done by Japanese surveyors and scholars, sent by their government after the 1910 annexation to demonstrate that the Korean culture was inferior or, that if it had once been advanced, and was a forerunner of Japanese civilization, then Korea should be shown to have degenerated from that higher point (Pai 2012).

Everything Koreans told me about the Japanese occupation that they had suffered in their own lifetimes concerned their second-class treatment. Among other humiliations, children were forced to speak Japanese in school, and everyone had to take Japanese names. When the National Museum was to be established in 1945 in Seoul, South Korea, no Korean with archaeological training was available to become the director, although Japanese archaeologists had excavated tombs in the ancient Korean cities of Kyongju, Puyo, Pyongyang, and Jian, capitals of early Korean states (Pai 2012).

I learned all this, and much more, after I arrived in Korea. There was a mismatch between my expectations of what could be done and the reality of Korean archaeology. My head was full of processual archaeology, but Korean archaeology was struggling to reach its stride. In spite of that, from my point of view, becoming a Korean archaeologist was serendipity at work. And in spite of logistical problems and occasional miscommunications, my work with Korean archaeologists was fruitful. They must have been pleased with my efforts too, since I keep being invited back.

GETTING TO KOREA

In 1969, I had passed my PhD prelims at the University of Michigan (UM) and had moved with my husband, Hal, and our sons to Denver, where I was hired as an adjunct to teach Introduction to Anthropology at the University of Denver (DU). We had been in Denver only a few months when my husband, a lieutenant colonel in the US Army Medical Corps, received orders to spend a thirteen-month "unaccompanied tour" (meaning without family or "dependents") in Korea. When this news arrived, I wrote to various potential mentors at the University of Michigan, explaining that I was willing to participate in any archaeological project any time during that year, in order to gather material for a dissertation. But there was a hitch—my three sons had to come with me, as there were no relatives to leave them with. I would bring materials to tutor them if necessary. The boys were then nine, twelve, and thirteen years old. It may not be surprising that there were no offers.

I don't know if there was any sexism in the lack of interest among the professors at Michigan in helping me find a dissertation project. At the time, I didn't feel that was the case; nevertheless it was crystal clear that the UM students who were allocated projects of their own, or who were given a facet of their advisor's project to work on, were those deemed most likely to succeed, to bring honor and glory to their advisor by their success. In those days, such students were all male, and they have indeed advanced archaeology in data, method, and/or theory, as predicted.

I thought I wasn't discriminated against as much as neglected, but even I could see the lack of advantages for any faculty member to invest effort in my future career. Why bother with a mother of three who will never have time to amount to anything, even if she has the skills and the will? Although none of the Michigan professors ever confessed to being surprised at my work in Korea, I admit that, after the fact, I was surprised myself.

I almost had an archaeological project in Taiwan instead of South Korea. A member of the DU Anthropology Department knew a priest who had found some ancient burials in Taiwan in the region of the former head-hunters who constituted his parish. Would I go to the eastern side of Taiwan and help him excavate? Wasn't Taiwan somewhere near Korea? I agreed. I began to study Chinese and corresponded with professor K.C. Chang at Harvard. I collected materials needed to tutor my children, since there were would be no English-speaking schools in this region.

We rented our Denver house for a year and drove to San Francisco with the boys and George the Poodle, to stay with my sister in Mill Valley while doing the necessary rounds of passports, visas, and shots. We made quite a houseful, with Eleanor and Barry, their five children—all of them younger than the three Nelson boys—as well as an au pair couple who lived in rooms created from half of the garage. The fire department came by to check one day, asking "Do all these people live in this house?"

But an unexpected snag rerouted my plans. Whoever was in charge of granting visas to Taiwan appeared to be horrified that a mother would take her children to a place where there were no schools and no health care. No attempted pulling of strings budged the decision that the boys could have visas for only three months, which would mean costly flights to and from Hong Kong to renew their visas thrice in one year.

In the meantime, Hal had arrived in Korea and learned that children who were "unauthorized dependents" were allowed to attend school on Yongsan Post in Seoul. The downside was that schooling was the only concession to our status. As "unauthorized" dependents, the boys and I couldn't live on the army post or shop on post. But we couldn't keep crowding our relatives in Mill Valley, and our house in Denver was rented.

Leaving the poodle and the car with my sister, the boys and I flew to Korea, where Hal had made living arrangements for us in Itaewon, a part of Seoul set aside for foreigners. We bought beds that folded out on the floor, a low table and five pillows for dining, a lamp to read by, and called the place furnished. Water was piped in, a good thing when only half of Seoul, then a city of 4.5 million people, had running water and sewage piped out. But our water, welcome as it was, came unmitigated from the Han River. A shower left one covered with fine brown particles of unknown origin. I was grateful when a new friend who lived on post invited us all over for showers.

It was mid-summer, with hot, drenching rains. All of us got outfitted with rubber shoes in the market—I was charmed that mine had upturned toes, one of the many connections I saw between Koreans and peoples of the steppes. Umbrellas, made by hand from thin plastic and bamboo sticks, were just a human-sized version of the tiny wooden umbrellas that come in mai-tai glasses, attesting to Korean ingenuity.

THE HAN RIVER SURVEY

I discovered that I could upgrade my status from "unauthorized dependent" to government employee by teaching at the University of Maryland, Far East Division, Seoul Branch. This position bestowed privileges at the Post Exchange and Commissary on Yongsan Post, which made my life much easier. My job even allowed me to have a car, a rare concession for American dependents not living on post. We found a used yellow Nissan Cedric station wagon that we called "Yellow Peril." It broke down often, but Korean mechanics kept it running with great ingenuity. From a departing unauthorized wife I inherited an *ajuma*, literally "auntie," who cleaned our small living quarters, washed our clothes, and sometimes cooked for the kids if I got home late from the field.

Hal was assigned to monitor the medical facilities along the DMZ—the demilitarized zone—for there had never been a final settlement of the Korean War, although a cease-fire had been declared some twenty years earlier. Although Hal had to live at Camp Howze near the DMZ, we could see him on weekends. On alternate weekends he came to Seoul, and the weekends between when he had to stay at Camp Howze, the kids and I rode an army bus to visit him, an hour-long adventure on a narrow road filled with pedestrians and livestock. On weekends when Hal could join us, we explored the beautiful countryside of Korea, visiting many Buddhist temples and other historic sites of South Korea.

None of this was leading to an archaeological project or a dissertation topic. I was thirty-eight years old and felt the passing of time and opportunity quite keenly. And, of course, my Chinese studies were now irrelevant. Dr. Griffin, director of the archaeology museum at the University of Michigan, had kindly provided me with a letter of introduction to the director of the Seoul National Museum, Dr. Kim Che-won. Dr. Kim told me he was on the verge of retirement and passed me along to his successor, Dr. Kim Won-yong. This proved to be a vital connection, not the least because the younger Dr. Kim was also chair of the Art and Archaeology Department at Seoul National University (SNU). I was sent around to other universities to meet archaeologists. Dr. Sohn Pow-key at Yonsei University shared his laboratory and his writings with me. Dr. Hwang of Kyunghee University was also generous with his finds and his opinions.

Dr. Kim and Dr. Sohn were the most eminent archaeologists in South Korea, but their degrees were not in archaeology—Kim Won-yong had earned a PhD in Art History from New York University, and Sohn Pow-key a doctorate in History from UC Berkeley. Both were brilliant men, but they had to learn excavation as on-the-job training. Not surprisingly, given their backgrounds, their orientation to archaeology was as an adjunct to history.

In the meantime, I joined a Korean class on the army post and discovered that the Hangul alphabet is logical and easy. Very soon I could pronounce any sign I saw on the street, although I didn't necessarily know its meaning. Often the sign would turn out to be English words, like *syo-ping-sen-to* (shopping center). After a few weeks, I had exhausted all there was to learn from lessons on post. The Korean teacher recommended a tutor, who miraculously turned out to be an assistant professor of geography at Seoul National University. Pak Dong-won was an excellent language teacher, and better yet, he brought site reports to pore through with me for my lessons. I struggled to read them with his patient prompting.

More serendipity came my way when I learned that Mr. Pak's college classmate and best buddy was also an assistant professor at SNU—and his field was archaeology. When I met Im Hyo-jai (Figure 1), neither of us was

FIGURE 1. The author with Im Hyo-jai at Osanni

fluent in each other's language, but I managed to understand that he had a permit for a survey looking for archaeological sites along the Han River. He had surveyed along the east coast of Korea with L.L. (Tish) Sample and Albert Mohr (Sample 1967). New methods of survey were being tried out at UM, so I offered to make a plan for an archaeological survey project that would include test pits and a new process called flotation. Mr. Im had students and tools and the all-important permit, and I contributed transportation, access to detailed maps of Korea, and new ideas. Post Exchange beer and cigarettes sweetened the deal.

My station wagon was unreliable but big enough to carry field crew and equipment. In those days, the only paved roads were within the larger cities, between military installations, and the highway between Seoul and Pusan. To get to the Han River and survey for archaeological sites meant driving on rocky roads, muddy roads, narrow roads, and sometimes on berms between rice fields. Each time my car got stuck in the mud, several young men would appear from nowhere to heave it out. Once I came to a stream too deep to ford with the car, so we parked and sloshed across. Another time our survey plan came too close to the DMZ and a warning shot was fired at us—which got our immediate attention and left a gap in the survey map.

New friends were important assets, making this survey all the more feasible and enjoyable. Ever the joiner, I had new pals from the International Women's Club of Seoul—mostly diplomats' wives—and from the American Women's Club of Seoul—mostly wives of civilians who worked for the US government as well as wives of businessmen and geologists. South Korea in those days was not especially welcoming to foreign women. Most social events for businessmen and diplomats were for men only, often banquets where beautifully dressed *kisaeng* served the men many courses, crouching beside them and putting bites in their mouths with chopsticks, and perhaps performing after dinner.

Another difference for foreign women in Korea was that servants were easily available and inexpensive. Some of the American families I knew employed a house boy, an *ajuma*, a sew girl, a chauffeur, and a gardener. Perhaps this seems like the lap of luxury, but it left the wives essentially unemployed. The women wanted something to do, and it happened that I could provide it.

I found the Korean women I met to be forthright and smart. I could not understand how they could be downtrodden, but I did observe that on the streets women walked several paces behind their husbands. I heard that Koreans seldom socialized as a couple. In one of my Korean lessons, I learned to say in Korean, "Yobo, bring me my shoes." And then I learned the words to berate the wife for not having the shoes shined brightly enough. This lesson worried me for several reasons. For one thing, in the lesson, *yobo* was translated into English as "honey," or "dear," but my understanding of its literal meaning was more like, "you there." When answering the telephone, one says "*yoboseyo*," in which the ending is a verb form. And I have never even considered polishing my husband's shoes. Anyway, what mind-set would include this vignette in a language lesson? I've never been able to process the disconnect between women's status when men are present and their behavior when men are not present. One Korean woman told me, laughing, that she had to take care of four boys—three sons and her husband.

After I met the international women, I offered to teach them to be docents at the National Museum, so that visitors who spoke various languages would have knowledgeable guides. When our Han River survey project was planned, I mentioned it at a meeting, and several women asked if they could help with the project. I had volunteers! One of my new friends also had access to a large four-wheel-drive van and driver. We needed all that space for the crowd I began to train to help with the survey. Jean Cronk's driver, Mr. Oh, drove us to many locations, neatly dressed and wearing short white gloves, which he kept on even to help us dig test pits.

To learn about Korea, I joined the Royal Asiatic Society, Korea Branch, and found members whose knowledge of Korea was wide and deep and who could offer such helpful things as botanical knowledge and photography from a helicopter. Yet more help appeared in the person of Martha Sloan, a Korean-American who volunteered to read Korean archaeological journals with me. Without her explanations of the meanings of words and the structure of sentences, I would never have grasped the content thoroughly. In these sessions, I also came to appreciate how few prehistoric sites had been recorded and how little was known about them.

I had decided to focus on the Neolithic period in Korea for a number of reasons. Some of my student digs dealt with early agriculture. I had briefly worked at Tierras Largas in Oaxaca and the Turner-Snodgrass site, a Middle Mississippian site in Missouri, so I had some data with which to think about differences among small farming sites. I was familiar with the worldwide literature on early agriculture, and I was interested in the whys and hows of early plant cultivation. I had been drawn to Carl Sauer's (1952) perspective on the way agriculture might have begun in wet climates rather than dry ones, stressing tubers instead of grains. Korea seemed to be relevant, with its seasonally dripping climate.

Thus I had some limited experience to guide interpretation and to look at the distribution of small early sites in Korea. But there was another, more devious reason for choosing to study the Neolithic in Korea. Few Korean archaeologists had any interest in that period of Korean archaeology, but other time periods were overcrowded. Paleolithic archaeology in Korea had rival archaeologists each trying to prove his own theory. Early state-level tombs contained artifacts made of pure gold, and there was little chance that an unknown foreigner would be allowed anywhere near those digs. Even Bronze Age sites produced collectible finds. Maybe there was a message in the fact that few of the known bronzes had been excavated properly. Bronze artifacts just turned up in private collections. But Neolithic Korea had basic pottery and undistinguished stone tools, from villages with twenty or so semisubterranean houses. Nobody cared if I stuck in my trowel at that level—or even noticed.

One big Neolithic puzzle had to be solved before more could be learned about early farmers. Two kinds of pottery had been found in sites with small house floors. One type had no decoration, the other had patterns incised or impressed in geometric patterns over the exterior of the pot. These types, called Mumun (no pattern) and Chulmun (comb-pattern), were usually found in different locations, so there was no superposition of layers. Mumun tended to be on hillsides, and Chulmun was mostly near rivers. Discussions about which style was earlier were not based on stratigraphy but on opinions about which type was more primitive. Most archaeologists thought the plain pottery must have come first, reasoning that it was simpler and therefore earlier. This, of course, had nothing to do with social archaeology, but we couldn't begin to understand agricultural beginnings without at least a sketchy chronology.

One of the places that Im and I decided to investigate with a test pit was Misari, a site on a sandy island in the middle of the Han River. Over the ages, sand had piled up to make the island, which was large enough to have some habitation and even small farms. The river had cut back through the sand bank on the north side, and both Mumun and Chulmun potsherds and artifacts were scattered on the ground near the water. Misari seemed to be a likely place for a stratigraphic test to solve the Mumun/Chulmun problem. I parked the Yellow Peril on the south bank and looked at Im for a suggestion about how we could get to the island. He whistled up a wooden plank boat, which, for a small fee, ferried Im and me and a student, along with our buckets, bags, shovels, and trowels, across to the island.

When our test pit revealed that the two kinds of pottery were in separate layers, with more than a meter of sandy deposits between them, we were ecstatic. Mumun was above, Chulmun below. We had demonstrated that Chulmun was older than Mumun.

We floated the dirt from several of our test pits, but when I sent the sieved remains to be analyzed, I was told that most of the black spots were ants, with a few bits of identifiable wood. There were also some impressions in potsherds that I thought could be grain impressions, but I couldn't find anyone to identify them. East Asian grains, especially millets, were almost unknown among Western botanists at that time.

I was interested in the possibility that gathering wild plants had been a strategy to extend the subsistence base when harvested grains had run out, even in Neolithic times. I had read that if the rains didn't come early enough to plant their rice, farmers in Korea suffered from "spring hunger." When all the rice from the fall harvest and the *kimchi* prepared in the fall had been eaten, women had to scratch together meals out of plants in the forests and marshes. Sometimes people ate the inner bark of pine trees. When I learned that many plants of the forests and swamps were collected and eaten, Martha Sloan arranged for an informant to show me which plants she used. I collected the plants my informant pointed out, as she explained to me which parts of the plants were eaten. Later I asked a botanist to identify the plants by their Latin names. Although the resulting chart was omitted from the published version of my dissertation, it was republished in *Korean Social Archaeology* (Nelson 2004b).

Against the received wisdom, I argued in my dissertation in favor of some plant cultivation in Chulmun sites. I concluded that the sites were year-round settlements because the dwellings were habitable in winter. I didn't yet think about the ramifications for gendered labor, but such an argument was implicit in my research. Large jars in groups on house floors were probably used for storage of food through the winter. I suggested that wild vegetables could have been used for a prototype of *kimchi*, a vegetable preserve made of turnips or cabbages, with flavorings added and preserved in brine. Each fall, Korean women make enough *kimchi* to last the winter, storing it in earthenware jars half-buried in the ground, just as jars were buried inside dwellings at the site of Amsari. Of the stone tools we found, 49% were probably used for vegetable food preparation, which also suggested more emphasis on farming and food storage than on hunting.

I didn't argue specifically that women were making the food to be preserved in the group of large pots found inside the dwellings. Stereotyped gender activities were routinely assumed in those days. The fall processing of cabbage and turnips, called *kimjang*, was women's work—no need to argue that point. Of course, I assumed that women made the pottery and were responsible for the food. I hadn't begun to analyze gender stereotyping even in the present; how could I analyze it in the past?

Chitamni, a site in North Korea, had reported grains of millet in a Chulmun jar similar to those in our survey, but that was thin evidence on which to hang millet cultivation. Nevertheless, I bravely wrote a paper, "Early Settled Villages in Korea, Evidence of Incipient Food Production" (1974; reprinted in Nelson 2004b) arguing the case for plant cultivation in the Chulmun period. Since then, however, several cultivars (especially millets and soy beans) have been identified in Korean sites (Lee 2011), and I would now propose that ancient women in the Korean peninsula were responsible for the preservation of these crops for winter food, aand probably took part in their cultivation. In 1970, I observed that whole families, men and women, children and grannies, together planted, weeded, and harvested rice. Women are in charge of households in current Korea—that, too, seems a likely continuity from the Neolithic.

DISSERTATION

I hadn't had much field experience, so at each stage of my project I wrote to my mentors at UM to ask for advice. The only response I received came almost at the end of my year in Korea, too late for me to make any additions or changes. This lack of interest in my project reinforced my notion that I was an "orphan" student and that I would have to persevere on my own.

In the meantime, during the year in Korea, I had to pay attention to my sons, travel in South Korea every other weekend with Hal and the kids, and teach my University of Maryland classes. We also traveled when we could, taking the boys to Japan, Okinawa, and Taiwan, and going without them to Hong Kong. It was a breathless year, ending with enough material for a dissertation, important insights into Korean archaeology, and many new friends.

After I submitted my dissertation, a year went by before any member of my doctoral committee responded to it. Finally Dr. Griffin sent a few suggestions for fixing typos and changing wording, and scheduled my oral defense.

The most critical moment of my oral examination seemed to be when a faculty member on my committee, an expert on Japanese ethnography, handed me a scrap of paper with three handwritten Chinese characters on it. "What does that say?" he demanded. I instantly recognized that the last character meant village, so I knew it was the name of a place. Fighting down panic, I realized that the middle character meant "shrine" or "temple." Oh, yes, and the first character meant "granite." Literally translated, it would mean Stone Temple Village, but I recognized it as the name of one of the sites on the Han River. "Amsari," I read aloud, with some relief. Apparently those characters are pronounced quite differently in Japanese, and Dick Beardsley thought I had missed a major site along the Han River. I wondered if he hadn't believed that I had learned to read Chinese characters in a year, but I tried not to focus on that facet of his challenge. I had indeed learned all the Chinese characters that I needed to know to read archaeological reports. So I passed a big hurdle.

RETURN TO KOREA

My first chance to return to Korea did not arrive until 1978. I felt lucky to be employed at a time when new jobs in academia were extremely scarce. My first teaching post as a PhD was as an adjunct professor at the University of Colorado in Boulder (CU), a temporary job. Although I moved to a tenure-track position at the University of Denver (DU) in September 1974, I had not been forgotten in Boulder. When CU was providing the academic deans and most of the faculty with a Semester-at-Sea adventure around the world, they needed a Koreanist to be an Interport Lecturer, because the ship's first port was Pusan, South Korea. I could just squeeze this adventure between winter and spring quarters at DU by flying to catch the ship in Honolulu and disembarking at Pusan. It was fun to lecture about Korea for ten days, and poignant to wave good-bye and watch the ship sail off to cruise the rest of the world without me. Wanderdust [sic] must have been sprinkled on me in my cradle.

I bootlegged a few days in Korea to become reacquainted with my archaeological friends whom I hadn't seen in seven years. With some of them I discussed writing a book on Korean archaeology, a topic too little known to

English readers, and found encouragement. At the time, I had in mind writing the usual kind of text that described the sites and the changes through time, but as I worked on the book, the notion of Korean ethnicity began to demand attention. I wanted to call the book "Ethnicity in Retrospect" and to tell the archaeological tale from present to past, but instead it was published as *The Archaeology of Korea* in the usual ancient-to-modern order. It is not gender in archaeology, but it is an approach to social archaeology. Many of my papers on the Korean Neolithic were subsequently republished in a book called *Korean Social Archaeology* (Nelson 2004b).

In 1983 and again in 1986, I was awarded research grants, each to spend a month in Korea to collect data for the Korean archaeology book. North Korean writings were forbidden in South Korea, which brought some problems for my understanding of the whole Korean peninsula. However, staying at the Academy of Korean Studies gave me access to North Korean publications. The journals were in a locked attic room, illegal to read without special permission. I found the differences in the reporting of archaeological sites between the north and south fascinating, and later would write about it (Nelson 2006). North Koreans followed Marxist lines and assumed that Neolithic sites represent matriarchies, while in the south little theory was evident, except organizing sites into typologies based on pottery styles.

In 1989, I took a group of Earthwatch volunteers to Korea, still concentrating on subsistence issues. We surveyed catchment areas around three Neolithic sites, one in the central east coast, one on the southeast coast, and one on the Han River in central Korea. That project is also briefly described in *Korean Social Archaeology* (2004b). I still didn't have a clear gender concept, but I was working on it through writing a novel about Neolithic Korea (see Part VIII).

I have returned to Korea more times than I can count, each time learning about new excavations, new dates, and new interpretations of the data. Korean archaeology is vibrant and changing. On one of my visits to Korea, Dr. Bae Kidong pointed out that there were only twelve archaeologists in Korea who had earned a PhD. Most of the advanced degrees were from the English-speaking world, although one early archaeologist had trained in France and another in Denmark. I am pleased that more women are now becoming archaeologists, but they are far from equal in numbers. Most of the men have PhDs from England or America, but as far as I can recall, Gyoung-Ah Lee is the only Korean woman who has earned a PhD abroad.

PART III

Figurines and Equity Issues: Measuring Gender

I didn't expect to be able to return to excavate in Korea, so after my dissertation was accepted, I sought other research opportunities. I explored the archaeological sites of Colorado and Utah for fieldwork possibilities. Although I was quite unschooled about archaeology in the southwestern United States, nevertheless I was invited to organize a field school in Butler Wash, Utah. Well, I thought, I didn't know anything about Korean archaeology when I started. But I knew my limitations. I asked Paul Nickens, a University of Colorado (CU) graduate student (who knew a lot about the Southwest and had done very well in the Quantitative Methods class I taught at CU; see below), to oversee the project. Paul was terrific. He had to deal with a challenging mix of high school and college students but managed the whole first summer of surveying and excavating without tearing out all his hair.

I had much to learn about Southwest archaeology, especially the basic fact that some of its practices were different from those of the eastern US archaeology that I had learned at the University of Michigan. Butler Wash amazed me, littered with Pueblo II sites between two dry washes. Not wanting to be left out of the field school discoveries, I claimed a small area for myself. I chose to search for the kiva (I supposed there had to be one but, if so, we didn't find it) in an area with painted potsherds scattered profusely on the surface. When Bill Lipe visited us at Butler Wash, I'm afraid he thought I came from outer space, because I gridded this Pueblo II site, and we were digging a random sample. Bill was very polite about my bizarre approach.

For readers who don't work in the American Southwest, and are not laughing yet, I should explain that Pueblo sites have architecture, much of which can be seen above the ground. In Korea, we had gridded sites that were

Shamans, Queens, and Figurines: The Development of Gender Archaeology, by Sarah Nelson, 33–47.

detectable only from artifacts on the ground, in order to make it easier to quantify the artifacts and ecofacts in each square of identical size, to allow for statistical robustness. But in Pueblo sites, each room provides a meaningful statistical sample. Grids would cut across rooms, muddying the counts rather than clarifying them. I had a lot to learn about Southwest archaeology.

To make up for my deficiencies, I pored over artifact collections in local museums, visited archaeological sites in the Southwest, and read site reports and syntheses of Southwest archaeology. As a volunteer, I recatalogued part of the Wetherill Collection that resides in the Colorado History Museum in Denver. The next two summers I managed a modest field school myself in Butler Wash (Nelson 1976, 1978).

Since I've raised the matter of statistics, I should briefly step further back into my UM years. I took a class in statistics during my first summer, and it happened that Hal was in the same class. We are both good at math, and the class was easy for both of us. We always did our homework separately and then compared answers. If our answers were not identical, we went back through the exercise to see who was right. Usually our answers agreed, but twice we had to revisit our answers. The results split 50/50 in terms of who was right the first time. We both aced the exams. When our grades came in the mail, I opened mine and was pleased to see that I got an A. I wasn't so pleased after Hal opened his grades, with A+ in Biostatistics. I was furious and stormed the professor's door. And what did he say? "Oh, I thought your husband must have done your homework for you." It was my first undeniable brush with sexist thinking. The professor changed my grade to A+ (the Michigan grade point system had 9 points (from C– [1] to A+ [9] instead of the usual 4-point system—D [1] to A [4]), so the + made a difference to my grade point average as well as my pride).

The next trimester I did an independent study in statistical applications to archaeology, some of which I used in my dissertation. However, my quantifying skills were not universally appreciated in Colorado. As a new PhD, I taught a seminar in quantitative methods in archaeology at the University of Colorado. Although I omitted some of the more obscure statistical techniques I had learned, the course was still difficult. The lessons were understood and appreciated by only a few of my students. The rest, the majority of the class, considered statistics unnecessary and obscure. My usages of statistics were to have additional untoward consequences.

EQUITY IN THE UNIVERSITY

I would like to pretend that my conversion to gender archaeology was entirely intellectual, but that would be inaccurate. In fact, my understanding of what feminists at that time called "The Patriarchy" came about in the usual painful, personal way. The reader of this book will be spared the details, but I can reveal that by being denied tenure, not once but twice, I learned that women were measured differently from men by the decision-makers at DU. The first time my tenure was denied, I protested and the process was declared to have been flawed by a "procedural irregularity." Therefore, the tenure process had to be repeated the following year. The result was the same. After my appeals to fairness and the Faculty Senate were successful, three attempts were made to eliminate the Anthropology Department completely. In the meantime, I had become department chair. In waging these battles, I had to dig in and learn the university systems—how they really work rather than believing the information on organizational charts.

Reading the burgeoning feminist literature helped me cope with setbacks: I could see that what I perceived as persecution was not (entirely) personal, but it seemed that the system was rigged so that if women professors had to be hired, not tenuring us would be a win/win situation for the Old Boys—we could be replaced by women faculty who were not only younger but also cheaper. By the time those young women understood the system, they would be gone and a new crop of young, talented, and hopeful women would join the faculty. Furthermore, the Old Boys wouldn't need to worry about gender fairness in the salaries of associate and full professors if all the women were in the lower ranks. We called this the "revolving door policy for women faculty."

In protesting the tenure decision, I could have pressed the case that I had experienced retaliation for activities with the Committee for Women on Campus, but I preferred to show that my case for tenure and promotion was at least as good as those (males only) who had been promoted and tenured at the same time I was denied. Still, when it looked like I really might be out on the street, I realized that since I had traveled widely in Europe and Asia, I might be able to learn enough to qualify as a travel agent.

Mine was not the only egregious tenure case among women faculty, and there were other issues for women that we had been unsuccessful in ameliorating through the designated channels. Reluctantly, the Committee for Women on Campus hired a lawyer from Washington, DC, resulting (after much negotiation) in a conciliation agreement. I was, and continue to be, very grateful to the cadre of women lawyers who agitated for Title IX and Title VII, without which I would be writing a very different story. I recently learned that a DU colleague, Diane Wendt, was a member of the committee that wrote Title IX. Although at the time the *Denver Post* described her as a "militant feminist," DU has just named new sports fields for her. The truth is she was far from militant but very effective.

EQUITY ISSUES IN ARCHAEOLOGY

Even after the tenure trials at DU were behind me, I had more lessons to learn. In 1983, I wrote a proposal to apply computers and quantification to the archaeological record at Piñon Canyon in southeastern Colorado, where 367 square miles of ranch land had been divided into three tracts to be surveyed and tested for archaeological remains before the land could be used by the US Army for tank training. My proposal was given the highest marks and I was chosen by the selection committee to do all the archaeology on all three segments of land. However, the techniques I proposed were not appreciated by the supervising agency. I had thought that my prowess in quantifying would be an entrée into the male world, but understanding computers and statistics turned out to be resented by those who preferred "old" archaeology. In this case, I'm not sure which rule I broke but the consequences were dire. I was dismissed from the project, and eventually the archaeology of that large region was not well served. Outside archaeologists were hired to continue the mapping program I had designed and to interpret the results, but the innovative laboratory procedures I had established were abandoned. I cannot say how it ended, because I was forbidden to talk to anyone involved in the project or to see the data, and my students were forbidden to speak to me. Some students would call late at night, whispering, with news of the latest problems with the project. When I entered the Anthropology office, everyone else melted away. It was a tough time—so tough that seven years later, one of the students made a special trip to Denver to apologize to me for not having spoken up. Of course, I assured her that I didn't blame her or any of the students, and it was ancient history. By then I had been promoted to professor. But it had been a difficult time.

FEMINISM

In spite of searing experiences, I did not yet call myself a feminist. The press had depicted such women as man-haters, opposed to children, harsh. But as I read, I found that many exciting things were occurring in the world of academic feminism, utterly unlike the popular view. I read about how to dress like a mannish woman ("dress for success"), and how women's ways of speaking were hindering us not only from success, but from even being heard by male colleagues at all. Historians were substituting where archaeologists should have been, discussing the long sweep of male dominance, often using archaeological data. Elise Boulding's (1976) masterful history, *The Underside of History: A View of Women through Time*, is a particularly thorough and insightful example.

But in my view, cultural anthropologists were more trenchant in their criticisms of gender stereotypes than historians. Since the US Army classified me as a "dependent," I was personally interested to read that "the definition of women as wife-mother-dependent as circumscribed by a nuclear family sphere is less than two hundred years old" (Sacks 1979:65). Only two hundred years! To archaeologists, that is scarcely more than the range of error for a radiocarbon date. An invention of the eighteenth century! I suddenly understood why Taiwan officials had prevented me from taking my sons to the east coast of Taiwan by granting the children only three-month visas. I was defined as wife-mother-dependent rather than as an archaeologist. On a less personal note, the notion that women's subordination had been rather recently invented meant that archaeologists should have important perceptions about the deep past.

Thus, a feminist anthropological perspective for me became key to the ability to explode the gender myths we were living with, but at the same time the long perspective of archaeology was vital to demonstrate variety in women's lives through time and place. I had heard too much in my anthropology classes at UM about universal female subordination. It was a topic that had been both commonly implied and baldly stated. Karen Sacks (1979 [1982]) began *Sisters and Wives* with a chapter called, "Anthropology against Women," and the next chapter is entitled, "The Case against Universal Subordination." I was astonished and intrigued. The notion that women were subordinate in all times and places, as decreed by evolution, may seem extreme now, but at the time it well described the underlying beliefs within anthropology.

The opening sentence in Sacks's book struck me so forcibly that I underlined it when I first read it, and marginal comments written in at least three different inks show that I came back to it often. I quote the sentence here, set off by itself, because the archaeological implications simply screamed at me.

> The search for women's overall or fundamental position *long ago or far away* [my emphasis] is an outcome of the confrontation between social Darwinist anthropology and the feminist and socialist movements over sexism here and now. (Sacks 1982:3)

Long ago? Far away? Of course, archaeology should weigh in on this discussion. But so far, we had been ducking our responsibilities. Sacks suggested that we needed to know "how the history of humanity looks with the female half at center stage" (p. 3). What an electric challenge. Eleanor Leacock's (1981) book, *Myths of Male Dominance*, using her own fieldwork on the Montagnais-Naskapi during the time of the fur trade as the centerpiece of her argument, was another inspiration for me as I tried to imagine an archaeology that put women in the center. I didn't think that I, personally, could do anything about inserting the female half of humanity into archaeological discourse, but I did think that archaeology had an important role to play, and began to wonder how I could contribute. First we had to imagine it, and then we had to make it possible.

Women in many fields of academe were inspiring, but while women in cultural anthropology provided the best models for me, I needed to figure out how archaeologists could use them. I looked for inspiration to women who were reanalyzing the foundational work of earlier anthropologists and in the process overturning many cherished beliefs of the field. Annette Weiner (1976) revisited the Trobriand Islands, made famous by Bronislaw Malinowski's raptures about the kula ring. Weiner asked Trobriand women about their own ceremonies and social activities and uncovered an important part of the culture that Malinowski had overlooked in favor of male magic in coral gardens and fancy kula canoes decorated lavishly with giant cowrie shells.

Jane Goodale (1971) revisited the Tiwi of Northern Australia, reported as patriarchal in the extreme, and discovered that the system wasn't as skewed toward males as had been reported. I devoured any cultural anthropology that reanalyzed women in a specific culture and pondered how material culture might allow archaeologists to reanalyze the past. As I write this, I realize I had forgotten what fun it was to be a feminist in those days. My bookshelves filled up rapidly with provocative new ideas. My classes were full of excitement and discussion. My writing was lagging behind.

In 1976, I organized a seminar called "Cross-Cultural Perspectives on Women," and two years later created another seminar, "Women in Prehistory." To plan these classes, I read all the feminist literature I could find in any field for the cultural course, and for the archaeology course I tried to figure out how each text could be applied to archaeology, and challenged the students to do so as well. I asked each student to read and critique any archaeological report and write down everything they learned about the women at that site. It was a surprise to the students that most of the time the answer was, "nothing." Blank pages would be handed in with embarrassment. Once they realized that lack of attention to women was typical, the class became eager to critique everything they read, rather than just accepting whatever the author wrote. The class would freely brainstorm ways the archaeological reports might have been improved.

After the Committee for Women on Campus brought some of the university's practices to the attention of the US Labor Department (see above), one of the demands of the conciliation agreement was to create a Women's Resource Center on the DU campus. Under the leadership of Jodi Wetzel, seminars were organized in which women faculty could try out new feminist applications to our fields in a safe and supportive atmosphere, without the inevitable sniping of male faculty.

Feminist colleagues in other fields became outstanding resources for one another. Diane Waldman directed me to a powerful book in her field, *Patriarchal Precedents*, by Rosalind Coward (1983), which I found many subsequent reasons to quote.

After we created the Women's Studies Program, the next year we had funds to create a new course. Susan Stakel suggested a course to be called "Biology of Women." We advertised the job in Women's Studies, interviewed three candidates, and then told the Biology Department that we had hired Susan Sadler to teach the course, and asked if they would like to cross-list it. They did. This procedure was breaking a huge rule. University departments are small fiefdoms with guarded borders. To our delight, course enrollments overflowed, the class got rave reviews, and eventually Susan Sadler became a permanent addition to the faculty. Similarly, the Women's Studies faculty members each designed new courses in our own fields and made them do double duty for our departments and Women's Studies.

I sometimes lectured to M. E. Warlick's art history classes about ancient figurines (and learned about art and alchemy from her on walks along the Denver Highline Canal). Diana Wilson spoke so elegantly about "Ariadne's Thread" at a symposium we organized for the chancellor that he became an enthusiastic supporter of Women's Studies. Sieglinde Lug, who taught German and read the German feminist literature, organized thirteen of us into a dinner group that met once a month. We called ourselves the "Loose Canon." For several years, members of the Loose Canon took turns chairing the Women's Studies Program we had created in 1984. The program is still flourishing, now under the name of Gender and Women's Studies, and the Loose Canon dinner group still meets, although less regularly, now that half of us have retired. Most members of our group have taken a turn as chair of their departments, recognizing it as a responsibility.

FIGURINES

Beginning to ponder ways to approach gender in archaeology, I considered representations of women in the past. I wondered what I could learn about the women who lived in the Paleolithic by studying figurines. Explaining how I chose the particular groups of figurines to study requires a bit of back-story. When I began my graduate program at UM, I had thought I would concentrate on either Near Eastern archaeology (building on my undergraduate degree in Biblical History) or European archaeology (since I had lived in Europe for six years and had traveled widely in western Europe, and I could speak and/or read most of the languages I would need). But I was warned by professors who worked in those regions that neither Europe nor Southwest Asia would welcome a female archaeologist as a chief excavator. Of course, there had been famous women who worked in these regions, but times had changed. I was discouraged from pursuing the archaeology of these areas and so began to search for other kinds of archaeological projects.

Korea had been a lucky beginning for me, but it seemed too far away to plan another project there, and anyway I hadn't yet come across any Korean archaeological data that seemed to lend itself to gender archaeology, which I was eager to pursue. I wanted to find some solid data that could be measured and quantified, and to prove something.

When it came to considering female bodies, the Upper Paleolithic female figurines in Europe, widely referred to as "fat ladies," were numerous enough that one could apply statistical methods to their shapes. Could I learn anything about social structure from the way their bodies were portrayed?

I read everything I could find in German, French, or Italian, including the circumstances of the discoveries, the locations (mostly caves), and the possible meanings of the figurines. I was horrified to learn that the famous Brassempouy figurine had been found in pieces, shattered by a workman's pick! What kind of archaeology was that? Others figurines had been found in caves but with very little cultural or environmental context.

Pronouncements about the figurines had some characteristics of responses to a Rorschach test. Males were assumed to have carved the figurines, for their own purposes. Many men who wrote about the figurines said they were "stylized" and did not represent real women. The notion that they represented goddesses was reiterated, but it was also said that they were made to frighten off enemies. Supposedly the women were all fat, but only a few figurines looked obese to me.

I wrote several papers quoting these early writings, but none of them were published, and they have been lost from my files. The first of these considered the comments of the men who discovered the figurines or generalized about them. From a feminist stance, the attitudes of most male scholars who had written about the figurines were appalling—or hilarious, depending on one's sense of humor. I was particularly amused to discover that E. B. Renaud, a retired DU anthropology professor, had written about the "Venus of Willendorf" with a headline, "The First God Was a Goddess!"

One day when I was teaching a class in European Prehistory and the topic was the Upper Paleolithic, I passed around a model of the Willendorf statue that had come in a teaching kit. I gave the usual spiel about the figures being stylized. But after class, a student wanted to talk. She told me, "That figurine is not stylized. It is a representation of one pattern in which women deposit fat. It depicts exactly the deposition of fat on some women's bodies." She convinced me that she knew what she was talking about.

I had learned to question the usual spiel, and I was intrigued with the student's point, but I needed an expert opinion. I sent photographs of the figure from several sides to Dr. Robert Hermann, an MD/PhD endocrinologist who studied obesity, asking him if he thought the carving portrayed a real woman or if it was imagined. He replied that the artist was so correct in the portrayal of an obese woman that a person who had never seen a fat female couldn't have invented so precisely the fat depositions on this female body. In other words, a real woman had to have been the inspiration for the artist.

My next question was, What could it mean if some women could become so obese in the Upper Paleolithic? They were, supposedly, hunter-gatherers who roamed widely to hunt for their dinner. If there was even one truly obese person, didn't that puncture part of the hunter-gatherer story? To question the received wisdom of the archaeological clan about hunter-gatherers would be to break another rule. A big taboo this time.

My first sabbatical was approaching, and I began to form a plan. A return to Europe was a pleasant prospect. I applied to the National Science Foundation for a grant to visit the European museums where the Upper Paleolithic figurines were curated. For my NSF proposal, I hypothesized that the figurines, if they represented real body types, suggested that there had to be some sedentism even in the Paleolithic—women as obese as some of those sculpted could not have walked the distances nomadic people were ethnographically known to cover. A home base must have been occupied by some of the inhabitants year-round, I concluded. My plan was to photograph all the figurines I could find from several angles, measure them, and run statistics. I wrote to the appropriate curators for appointments, and they responded cordially.

Alas, my proposal was not funded, receiving low grades. Some comments by reviewers were downright insulting. For example, one reviewer gratuitously suggested I could not have read the articles I cited in German, French, and Italian. However, the curators of the museums I wanted to visit were welcoming. I went to Europe at my own expense. The rule that one has to have a grant to brag about one's research was one I gladly broke, but I do understand that I was lucky to be in a position to break it.

It was a delightful sabbatical—six weeks tooling around Europe in a diesel Mercedes picked up in Stuttgart—with Hal as my photographer and chauffeur. My visits with Prof. Henri Delporte outside of Paris, and Herr Professor Wilhelm Angeli at the Natural History Museum in Vienna, were particularly productive. Hal and I visited museums from France to Italy to Malta, and back north to Czechoslovakia and Austria. Our adventures were too many to relate here, but the oddest was the night spent in a wine barrel. I knew that Dolni Vestonice, a site where an unusual ceramic figurine uniquely had a belly button, had been found near Brno, Czechoslovakia, but the village with the site and museum was hard to find, and it took time to photograph and measure the figurines in the museum and then walk around the site.

The sun was setting as I began to inquire about vacancies at hotels in Prague; in our reckless youth, Hal and I didn't make reservations, even in communist countries. After receiving negative answers at several hotels (in German, which was widely understood; I don't speak Czech), I learned that all the hotels in Prague were completely full. It turned out that outstanding Russian workers were being rewarded for their industry with a weekend in Prague. A sympathetic desk clerk directed us out of town to a hotel a few miles north, but by the time we found that hotel in the pitch dark with no streetlights, it had also filled up.

We were told to try farther up the road where there was an auto camp. The manager there greeted us with a shake of his head and "*Keine kabine*." The Czech army was occupying all the cabins. I must have looked weary, maybe even eked out an exasperated tear, for the manager looked thoughtful and then asked diffidently if we were willing to sleep in a "*wein fass*." Of course, I knew that meant wine barrel but what the heck. Whatever he meant must be better than sleeping in the car. Indeed, he showed us to a row of wine barrels on their sides with the lids in the front, about six feet in all dimensions; into each lid a door had been cut. On the inside, benches had been built on both sides, which could be used for seats, and later the benches made supports for a foldout double bed that took up most of the space. It cost two dollars a night, and for another fifty cents we could rent a heater.

Dinner at the auto camp was another adventure. The young men of the Czech army sang while one of them strummed a Western-style guitar. They began with "Oh, Susannah!" and ran through many other American songs. We joined in, to their delight. They knew all the words, in English. The manager's English turned out to be fluent, as well. He told us he had learned English listening to the BBC.

A different kind of adventure in Vienna involved the new car. We read in the newspaper that very morning that a ring of car thieves was stealing Mercedes cars in Vienna and sending them to Saudi Arabia. Imagine our horror when our car was missing after we had held, photographed, and measured the Venus of Willendorf, the fattest of all the figurines. Hal went to report the missing car to the police, but it turned out we had parked illegally, and the car had been towed away by the police. What a relief!

Heading back toward Germany, we drove along the Danube River to visit the town of Willendorf, where the figurine had been found. The Venus of Willendorf had been commemorated with a supersized statue of the tiny figure.

When I returned to DU after my sabbatical, students helped to carefully measure front and side views of each figurine, the measurements covering bellies, breasts, and buttocks (Figure 2). I had to use photographs of the figurines from the Soviet Union, because I had not been able to gain access to the originals—and we couldn't have driven into the Ukraine in any case. I standardized my sample, and students punched the data on computer cards. Using SPSS, I looked at histograms of each variable. I tested whether the figurines would cluster into body types based on the measurements, and they did! I labeled the three groups, "obese," "steatopygous," and "normal" (Figure 3).

I found the variability in the figurines not only interesting but also contrary to what I had learned about them. Textbooks usually illustrated the obese Venus of Willendorf (no wonder they were nicknamed "fat ladies" since that figurine was so widely reproduced). I looked into the literature on obesity and rewrote the paper several times, each time answering reviewers' comments, although they were often dismissive. I finally gave up, in the mid-1980s, and simply circulated the paper to my friends, receiving interesting and innovative (but also unpublishable) feminist papers in return.

After my purple-ink mimeographed papers about the figurines vanished when a leak from above my office turned all copies to mush, I did manage to get one version of the work into print, by using the kind of subterfuge then necessary to publish anything about women in the past—we didn't use the term "gender" yet. Alice Kehoe and I had each written rejected papers, and we despaired of ever making our works available to our colleagues.

Publication problems were not unique to archaeologists. Eleanor Leacock reports in the preface to *Myths of Male Dominance* that "it took fifteen years after I obtained my PhD before I achieved a full-time academic job that allowed me to choose my areas of research" (Leacock 1981:5). Thus, even such a respected scholar as Eleanor Leacock had similar problems. I was delighted to meet her at a Wenner-Gren symposium in Mijas, Spain, but I was too shy to ply her with as many questions as I would have liked.

Alice Kehoe and I were tired of lurking in the shadows of the gray literature. It is frowned upon to publish one's own papers (disparaged as "vanity press"), but desperate measures were called for. We decided to organize a symposium that would accommodate two papers that had been rejected recently,

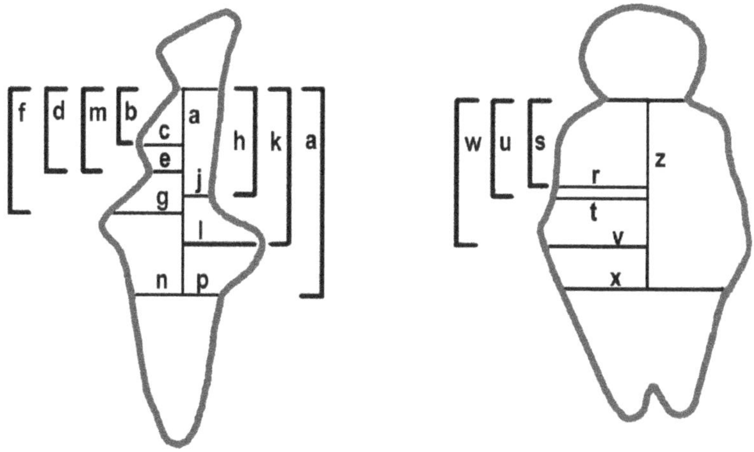

Measurements on Profile
a. Distance from neck to thigh.
b. Distance from neck to maximum breast width.
c. Maximum breadth to midpoint of vertical line.
d. Distance from neck to minimum width.
e. Minimum width from vertical line.
f. Distance from neck to maximum abdominal width.
g. Maximum width of abdomen from vertical line.
h. Distance from neck to back minimum width.
j. Minimum width of back from vertical line.
k. Distance from neck to buttock maximum width.
l. Maximum width of buttocks from vertical line.
m. Distance on central vertical line from neck to maximum breast length.
n. Distance from vertical line to front of thigh.
p. Distance from vertical line to back of thigh.
Measurements on Frontal View
r. Maximum breast width to vertical line.
s. Distance from neck to maximum breast width.
t. Line drawn at waist.
u. Distance from neck to waistline.
v. Maximum width of hips.
w. Distance from neck to maximum hip width.
x. Distance from vertical line to front of thigh.
z. Distance from neck to thigh.

FIGURE 2. Measurement of figurines

and proposed a session for the American Anthropological Association (AAA). Alice invited several male archaeologists who had innovative ways of perceiving their data, in addition to several women we knew with feminist perspectives. The session was accepted, well attended, and well received. Our

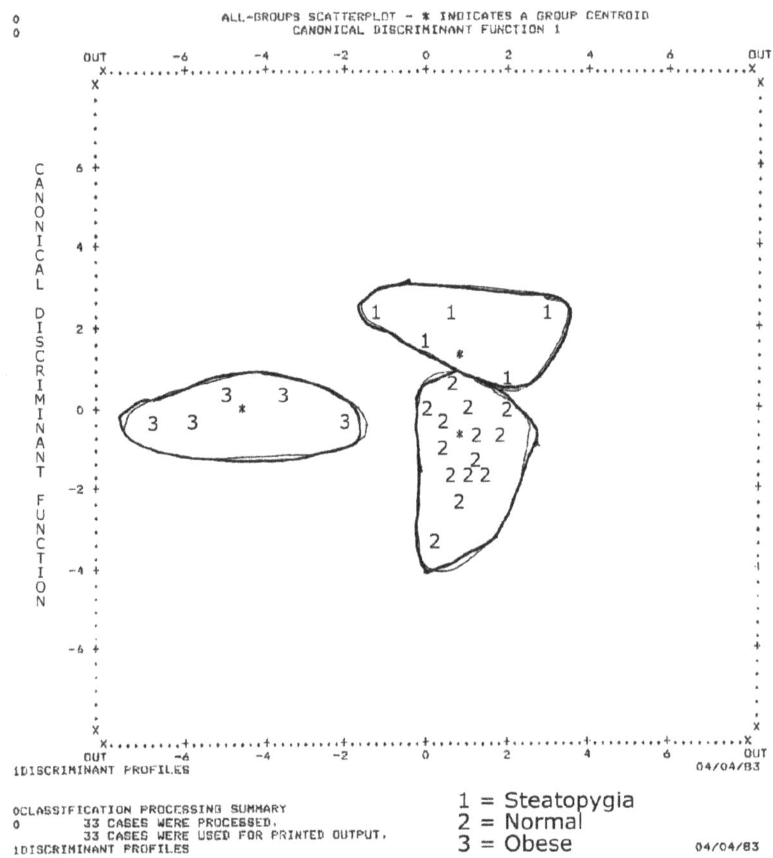

FIGURE 3. Discriminant analysis of figurines showing steatopygous, obese, and normal groups

symposium papers were published as *Powers of Observation: Alternative Views in Archeology*, the second in a series still being published by the Archeology Division of AAA. Another rule broken, another taboo sidestepped without supernatural or human consequences. In fact, that paper has been reprinted in at least two anthologies, and it deserves another exposure here (Chapter 1).

EQUITY ISSUES: MORE USES OF STATISTICS

Bill Zaranka, the new and wonderfully perceptive provost at DU, allocated funds to the Women's Studies Program to invite an outside scholar to lecture and teach for two quarters. It was an enormous boost for the program. Alison Wylie was the perfect choice to be our visiting scholar. She brought new perspectives, impeccable credentials, and boundless energy. I was particularly delighted to be introduced to papers about science and feminism. In Alison's seminar for faculty, both facts and strategies were showered upon us. Her ability to articulate the Women's Studies position clearly and persuasively convinced many male faculty members that this field was both necessary and sound. Her time as a visiting scholar at DU was a triumph for Women's Studies.

Alison had begun collecting the many circulating feminist papers about equity for women in archaeology, and she was inspired to collect and publish this "gray" literature. Several papers quantified the imbalances between males and females among students as well as faculty. We women in North America were not alone—papers came from several countries around the world. Although the papers were not acceptable for any standard journal, the multiple problems of being a female archaeologist were articulated in different and overlapping ways so that the aggregate made the point loud and clear.

At a board meeting of the AAA's Archeology Division, Alison suggested that these papers should be published in a book. Many board members agreed that it was important for the voices of women archaeologists to be heard. Alison easily persuaded Peggy Nelson and me to help edit the papers and produce the book; my student assistant typed the contributions on my office computer, and the volume, *Equity Issues for Women in Archeology*, was published as No. 5 of the Archeological Papers of the American Anthropological Association. Alison wrote an introduction to the volume, and Peggy and I together wrote the conclusion, with some thoughts on what women could do to succeed in archaeology. Our conclusion is a summary of the issues raised, as well as the collected wisdom and advice from the chapters. It is reproduced in this volume (Chapter 2), as a reminder of what women had to cope with to become archaeologists, and gives us a chance to wonder at the stamina of those earlier women archaeologists and to admire what they had already accomplished. It also seemed important to keep improving archaeology and to make sure the field never slides back to where it was for women as late as the 1990s.

By the mid-1990s, the time was ripe for a book-length summary of gender in archaeology. I roughed out some ideas and discussed them with Alison. She recommended sending the book proposal to Mitch Allen for his newly founded AltaMira Press. Mitch liked it. With a contract for the book, I applied to and was selected for an idyllic five spring weeks in 1996 as a resident scholar at the Rockefeller Center in Bellagio, on Lake Como, Italy. The azaleas were blooming in neon colors and all was bright with the world.

The experience at Bellagio was one of the highlights of my career, with (at any one time) eleven other scholars in various fields and from around the world, with their spouses, most of whom were also scholars.

The Rockefeller Foundation Center occupies an old villa near the top of a hill, with views of Lake Como that are so picturesque they hardly seem real. Hal and I have each had a poster of Bellagio hanging in our respective offices all these years. It is a place to sigh for. The Villa Serbelloni provided gracious living at its best, and the month was as productive as it was pleasant. The other scholars were working on their own projects by day, and were great company in the evenings, after we had all spent a day grinding out our work.

A few days into the Bellagio experience, it dawned on me that I was experiencing what life must be like for males in our culture. It seemed heaven-sent that for five weeks I never had to think about meals. I didn't have to decide what food to prepare, or shop for it, or cook it, or clean up after it. I wrote the entire first draft of *Gender in Archaeology* during my month at Bellagio. I had never been so productive.

Collaborations arose from this ferment. Prof. David Ayalon, from Hebrew University in Jerusalem, was a fellow resident scholar. His wife, Miriam Rosen-Ayalon, is an archaeologist of the Middle East. Miriam and I had great evening discussions at the villa. Before we parted, we decided to jointly organize a meeting on gender in archaeology on a worldwide scale.

Miriam and I invited our archaeologist friends from as many areas of the world as we could. Our proposal for a conference, "World-Wide Archaeological Perspectives on Gender," was accepted by the Rockefeller Foundation, and Miriam and I found ourselves again at beautiful Bellagio in 1998, with participants from Thailand to South Africa. The discussions enriched all of our thinking. Several of the participants began to do even more stimulating research on gender in archaeology in many places around the world. Miriam and I felt we had seeded the topic widely and well.

One of the interesting facets of the Bellagio discussions was discovering the unevenness of interest in gender in different parts of the world, and the varied ways that the participants found to discuss women and gender in the past. The deliberations resulted in *Gender in Archaeology: World-Wide Archaeological Perspectives* (Nelson and Rosen-Ayalon, eds. 2002).

Chapter 1
Diversity of the Upper Paleolithic "Venus" Figurines and Archeological Mythology

AMONG THE EARLIEST DEPICTIONS of human beings, dating back to perhaps 30,000 years ago, are small figurines of nude females, which are found across a broad belt in Europe from the Pyrenees in southern France to the Don River in the USSR, with outliers in Siberia. Every anthropologist is familiar with these Upper Paleolithic "Venus" figurines. They are used to titillate freshman classes, and photographs or drawings, especially of the figurines from Willendorf and Dolni Vestonice, routinely enliven introductory textbooks.

Current trends in literary criticism lean toward deconstruction of "texts," in which both words and situations may serve as the text for analysis. In this chapter I would like to deconstruct some texts in a narrower sense, using the example of the Venus figurines to demonstrate that introductory textbooks of archeology and physical anthropology produce gender metaphors which, by ignoring much of the scholarship on the figurines, reaffirm the folk model of gender preferred by our culture.

Figurine Descriptions

The figurines themselves have only gender in common. They are diverse in shape, in pose, in the somatic details depicted, and in ornamentation (Soffer 1988, Fleury 1926, Abramova 1967, Luquet 1926, Delporte 1979). They seem to represent differences in age as well (Rice 1981). Yet the textbooks tend to represent the figurines as all the same, and then to leap from this purported

Sarah M. Nelson (1990a). In *Powers of Observation: Alternative Views in Archeology*, edited by S. M. Nelson and A. B. Kehoe, pp. 11–22. Archeological Papers of the American Anthropological Association No. 2, Arlingtin, VA. Republished in *Shamans, Queens, and Figurines: The Development of Gender Archaeology*, by Sarah Nelson, pp. 49–58 (Taylor & Francis, 2015).

sameness to a supposed function for all figurines over their 3000 mile and perhaps 10,000 year spread (Soffer [1988], although Gamble [1986, 1987] asserts that most figurines fall within a 2000 year range). We need to explore this phenomenon of perceiving sameness in the diverse figurines, and ask why it occurs.

The texts our students read describe the figurines and frequently ascribe a function to them. There is little indication in the bibliographies that the authors of the texts have read any primary sources about the figurines, or that they are conversant with the rich literature which explores the variation in both the figurines themselves and the possible meanings and functions of the figurines. Rather, it seems that a kind of folklore is repeated, a folklore of the anthropology profession, too well known to require documentation.

The textbooks utilized in this study represent an unsystematic nonrandom sample—all that happen to be on my bookshelves—supplemented with those of my colleagues. Of 20 introductions to archeology or archeology and physical anthropology textbooks thus examined, eight concentrate on methodology and do not mention the figurines, while the other twelve contain cursory remarks on one to three pages. It is these twelve texts which constitute the study sample.

Table 1 shows the distribution of what is written regarding the physical characteristics of the figurines. Six of the textbooks mention exaggerated sexual characteristics as a prominent feature, whether or not they specify which traits are meant. The most common feature to be singled out is the breasts, described as "large," "generous," or "pendulous." All but one of the texts characterize the figurines as having either exaggerated sexual characteristics or large breasts, and four include both. Buttocks are mentioned five times, once described as "protruding," while hips, once with the adjective "broad," are specified three times. Only one author mentions both, showing that he makes a distinction between hips and buttocks. We are left to guess whether these terms are intended to refer to hindquarters in general in the other cases, or whether one set of authors indeed has protruding buttocks in mind (i.e., steatopygia), and the other really means broad hips (i.e., steatomeria) (Boule and Valois 1957:318). In one confusing case, an illustration of Willendorf, without a trace of steatopygia but with undoubted steatomeria, is pictured side by side with a Khoi-San woman, of whom the reverse is clearly the case—that is, protruding buttocks without broad hips (Campbell 1988:508).

The assertion that pregnancy is depicted in the figurines occurs in the textbook sample three times, and one additional author points out the exag-

TABLE 1 Description of Figurines

Author	Sexual	Abdomen	Breast	Buttocks	Hips	Pregnant
Barnouw (1978)	x	x	x		x	x
Campbell (1988)		x	x	x		
Chard (1975)			x	x	x	x
Clark (1977)			x	x	(thighs)	
Eddy (1984)	x		x	x		
Fagan (1986)	x		x			
Hester & Grady (1982)			x		x	
Jurmain et al. (1981)	x					
Pfeiffer (1985)	(stylized)					
Poirier (1987)		x	x	x		
Smith (1976)	x		x	x		x
Wenke (1984)	x					

gerated "belly," allowing him the satisfying alliteration of "breasts, belly, and buttocks." Three of the authors describe the figurines as fat. The only author to refrain from asserting or implying fatness does not describe the figurines at all, but contents himself with an illustration of Willendorf (Pfeiffer 1985: 203). Reading these descriptions, one would suppose that the Willendorf statuette, easily the most familiar, was typical or normal or modal. Instead, it is one of the least stylized and the most obese—referred to in another context with admiration as representing "resplendent endomorphy" (Beller 1977:78).

The generalizations in the textbooks do some violence to the facts. Few of the statuettes represent gross obesity, and some are quite slender. Even the first figurines found in the 1890s were classified by Piette into svelte and obese classes (Delporte 1979:73). Half a century ago Passemard (1938) examined all the then known figurines to see whether they were steatopygous, a description quite popular at that time, and came to the conclusion that most were not. Saccasyn della Santa (1947:9–13) reviewed the literature on the figurines again, and also concluded that they were not meant to represent steatopygia.

An unpublished statistical study of the variation in body shapes made 22 measurements on each figurine for which both frontal and profile photographs could be found—24 measurable figurines in all. The statuettes sorted into distinct groups of 5 obese (wide hips and thick body), 5 steatopygous (protruding buttocks), and 14 normal (Nelson n.d.). Another study shows that only 39 percent of these figurines could possibly represent pregnancy, slightly over half (55 percent) have pendulous breasts, 45 percent have broad hips, and 13 percent have protruding buttocks. Twenty-two percent have none of these characteristics. Body shapes depicted in the figurines have been divided into three or four categories by intuitive studies as well, such as those by Fleury (1926), Abramova (1967), and Luquet (1926).

Rice (1981) has suggested that this variability in body shape reflects different age groups, and has shown that different body characteristics can be so interpreted, with a high correlation between ratings. The distribution of the figurines in these age categories corresponds to the expected age pyramid for foraging societies.

Failure to acknowledge the variability of the figurines makes it easier to produce sweeping generalizations about their probable meaning or function. This is evident in the textbook interpretations. By far the most common function ascribed to the figurines is that of "fertility" (Table 2), specifically so des-

TABLE 2 Functions of Figurines

Author	Fertility	Goddess/Cult	Erotic	Artistic/Stylized
Barnouw (1978)	x			
Campbell (1988)	x	x		
Chard (1975)	rejects		x	
Clark (1977)	x (maternity)			x
Eddy (1984)	x	x	x	
Fagan (1986)	x	x		
Hester & Grady (1982)	x			x
Jurmain et al. (1981)	x	x	x	x
Pfeiffer (1985)				x
Poirier (1987)	x	x		
Smith (1976)	x		x	x
Wenke (1984)			x	x

ignated in seven of the 12 texts, and called "procreation" and "maternity" by one text each. This ascription is usually not explained at all, or weakly expressed at best. For example, "It seems unlikely that Upper Paleolithic women actually looked like that, but perhaps it was an ideal type or expressed a wish for fertility" (Barnouw 1978: 176). Apparently in conjunction with the fertility function is the idea of a "cult" or "Mother Goddess," since the five authors who use one or both of these expressions attach them to the fertility notion. Only one author rejects fertility as an explanation, on the grounds that hunters are not concerned with human fertility. Rather he explicitly suggests that the figurines are erotic: "Pleistocene pinup or centerfold girls" (Chard 1975:182).

Hidden Assumptions

The brief descriptions and interpretations of the female figurines contain and to some extent conceal unexamined assumptions about gender. Among them are: that the figurines were made *by* men, that the figurines were made *for* men, that nakedness is necessarily associated with eroticism, and that depiction of breasts is primarily sexual.

Underlying the description of the female figurines as erotic or reproductive is a masculist construction of the world, in which females are assumed to exist primarily for the use of males, sexually or reproductively. The scholarly literature is replete with explicit examples of this worldview, which the textbooks reflect.

A few quotations from the scholarly literature will demonstrate that males are usually assumed to be the sculptors of the figurines. The italics are mine throughout. "How did the artist's vision, which reflected the ideal of *his* time, see her? For as with man, we can never know what she really looked like . . . so we have to make do with the version her companion, man, had of her" (Berenguer 1973:48). The possibility that it was *her* version appears not to have crossed Berenguer's mind. Although this mindset focuses on males exclusively, it is not confined to males only, as shown from this quote from a woman, "He [the artist] desired only to show the female erotically and as the source of all abundance—in her he portrayed not woman but fertility" (Hawkes 1964:27). Referring to the not uncommon find of broken-off legs, Campbell (1982:410) suggests that "they may have cracked off in the baking, or when the ancient ceramicist tossed aside a work that failed to please *him*." (Most of the figurines of course are carved.) In case there is any doubt about the use of the specific rather than the generic use of the term "man", Leroi-Gourhan (1967:90) makes it crystal clear that "prehistoric man" doesn't include females, speaking of "the first figurines representing prehistoric man—or at least *his wife*."

If the figurines are assumed to have been made by men, then it follows that they were created for male purposes. Even when they were first discovered, the Abbe Breuil (1954, cited in Ucko and Rosenfeld 1973:119) said they were for "pleasure to Paleolithic man during his meals" (do we have a euphemism here?). Berenguer (1973:52) focuses on reproductivity: "we may deduce man's obsessive need for women who would bear *him* lots of children to offset the high mortality rate caused by the harsh living conditions." Von Koenigswald (1972) worried about other possessions: "It certainly is an old problem: how could man protect *his* property, mark a place as 'his home', 'his living site' so that others would recognize and respect it, especially in a period where there were no houses, just *abris* and caves?" He concludes that men made the "grotesque" figurines to guard their property, and scare off intruders! Delporte (1979:308) muses more philosophically, "for [paleolithic men] as for us . . . the mother who gives and transmits life is also the woman who gives and shares pleasure: could the Paleolithic have been insensitive to this novel duality?" [my translation]. Could the present be insensitive to the fact that there were paleolithic women as well as men? Are women to be denied their own sensitivity, or indeed their own existence as sentient beings?

The fact that the figurines were unclothed, or scantily clothed, for several wear belts and other decorations (a fact that is noted only by Clark [1977:105] among our textbook sample), surely has been essential to the interpretation of eroticism, in spite of the fact that there are many other possible reasons for the depiction of nudity. For example, people may have been usually unclothed inside the cave or hut, so that nakedness was not a special condition. The figurines could have been teaching devices for girls' puberty rites, as Marshack (1972:283) has suggested.

Nakedness frequently has different connotations when men rather than women are the sculptor's subject. For example, a naked male torso from Harappa is shown under the heading "Figures of Authority," in *The First Cities*, a widely used book from the Time-Life series (Hamblin 1973:133). The text tells us:

> Although male figures rarely appear among sculptures dug up at Mohenjo Daro and Harappa, the few that do all seem to represent men of importance. In the three works reproduced here, there is a common theme, however varied the pieces themselves may be: regality or godliness.

As Conkey and Spector (1984:11) point out in another context, changing the rules of interpretation according to sex will not reveal anything about prehistoric gender roles. Rather it comforts us in supposing that things have always been the same.

In spite of being naked, however, it would seem that the fat figurines have little sex appeal to modern male scholars. This has called forth various explanations, ranging from assertions that they are stylized, to a suggestion that you cannot tell *what* might have turned on those prehistoric men (you can almost see the shrug and the wink), to a rejection of the erotic argument on the grounds that the figurines are simply too grotesque! In all of this discussion, passivity of women is assumed.

It is deserving of some comment that breasts are equated with eroticism in the textbooks, more by juxtaposition of words than by explicit statements. Sometimes, though, the equation is specified. There is one carving, referred to as the "rod with breasts," which evoked the following paean: "This statuette shows us that the artist has neglected all that did not interest *him*, stressing *his* sexual libido only where the breasts are concerned—a diluvial plastic pornography" (Absolon 1949). Surely anthropologists of all people know that exposed breasts are not at all uncommon in the warmer parts of the world, and cause little comment or excitement except for visiting tourists and perhaps a segment of the readership of *National Geographic*.

The "rod with breasts" is an interesting example of the extension of the underlying attitude toward women that is revealed in some generalizations about the figurines. Enigmatic carvings are declared to represent breasts, buttocks, or vulvae, reducing women to their "essentials." Especially the notion of the "vulvae" (some of which look rather like molar teeth), "has become an *idée fixe* and one of the most durable myths of prehistory" (Bahn 1986:99). The "rods" from Dolni Vestonice could be as easily perceived as stylized male genitalia, but if they were so described the eloquence would probably be in a different vein. It is hard to imagine exchanging the genders in the quote by Absolon above.

Alternative explanations, based on variability rather than generalizations, are not lacking in the scholarly literature. The figurines have been argued to represent priests or ancestors or clan-mothers, to show women as actors with a ritual function (Klima 1962:204, Abramova 1967:83, Hancar 1940). These possibilities are not even hinted at in the texts, with one sole exception (Campbell 1988:481).

ARCHEOLOGICAL MYTHOLOGY

What are the possible reasons for the selective reporting found in the textbooks? First, to be fair, is the summary nature of the texts. Little space is given to the figurines, and it is necessary to paint a broad picture with a few strokes. But the selection of this particular way of viewing the Upper Paleolithic figures as fat, as sexual, and as representing fertility can be linked to our own cultural stereotypes and assumptions about the nature of men, women, sexuality, and reproduction. I suggest that our own culture makes these generalizations seem so natural, so satisfying, that there is no reason to examine them. The "text" read into the figurines is ours.

Several archeologists have commented on the problems of reading our unconscious assumptions about the present into the past. "History and prehistory constitute bodies of knowledge used to legitimize social policies and to validate social trajectories" (Moore and Keene 1983:7). This tendency has been traced to the dominant paradigm in archeology: "Because of the logic of empiricist epistemology, theories rising on empiricist foundations potentially serve only to recreate in the past the dominant cultural ideologies of the present" (Saitta 1983:303). We must recognize "the importance of taking into account the conceptions we hold of our own society which inevitably mediate our understanding of the past" (Miller and Tilley 1984:2).

Recent research on gender roles in cultural anthropology proposes that "male and female, sex and reproduction, are cultural or symbolic constructs" (Ortner and Whitehead 1981:6). These constructs are often reflected in origin stories as "metaphors for sexual identity" (Sanday 1981:56), which Sanday calls "scripts." I am suggesting that culturally constructed gender roles, and our attitudes and beliefs about sex and reproduction, enter into the selectivity of reporting on the Upper Paleolithic figurines. The reading of the metaphors of the figurines derives from a masculist script.

I do not wish to impute either evil intentions or inferior scholarship to the authors of these textbooks. It is important to note the unconscious nature of the acceptance of cultural scripts. But that does not make them less pernicious. Reinforcing present cultural stereotypes by projecting them into the past allows whole generations of students to believe that our present gender constructs are eternal and unchanging. Especially those who deal in prehistory need to be alert to our cultural biases, and not imply that present gender roles are eternal verities.

Marvin Harris points out that "our ordinary state of mind is always a profoundly mystified consciousness. To emerge from myth and legend to mature consciousness we need to compare the full range of past and present cultures" (Harris 1974:5). The trick is to examine the past without the mystification.

I am not proposing that alternative explanations are necessarily better, only that the diversity of the figurines should be taken into account. Maybe women made some of the figurines. Maybe the figurines were used for women's purposes. Maybe it isn't relevant whether men find them sexy or not. If an explanation feels intuitively right, perhaps that is the best reason to re-examine it.

CHAPTER 2

EQUITY ISSUES FOR WOMEN IN ARCHEOLOGY: CONCLUSION

with Margaret Nelson

PROGRESS, SUCCESS, AND PROMOTION of women in archeology does not parallel that of men. Women have lower status than men, resulting in lower income and prestige. The studies reported here offer a coherent picture of this difference. Many argue that "times have changed." Women are growing in numbers, are successful in various ways, and do make significant contributions. Women are entering archeology as trainees, both graduate and undergraduate, in much higher proportion than a decade or two ago. Their numbers are nearly equivalent to the enrollment of men. This is true not only in general, but in specialized areas of archeology. These women and men are equally successful while in training, as measured by research performance, funding, and publication, among other dimensions, although they tend to drop out at a higher rate than men.

Times may have changed, but evidence for change is less clear when we examine the professional growth of women beyond their degrees. After graduate training, women proportionately hold fewer positions of leadership, publish fewer books, receive fewer grants, and receive less recognition for their work. The papers in this volume document these conditions, in some cases for the first time, for various subfields and professional tracks in archeology. This should disturb archeologists, female and male, because the design of our current system results in the loss of intellectual input from many fine professionals. Why?

Sarah M. Nelson, with Margaret Nelson (1994). In *Equity Issues for Women in Archeology*, edited by M. Nelson, S. Nelson, and A. Wylie, pp. 229–235. Archeological Paper No. 5, American Anthropological Association, Washington, DC. Republished in *Shamans, Queens, and Figurines: The Development of Gender Archaeology*, by Sarah Nelson, pp. 59–70 (Taylor & Francis, 2015).

Many women and men know some of the answers, but the papers in this volume offer a collection of studies and experiences that show the depth and breadth of the problem of gender bias and the need for network development for women. Archeological careers require fieldwork, publication, job placement and advancement. In all these areas, negative attitudes regarding women's capabilities and accomplishments hinder their career progress. It is also evident that networks play a key role in developing fieldwork opportunities, successful review and citation of publications, and obtaining jobs.

This conclusion offers an overview of the problems and some suggested solutions, along with an acknowledgement of missing voices. Finally, we leave you with some thoughts about the future of archeology, and the benefits of equity for women and other disadvantaged groups, as well as for the discipline as a whole.

Women still face a great many barriers to full participation. As much as we might wish for the issue to disappear, "gender is still an issue in archeology," to paraphrase the title on the first page of the *SAA Bulletin* in January, 1991, and while some gains have been made, equity is not a fact of life for most women archeologists.

Identified Problems

The chapters in this book [i.e., Nelson et al. 1994] describe problems for women in archeology along a number of specific dimensions: graduate education (Kelley and Hill), selecting a specialty (Gero, Chester, Rothschild and Wall) or subspecialty (Gifford-Gonzales), obtaining a job (Nelson and Crooks), getting tenure and promotions (Kramer and Stark, Gifford-Gonzales), salary (Wildesen, Ford and Hundt, Morris, Chester et al.), work environments (Goulding and Buckley), access to grants (Yellen), and publications (Bradley and Dahl), to name a few of the most obvious categories. Several chapters have addressed climate issues (Parezo and Bender, Wylie, Reyman, Smith and du Cros, Cane et al.), demonstrating that in some cases women have been marginalized, our voices not heard, our work considered trivial. But those are not the only messages in these chapters, nor are they necessarily the major ones.

These analyses show that the causes for the differentials between women and men are societal, not individual (although women have been taught to blame ourselves when things go wrong). It is the organization of archeology, including the institutional setting in which it is practiced (Gero, Morris, Ford and Hundt, Spencer-Wood, Hendon, Beaudry; Chester, Rothschild and Wall), and societal perceptions of women's abilities and appropriate roles (Parezo and Bender; Cane, Gilchrist and O'Sullivan) that are responsible for the dismaying experiences of women archeologists documented in these pages.

Even the constraints imposed by these social conditions, important as they are, are not the main finding of this group of papers, however. The fact that women have named the problems and have begun to find solutions, both individual and societal, is the most important message in these chapters, and it is a message common to most chapters. It is heartening that so many strategies for constructive change are suggested to improve women's status in archeology, that after each analysis is completed, specific remedies are generated to alleviate specific problems. We have come a long way from the days when many male archeologists would not take women into the field, when some women students were treated merely as toys for male faculty, when women were ineligible for tenure-track positions in archeology at "elite" institutions. But inequities remain, both individual and societal, and old behaviors are difficult to eradicate.

Successes have been engineered by women themselves, and by supportive men (Levine, Reyman, Anon.). Many creative solutions have been found by individual women in order to have productive careers in archeology. Some have found new niches or have exploited ones that were underrepresented, some have joined their interest in archeology with other disciplines, and women's networking has been important for many (M. Nelson). The support of other women and men, and the analysis of problems demonstrating that this is a societal issue, not a personal one (Kramer and Stark, Wildesen), have been important. Yellen notes that more women than men choose Old World subjects, possibly a specific example of what Levine sees as a strategy of looking for unfilled niches instead of competing for space in overcrowded areas.

For data on the status of women in archeology, Wildesen provided an important baseline in 1980, and Kramer and Stark collected and published a wider survey in 1988. These early surveys make it possible to chart a certain amount of progress. To examine the problems women face, it is useful to consider the trajectory of women's professional lives in archeology.

Inequities for women archeologists begin in graduate school, partly reflected in the fact that more women than men withdraw from their graduate programs (Kelley and Hill, Kramer and Stark). Graduate school barriers may account for the finding that, as recently as 1980, obtaining the PhD was the most important achievement for a sample of women in archeology (Wildesen). Goulding and Buckley report that many women perceive their graduate experience negatively, and that women's career aspirations differ from men's.

Women may be downscaling their hopes to match societal reality. On the brighter side, Yellen states that women have "complete equity" in receiving doctoral dissertation awards from NSF.

More women than men proportionately disappear from the job pool after they complete their degrees. Although other employment is possible, it is particularly telling that Kramer and Stark found a substantial gap between the number of women receiving PhDs and those employed in departments in the *Guide*. Whittlesey shows that women are more likely to make non-academic career "choices" than men, but such choices may be due to lowered chances at academic or other archeological careers as much as selection in favor of spouse and children, although family issues figure into the picture as well. Women's slower progress through academic ranks is also documented (Gifford-Gonzalez).

The problems are not confined to the US and Canada (Kelley and Hill) or even the English-speaking world (Cane, Gilchrist, O'Sullivan, Beck, Hope, Smith and du Cros, Morris). Papers from Norway (Engelstad et al.), Spain (Diaz-Andreu and Gallego), and Argentina (Bellelli et al.) demonstrate that similar patterns occur elsewhere, even in different social and jurisdictional contexts. Differences will be noted below, but in general these chapters reveal inequities that are common to women in archeology throughout their careers and wherever we do our archeology, including in various institutional contexts.

In spite of the folklore that insists that women are getting all the jobs, the statistics show otherwise (Hendon, O'Sullivan). While aggregate statistics in the US for academic hiring show that women now are hired in a slightly higher percentage of entry level positions relative to their presence in the relevant candidate pools (Wylie), this advantage does not carry over into more senior (and permanent) ranks, and is generally not true of higher status schools, especially those that do most of the graduate training. It is not clear whether this slight edge in entry level positions holds for archeology, but in each data set and subset, over and over again it is clear that the more highly sought-after jobs (tenure-track positions in large research universities) are disproportionately going to men, whether we look at women in subdisciplines such as zooarcheology (Gifford-Gonzalez) or in areas as dissimilar as Mesoamerica, where many work (Ford and Hundt), and Asia and the Pacific, populated by few archeologists (S. Nelson).

Within academic settings, women still progress through the ranks more slowly than do men, and few women hold the highest academic ranks. Women are conspicuously rare in the highest ranked departments of anthropology. It is not merely snob value that makes the research universities more desirable. As Yellen makes clear, research universities are the path to better funding, in addition to which they control much of the graduate training of the future generations of archeologists. Grant funding at a national level is the *sine qua non* for mounting large projects. This feeds into the preference for excavation over analysis so well discussed by Gero, and noted also by Morris. If grants are more available for excavation, and the ability of one's institution to support a large expedition and its analysis is a key to receiving grants, it is no wonder that women do less well at getting grants—particularly "senior" women, for the highly ranked departments rarely hired women at the time "senior" women began their professional careers. The creativity of this older cohort in designing projects that overcome the deficiencies of their places of work has not been recognized with funding. Few women "develop active careers in archeological research," because they have not held jobs that give them a reasonable shot at large grants.

The connection between large projects and book publication, an area where women do less well than men, is made by Bradley and Dahl. They demonstrate that women are behind men in number of publications and in type of publications. Chester et al. show that women in their data set also submit fewer papers for publication. For England, O'Sullivan finds that women are more likely to publish in journals of less distinction, probably for a whole spectrum of reasons. Women's publications are also less likely to be cited, and women cite each other more than men cite women (Beaudry). This reinforces the patterns observed by Beaudry; women are less acknowledged in print by those who publish the most and publish in more mainstream contexts.

Success in publication and acquisition of research grants is key to promotion. Various studies report that women receive fewer and smaller research grants and have fewer publications, especially books. This pattern can be understood in light of the bias against women as leaders of field projects and the lesser value placed on laboratory or non-field research. Women have not received the same opportunities for leadership training in fieldwork as have men. This has resulted in fewer women leading field projects. Receiving grants for fieldwork depends on establishing a track record. A cycle of failure is thus created from the beginning of professional training. Likewise, book publication often is the product of years of fieldwork. If the leaders of most projects are men, they will be the authors of books more often than will women. Again, the pattern begins in graduate training.

Fewer women lead field projects not only because graduate programs have historically tracked women into laboratory work, but because social conventions discourage such roles for women, especially those with male partners and children. In our society, it is men who "leave home and go to work." Women do not traditionally leave their male partners and children for weeks at a time to "go to work," which for archeologists includes going to the field. While we cannot change society as quickly as we might like, increased access to female role models can allow women to gain insight into the ways in which social concerns can be addressed.

Equity in rank and income is also lacking in virtually all cases in academe (Morris, Wildesen). Women's levels of compensation and recognition are less than those of men, even when the time since obtaining the PhD is held constant. Women often are second-class citizens in academic and other contexts. Small wonder, then, that women who have turned to government jobs prefer them, having actively sought this as a more supportive environment (Wildesen). Yet, comparing the income of men and women in non-academic work places, the studies in this volume report lower income for women in comparable positions to men.

Women dominate the non-academic workforce, but not as leaders. Many of these women are married to other archeologists and have not completed their graduate training to the doctorate. Women who marry have found considerable prejudice develop toward their work. They report attitude shifts of their peers and advisors toward a belief that they are not serious about a career in archeology. This bias is considerably amplified if a woman has children. Few men report the same attitudes applied to them. Bradley and Dahl report that marriage and children do not predict rank, but they examine only those women with PhDs in academic institutions. We believe that this climate in archeology causes many women to leave their training programs and contributes to the high proportion of women without PhDs in the non-academic workforce. Thus, women are underrepresented in the higher ranks.

Family responsibilities still "belong" primarily to women, as the chapter by Ford and Hundt indicates. In Britain, the practice of archeology favors single researchers of both sexes, if they are without family responsibilities (Morris). Whittlesey found that childless archeologists had more success in their careers. As is suggested by the survey of Asian/Pacific archeologists, distance from the field exacerbates this problem, no doubt as much from the cost of taking children far from home as the difficulties of leaving them behind. It is easier not to have any.

Wildesen notes that even marital status affects employment opportunities. Dual career couples have special problems (Nelson and Crooks). Lack of mobility is most frequently framed as the woman's problem, since more men than women of dual career couples have the primary job. Sometimes couples separate to pursue their career goals; sometimes women change their career goals to be more compatible with family responsibilities. It is interesting that few archeologists find these compromises acceptable. The finding that dual career couples have slower career development is an important one, because it sheds light on the societal nature of the problem, beyond even gender.

Parezo and Bender, Wylie, Cane et al. and several others address chilly climate issues directly, and a great many others allude to them. O'Sullivan in Britain also targets certain types of male actions which create in-groups and out-groups, for example at archeology meetings, where the chair may make it clear (by calling his buddies by name, among other behaviors) who are "in" and who are "out." In many situations women are invisible, their successes and indeed their words attributed to others, and their work evaluated by different standards than those applied to men. There is even overt hostility (Smith and du Cros, Anon., Reyman, Goulding and Buckley), and women (and men who support them) may be excluded from information networks and maligned when they challenge the inequities they encounter. Some of the most poignant examples of chilly climate behavior are catalogued under the heading of "advice" by Anonymous. It is no wonder that many women prefer jobs where they can function independently!

It is also interesting to note that while women frequently report chilly climate behaviors, men often do not perceive them as problematic (S. Nelson). Differing perceptions may result from the fact that women are the target of incidents, and thus would be more likely to pick up on subtle exclusions and put-downs. Although many men are well intentioned, they may feel defensive because they do not wish to see themselves as part of a problem they deplore. We all need our consciousness raised on these issues.

NATIONAL COMPARISONS

Reports from other countries are mixed. Some of our sister workers abroad have worse problems, others are better treated, but problems everywhere need solutions. In Britain, only three of every 100 academics is a woman (Gilchrist), in a place where 65 years ago Virginia Woolf (1992 [1929]) spurned the academic establishment and recommended instead a room of one's own and an independent income. This may be fine advice for those with literary ambitions, especially if you and your husband own a well-established publishing business (and of course the advice was delivered ironically), but it is not much help for most women who aspire to a career in archeology. The situation in Argentina is one where women are well represented in the archeological community, but few occupy decision making positions that affect the careers of all archeologists (Bellelli et al.). Spain has been slow to accept women in archeology, but they are emerging through individual efforts, although there is still some room for progress (Diaz-Andreu and Gallego). The historical dimension available in the North American studies shows that change in many areas can and does occur. All these studies indicate that, in spite of effective barriers, and against the odds, many women have made substantial contributions to archeology. The challenge now is to create institutions and environments which insure that the discipline does not continue to squander this resource, losing the commitment and contributions of this growing contingent of practitioners.

MOVING ON

Solutions for progress toward equity can be offered at both the individual and societal levels. At the most individual level a number of contributors consider ways of addressing problems that arise when women internalize the valuations and stereotypes that systematically demean women and underpin the chilly climate. Some women come to lack confidence, are (sometimes quite realistically) unwilling to reach for the stars, or are disinclined to plan for lifelong careers (Goulding and Buckley). Some solutions to inequity will require ways to boost women's self-esteem, and reinforce their commitment to long-term involvement in archeology. Several strategies have been attempted, and are described by various contributors to this collection. They include career-planning sessions and provisions for mentoring within the institutions where women are employed and trained, and, crucially, in the archeological societies and associations that constitute their professional communities (Spencer-Wood).

To be effective, strategies for change must be responsive to the particular situations in which women find themselves; there are no formulas or recipes for success. Many senior women choose to fight for all women in their universities, not merely for themselves (one of the respondents to Wildesen's questionnaire said she was "tired of being on the front lines, both as an archeologist and as a woman"), while others adopt a strategy of lying low and accepting invisibility as preferable to hostility, and still other women imitate men as closely as possible.

There is no second-guessing the viability of any of these strategies for opening doors to women in specific contexts. Women who are now students or early in their careers have different objectives. Performance assessments are critical to women's advancement. Tenure committees are not as gender neutral as we would wish, but probably fewer can now succeed in imposing a harsher standard on women, if only because several women are likely to be on the committee. Assessing the value and credibility of scholarship (Boyer 1990) in ways that acknowledge different approaches favor the styles to which many women have been socialized, rather than those which assume a single hierarchical standard. Parallel issues occur in non-academic contexts where qualifications for hiring, job-assignment, promotion, and so forth will likewise count against women if they are rigidly (even unintentionally) defined by gendered values or otherwise preclude the recognition that significant contributions may be made in many different ways.

Insufficient networks are a key element limiting career progress for women. Many women have smaller, weaker networks than do men in archeology. There are several reasons. As the studies in this volume indicate, women are rare in tenured faculty positions and in positions of leadership within businesses and government agencies. It is not true that the men who dominate these leadership positions only promote their male students, or that women who might hold these positions would only promote their female students. However, combining the pattern of prejudice against women's abilities to perform with this gendered pattern of leadership has restricted opportunities for women to develop networks of leadership. Women have traditionally been rare on boards and committees within universities, publication organizations, and professional organizations. Any woman who has tenure will attest to the onslaught of requests for her participation on university committees, which have few if any other females as members. Such committees are the breeding ground of networks.

Also important is the development of smaller local networks capable of providing support for women in the full range of contexts in which they work as archeologists. Such networks have been recommended by many of those active on women's issues in archeology, and are discussed here (M. Nelson, Wylie). Certainly those of us who toil in regions without close cohorts find ourselves very dependent on our far-flung correspondents. E-mail is a blessing, for those with access to it. We may live in a global village, but more women need to participate in it. The much-touted information superhighway may indeed contribute to lessening the isolation that many women feel in their places of work, but we need to develop creative ways of exploiting the potential of these technologies and make them more widely available to those most likely to be excluded from professional networks.

Another component to this strategy of building or expanding networks of support, breaking isolation, and challenging divisive and exclusionary stereotypes, may be to more actively engage men in some of the networks and community activities designed to "warm" the workplace environment and to change institutional policies or practices that systematically disadvantage women. Indeed, it is possible to make an effective argument that warming the chilly climate is beneficial to men and women. Not all men fit comfortably into the rigid mold ordained by research universities, and if the culture of archeology could recognize diverse kinds of contributions to our common endeavor it would benefit us all. Likewise, many men detest the effects of gender bias on their female colleagues and students.

Perhaps most important, in considering these strategies, is the recognition that the difficulties women face, often individually and in isolation, are very often not unique or strictly "individual". However idiosyncratic and personal they become, systematic patterns emerge along gender lines which require collective response. Changing individual attitudes and seeking local solutions is crucial, but collective responses designed to make institutional and structural change is necessary to avoid regenerating the problems of gender bias despite growing awareness of them. This point was brought home in particularly powerful terms in the discussion that followed the Equity Workshop at the 1992 AAA meetings where a number of women raised issues to do with sexual harassment; they described a system of practices that served not only to make them vulnerable to harassment, but to ensure that they would not take action against it (e.g., threats of retaliation; fears of losing their jobs or opportunities for further training). Individually focused solutions, such as strategies for building stronger self-esteem, will only be effective in a context where collective action ensures that women do have recourse against such forms of harassment and intimidation.

It is a component of this insight that the gender bias issues women face cannot be disentangled from those that they, and many men, face as visible and ethnic or religious minorities, as gays and lesbians, as people with disabilities, or along other lines of differentiation defined by class, race, sexual orientation, and community affiliation. For the most part we have not looked at the ways in which these various "differences" are mutually constitutive; they deserve investigation and attention not only as they shape women's experiences and opportunities in archeology but also in their own right.

This volume provides information on gendered difference in archeological careers. Many conditions of inequity remain in training and the workplace that are of concern to the archeological community. Changes have occurred over the past decade toward more equitable conditions in some areas, but the reality of the current composition and conditions of archeology as a profession leave women under-represented, under-salaried, and their work undervalued in academia and in non-academic settings.

There is general agreement that graduate training contributes to many of the professional obstacles that women face. Similarly, the lack of women in leadership positions within universities, businesses, agencies, and professional organizations creates a climate of limited consideration of gender equity issues and limited role models for women facing the traditional social environment unaccustomed to women as fieldworkers and leaders.

Reaching critical mass in these institutions is important for women, but what we learn from the case studies, analyses of the problems, and suggestions for change, is that critical mass is not a solution by itself. Occupying positions with tenure (or otherwise permanent/long-term employment) and the upper ranks of the administration or management structure is crucial in effecting change in the institutions which employ, fund, and train archeologists (Engelstad et al.). Women are earning their advanced degrees at the same age as men (Chester et al.), but the ranks of senior women are thin (M. Nelson). This has a negative effect on the mentoring of younger women. It is somewhat surprising to discover that many women students are "unaware of the gendered politics of their profession" (M. Nelson).

It is critical to have women in decision-making positions (Bellelli et al.). In fact, these strategies work synergistically, since a lone woman may be powerless to sway a committee, or rightly fearful of trying to, while women together on a committee can support equity concerns of each other; even more, they may hope to be supported by a woman manager or administrator, and women in senior positions may be able to count on support for equity goals from below. The tokenism that was characteristic of 20 years ago is slowly giving way to more gender mixed departments or work units where the climate is likely to be far less chilly, even with the "one-in-ten" (Anon.) hostile male who makes life difficult for everyone.

On the other hand, Chester et al. show that inequity is not merely a pipeline issue. We cannot just wait until there are "enough" women professors and administrators. Critical mass is not a solution by itself, especially if the system of training, hiring, compensation and promotion rigidly enforces values which are inimical to the changes in career structure and diversity of styles in research and management associated with women. As numbers increase, women in these institutions may face entrenched structural obstacles to change.

LAST THOUGHTS

In light of the work that has gone into these chapters, it is clear that we need to work simultaneously on many fronts:

- encourage women to pursue archeology as a career.
- increase the number and percentage of women in managerial and administrative roles.
- encourage women entering areas of research from which they have been excluded and revalue those areas in which they have been active and visible.
- encourage women to become more visible, through publication and original research.
- work to change the professional cultures of archeology so that we all break the grip of dysfunctional stereotypes, learn to appreciate the variation in women's talents and abilities and recognize in these a range of attributes which are valuable for archeology, including field archeology.
- eliminate institutional barriers to hiring dual career couples.
- raise concerns regarding gender and other biases in all contexts of work.
- create opportunities for gender bias concerns to be discussed.
- improve access for those in training to female role models.

These changes will be beneficial to everyone who practices archeology, and to our clients, associates, and colleagues. Improving the position of women in archeology is not a zero-sum game; giving women their due improves working conditions for everyone.

PART IV

QUEENS: WOMEN WIELDING POWER

AFTER MY WORK ON THE UPPER PALEOLITHIC figurines came to a dead end, I looked for inspiration to the approaches of cultural anthropologists, and I thought again about applying their approaches to the past. Before "gender in archaeology" became a common phrase, I relied on writings from feminist science studies, feminist history, feminist artists—in fact, anybody with a flashlight to shine into this vast darkness.

Writing as a feminist became an important topic for me. Of course, there was Virginia Woolf, but then what? I had a room of my own and a salary, but I seemed to be writing only for myself. Trying to recover those times from my memory, I recently scanned my bookshelves. Some of the books have heavy underlining—they must have served as important guideposts, even if I can't recall their precise influence.

While I struggled with trying to do archaeology as a feminist, I read about the ways feminist ethnographers had chosen to write. From this reading I learned that the inability to publish my figurine research was not about my research, not about my writing. It was a political game. Ruth Behar, in *Women Writing Culture* (1995), discusses the politics of publication. Those who are published are "victors in struggles for past and present recognition and the attribution of significance" (Behar's quote from Joan Vincent). My work was insignificant because it was about females, as well as upsetting to the received wisdom about the Paleolithic. Besides, my place of employment made me insignificant, a mid-size university far from the centers of action on either coast. As I thought about this, I didn't know whether to be less discouraged or more. But I tend to be an optimist, and my strategy is always to try, try again.

While new ethnographies based on the study of women in the field had been shaking up cultural anthropology, other studies on women in the present were rewriting anthropology in another way—especially concerning issues of

Shamans, Queens, and Figurines: The Development of Gender Archaeology, by Sarah Nelson, 71–78.

women's health, from the aborting of female babies through genital mutilation, to maternal death, among many other reported topics.

Barbara Miller, whom I met at a convention of the Association for Asian Studies, was doing leading-edge work in this arena, studying the health of girls in India. A poignant photo shows a mother in India waiting in a clinic with twins on her lap, a boy and a girl. The boy is fat and healthy, the girl undernourished. The girl is crying, but the mother is paying attention to the boy. The point is that the plight of many girl babies is neglect.

What could archaeology contribute to this level of cultural questioning? I wondered. How could discussing what women's lives were like in the past, whether their lot was better or worse than many women in the present, help those women who were currently leading lives that were unequal at best, if not damaging to their very existence and the lives of their daughters?

Barbara Miller produced a newsletter, *Gender in Asian Anthropology*, which I read avidly. I contributed a review of Irene Silverblatt's (1987) *Moon, Sun and Witches*, a book that provided a model for approaching women of power, especially in a society known from both archaeology and documents, such as the Silla polity. This book showed that understanding women in the past was important, not the least because inaccurate assumptions about women in the past lead to distortions about women and their abilities in the present. It inspired me to tackle the Silla Kingdom of early Korea.

Barbara invited me to contribute a paper to a session of the American Anthropological Association in 1985, when gender was still a relatively new topic at meetings, even in cultural anthropology. Although some anthropologists were still uncertain about gender as a viable topic, the session was successful.

The topic was further developed at a contentious Wenner-Gren conference in Mijas, Spain, in 1987 (Silverman 2002:15–23). I was invited to provide an archaeological perspective, along with Mark Cohen. Adrienne Zilman described women in human evolution, and Patricia Wright told us inspirational tales about primates in Madagascar where the male takes charge of an infant shortly after its birth. Elinor Ochs discussed sociolinguistics. The other ten conference participants were cultural anthropologists. The Wenner-Gren Foundation emphasized four-field anthropology, but we five in other subdisciplines were not central to the discussions. I felt like the lightweight of the gathering, and indeed I had much to learn from most of the other participants.

It would seem like name-dropping to mention all the famous anthropologists who were present, but a conversation I had with Marvin Harris about the Upper Paleolithic figurines is relevant. He understood my point and took the findings of my research more seriously than archaeologists had. Months later, wanting to cite that work in the latest edition of his textbook, he called to ask me for the citation. When I told him nobody would publish it, he cited the unpublished paper in a footnote, along with an explanation of my hypothesis. Some DU students noticed the footnote and were impressed, but I would have been more pleased if the whole research project could have found a receptive journal.

The Wenner-Gren meeting was contentious in part because of the spectrum of points of view that were expressed. The more activist faction was composed of younger women who wanted more action and, perhaps, less theory. I had so much to learn that I didn't belong in either faction, but I listened and found the discussions and disagreements fascinating. Elizabeth Colson, in her summation of the days of discussion, really captured this moment in time when researchers of gender in anthropology were trying to shake off an androcentric past and find new ways to think, to research, and to explore.

THE QUEEN IN TOMB 98, KYONGJU, KOREA

The paper I presented in Mijas was thoroughly rewritten as a result of the Mijas discussions, but it began with an archaeological site. Tomb 98 is the largest burial mound in Kyongju, Korea. It is a double mound. Double mounds are always interpreted in Korea as graves of a married couple. The two mounds were constructed at different times, with a small amount of overlap. The south mound was excavated first, but to the disappointment of the Korean archaeologists, the expected gold crown and belt, interpreted as the regalia of royalty, were absent. The male in the south mound had crowns of bronze rather than gold, but the amount of weaponry was impressive.

When the north mound was excavated, the anticipated gold crown and belt were not only present but stunning, the most elaborate gold crown ever found in Korea (Figure 4). It was definitely a woman's tomb. An inscription scratched on the belt reads, "belt for milady." Almost ten pounds of gold jewelry accompanied her. It was clear that the queen was the ruler, but who was she?

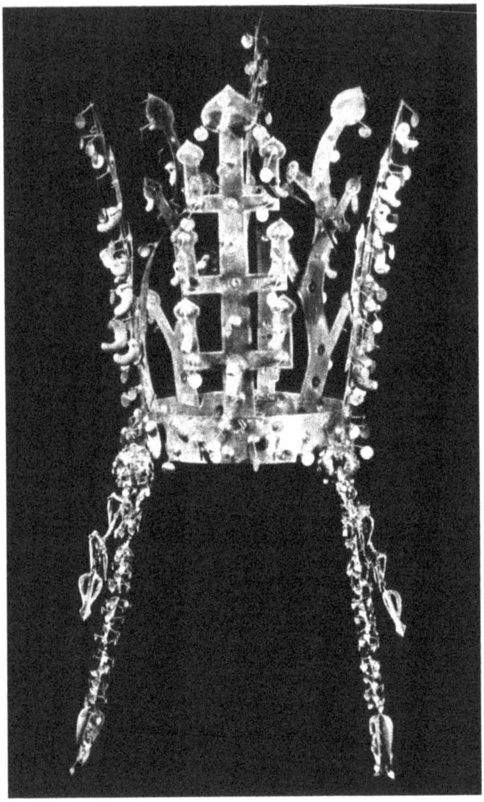

FIGURE 4. The Queen's Crown from Tomb 98

As I read the ancient Korean histories to learn who this couple might have been, I discovered to my surprise that this ruling queen was not listed among the kings, although three later queens do appear in the king list. Archaeology proclaims this woman to have been the monarch, but the histories have passed over her reign. I began to dig into the question of why she was not included in the list of Silla kings.

My contribution to the eventual book, *Sex and Gender Hierarchies* (Miller 1991), concerned this tomb. Several papers by cultural anthropologists had suggested that the origin of the state was the downfall of all women. The implications of this double mound suggested otherwise. I included virtually every scrap of information I could find about Silla and leadership, but in particular I addressed what was then the hot topic of whether women's status really was universally lowered with the origin of the state. Silla appeared to be a contrary case, and it seemed worthwhile to challenge the Marxist (or Engels-ist?) version of prehistory. Even though this kind of universalist question has been abandoned for more nuanced perspectives, my chapter *in Sex and Gender Hierarchies* is included here (Chapter 3) as my most complete discussion of the Silla tomb and what could be deduced from the tomb about the social structure of the Silla "kingdom."

"The Statuses of Women in Ko-Shilla" began as a paper for a biennial meeting of the Association for Korean Studies in Europe, at Dourdan, France, in 1990. I was still using Tomb 98 to discuss the Silla polity. Since none of the Koreanists present were archaeologists, I organized my talk differently, delving into the literature on the kinship system of the royalty who were named in the king lists—often including names of the king's parents and the queen's parents. This circumstance allowed me to create a partial kinship chart of the early royals.

Several of the Koreanists present encouraged me to offer the paper to *Korea Journal,* an English-language journal published by UNESCO. My talk was especially relevant to Martina Deuchler, who was finishing her award-winning book, *Confucian Transformations of Korea.* Martina had discovered that relative gender equality, such as I reported in Silla, continued in Korean history, with traces of gender equality even as late as 1392, at the beginning of the Chosun dynasty, when the influence of Confucianism began to swamp gender equity. For the first time, an audience understood the point of my work on the Silla queens.

I continued to probe the social system of Silla and found more evidence that rank was more important than gender for the selection of rulers. I was able to tease out the kinship system of the ruling elite of Silla, the Song'gol, or Holy Bone, complete with an anthropological kinship chart of the named rulers, showing that queens' daughters married kings, rather than kings' sons becoming kings, in the early days of Silla.

At every possible opportunity, I found an audience and discussed the gender implications of Tomb 98. I was not satisfied that I had explored all the gendered possibilities of this archaeological discovery. When I was invited to give a talk at Berkeley, Evelyn McCune, whose work on the art of early Korea had been groundbreaking (McCune 1962), came to hear my talk. I was delighted to meet her. I had heard that she had written a paper on the queens of Silla, but I couldn't convince her to send me a copy of that much earlier paper. If she had more to say about the queens, she didn't share it with me, to my regret.

I was pleased to meet David Keightley, historian of early China and a major authority on the Shang oracle bones. I had already read some of David's work and later would rely on it heavily for much of my third novel, which centers on Lady Hao of Shang (see Part VIII).

It felt like a big deal to lecture at Berkeley, all the way from Denver. My sister came with her daughter Eve, a student at Berkeley, for support and curiosity. Eleanor and Eve remember the questions after my talk as hostile, but I explained to them it was just the academic way to question a speaker. To me, the questions seemed more puzzled than hostile—apparently I didn't make it clear why would it matter if later historians had suppressed a ruling queen. Most of this audience wasn't yet used to gendered questions. I had a little time to chat with Meg Conkey, before meeting Linda Donley-Reid. Linda had been one of Ian Hodder's students at Cambridge, but she and I knew each other through our allergist husbands. Linda's marriage was a recent, second marriage for both of them, and Linda wanted to quiz me about how to juggle archaeology and a household.

I tried to make the most of my travels, since I felt isolated in Denver from the East Asian archaeology scene. On that California trip, I also lectured at Stanford, arranged by Lothar von Falkenhausen, where my small audience again seemed to be a bit mystified that I would think an overlooked queen of the Silla Kingdom was an important topic. Perhaps the all-male audience thought it was obvious that a queen would be overlooked in the histories, although they were perfectly polite.

All that bumping around was good for my career. It was important to know the players in Chinese archaeology as well as Korean archaeology. I met many of the gender crowd at conferences. Even though I was not altogether over my shyness, I pushed myself to get to know as many of the interesting people in the field as I could.

Many traits made it clear that the culture of Silla had much in common with cultures of the steppes. There is increasing evidence that women in the Central Asian cultures were equal and sometimes leaders. Could I argue that the gender equality of Silla was part of their heritage from Manchuria or the Xiong Nu?

There are two prongs to my argument. The first is to show that burials of Silla elites contain many indications of an ancient northern culture. Reverence for white horses is shown by paintings on mudguards in Silla royal tombs, for example. Actual materials, such as birch bark, suggest a northeastern connection. Echoes of reindeer, inappropriate in southern Korea, from golden antlers on crowns to the prohibition against anyone but the highest rank wearing boots of reindeer leather, suggest northern roots as well.

The other prong is made possible by a document describing Silla's sumptuary laws. Among other things, they show that horseback riding was not a privilege limited to the elite; rather, everyone in the society rode horses. Ranks were restricted only in the number of horses they could keep and the costliness of the accouterments, such as saddle, reins, and stirrups, but all, both men and women, were allowed to own horses. Laws were specified by rank and gender, but rank was clearly more important than gender. Gathering this material together, it became evident that women and men were equal not merely in the highest rank, but throughout Silla society, within any rank.

I was delighted when Kathy Linduff and Karen Rubinson edited a book about gender in the steppes of Central Asia (*Are All Warriors Male? Gender Roles on the Ancient Eurasian Steppe,* 2008). It was almost the last in the Gender in Archaeology series I edited for AltaMira Press, and it addressed a burning problem in steppe archaeology: are all warriors male? My paper, "Horses and Gender in Korea," showed that all genders and ranks rode horses in the Silla Kingdom, restricted by rank only in the trappings and number of horses they could own (Nelson 2008b).

By the 1990s, most scholars engaged in researching the archaeology of gender had long since realized that to study "the status of women" in any culture, as if status was static and all women were the same, was not a useful way to understand gender in the past. Women are not interchangeable in any culture. No overarching women's status could contribute to discussions of the origin of the state, or indeed any topic. Variables of class, ethnicity, and age, for example, entered importantly into the analysis of gender.

In this light, I began to wonder what characteristics of the queen in Tomb 98 might have been important to her selection as the ruler. Her crown implied not only connections with the north but suggested that she was a shaman. Shaman crowns in the steppes are often circlets with antler uprights.

Furthermore, the curved bead (*gokok*) implied sacredness or high rank. These beads had been found at the center of necklaces in the largest dolmens in the Bronze Age and, in that context, are interpreted as designating leaders.

I organized a session on archaeological queens for the Society for American Archaeology in 1997, in which a variety of queens, from Vikings to Aztecs, were discussed. Joan Gero encouraged me to arrange this session, and it was fun to find archaeologists from around the world who could discuss queens. I had met Elisabeth Arwill-Nordbladh of Sweden in Lisbon at the World Archaeological Congress (WAC 3), and recently shared the stage with her again at Chicago TAG (Theoretical Archaeology Group). Kathy Linduff's paper on Chinese queens is one I have often quoted since, and have found useful in writing my latest novel.

The variety of queens in these papers—not just the geographical distribution, but the size of the polities and the circumstances of the queenly rule in archaeological cultures—shows that there is no universal requirement that only males are eligible to rule. Women are quite capable of leading state-level societies.

When I was invited to offer a paper about power at a symposium at Southern Illinois University, I thought again about female power. It was a stimulating conference, with several feminist views on power. "Performing Power in Early China" is included as Chapter 4.

Chapter 3

The Statuses of Women in Ko-Shilla: Evidence from Archaeology and Historic Documents

It is generally agreed that in the Kingdom of Old Shilla[1] gender relations were less hierarchical than in later Confucian-influenced regimes in Korea (Kim C.S., 1977; Kim Y.-C., ed., 1977; Grayson, 1976). On the basis of a combination of archaeological and historic evidence, I believe that it is possible to go further, and to argue that women and men in Ko-Shilla (Old Shilla) enjoyed social equality. The evidence shows that women were not confined to the house, boys were not favored over girls, and a woman could achieve anything, including the rulership, as long as her aspirations were permissible within her social class. Although the historic documents, written long after the events recounted, describe a single ruler, usually male, it is consistent with the archaeological and ethnographic evidence to posit that in the early years Shilla may have been ruled by a married pair, with a woman of the *sŏnggol* (holy bone) as the ceremonial and secular ruler, while her husband (also *sŏnggol*) served as the war leader in a pattern similar to the war chiefs and peace chiefs of the Cherokees.

The evidence leading to this hypothesis is derived from several sources. First it is necessary to consider the archaeology of the Shilla period at its most basic level—the discoveries and the underlying assumptions used to evaluate the data from the excavations. A number of assumptions are built into the common interpretations of Shilla burials, of which the most important for this

[1]Korean names are transliterated into English according to the system used in South Korea at the time of publication.

Sarah M. Nelson (1991b). The Statuses of Women in Ko-Shilla: Evidence from Archaeology and Historic Documents. *Korea Journal* 31(2):101–107. Republished in *Shamans, Queens, and Figurines: The Development of Gender Archaeology*, by Sarah Nelson, pp. 79–86 (Taylor & Francis, 2015).

paper are: 1) that gold crown and gold belts indicate rulers, 2) that preferentially rulers were men, and 3) that double mounds contained the graves of a husband and wife, separately interred.

In the vicinity of Kyŏngju, several large impressive crowns made of sheet gold and covered with *kogok* (comma-shaped jade) and gold dangles have been excavated from Shilla tumuli. These pure gold crowns, along with golden belts with multiple pendants of varying lengths, have been assumed to be kingly regalia, due to their relative scarcity, their placement in the largest tombs, their imposing character, and the quantity, quality, and character of the goods found with them (Pearson et al., 1989).

Another important assumption has been that the rulers of Ko-Shilla, as listed in the *Samguk sagi* and *Samguk yusa*, were men (kings), with the exception of Queen Sŏndŏk (r. 634–647) and Queen Chindŏk (r. 647–654), the two final *sŏnggol* rulers, called "female kings" (although the English language literature calls them queens), distinguishing between the king's consort and a ruler with intrinsic power.

Finally, double burials are interpreted as those of wife and husband. Although there are separate interments, the second burial is spatially close enough to the first to cause the second mound to overlap the first, producing a gourd-shaped mound. This configuration is not common, but it is found sporadically in both the Shilla and Kaya regions.

The results of the excavation of Tomb 98 in Kyŏngju, the largest of Shilla tombs (120 meters long and 23 meters high [Kim and Pearson, 1977]), violated at least one of these assumptions. Since this was an example of two burials related by overlapping mounds, it was expected that a male would have been buried in one mound and a female in the other. Tomb 98 contained, as anticipated, separate burials with overlapping mounds. Complete skeletons were not found to allow conclusive sexing, although a few teeth and a partial mandible, described as belonging to an elderly male, remained in the south mound.

To the excavators' surprise, the north mound in Tomb 98 contained the gold crown and belt, rather than the south mound, known to be a male. It may have been tempting to think of the north mound as another male grave (violating the assumption of a husband-wife pair), but to clinch the designation of the north mound as the queen's tumulus was an inscription scratched on a ceremonial belt, "belt for milady."

Furthermore, the woman's burial gifts seemed to be of higher status than the man's. Although the southern burial boasted gilt-bronze crowns and a silver crown in the north tumulus (Kim C.K. and Yi, 1975; Kim and Pearson,

1977), the amount of gold jewelry was dazzling—not only the crown and belt already noted, but also necklaces, rings, earrings, and bracelets, amounting to several pounds of gold. Exotic imports, including silver bowls and glass vessels from the western world, probably as far away as the Mediterranean, accompanied the queen.

The amount of equipment for war in the south mound—more than 1,000 projectile points, 543 spears, 380 battle axes, and 30 swords, as well as armor with silver leggings—was overwhelming, even for a Shilla burial. In the largest mound of Shilla, however, the quantity seems not inappropriate. The king had glass vessel imports, as well.

Akio Ito (1971) found no gender difference in the amount or kind of jewelry or other grave goods in Shilla burials. The only distinction he noted was in the presence or absence of swords, which, being close to 50%, seemed to indicate that males were buried with swords and females were not. Furthermore, this difference was found in known male/female double burials, that is, double mounds. The south tumulus of Tomb 98, with many swords, therefore must have been erected for the male.

As noted above, ruling queens are recorded for Ko-Shilla, thus a woman buried with a crown could be interpreted as a ruler. Tomb 98 cannot be the grave of Queen Chindŏk or Queen Sŏndŏk, however, because the tomb is dated to the fourth or fifth century, while these known queens both died in the sixth century. If we are to believe the histories, the north tomb cannot be later than 502, when human sacrifice was outlawed, for bones of a teenaged girl were found outside the burial chamber of the south mound, as if thrown in for a sacrifice (Kim W.Y., 1983).

Archaeologists have offered an assortment of dates for Tomb 98. Morimitsu (cited in Pearson, 1985) believes it to be the earliest of the known gold-crown tombs, based on the presence of a Chinese jar. Similar jars in China have dated contexts of 364 and 349. Allowing for a time lag, Morimitsu places Tomb 98 in the late fourth or early fifth century. Ch'oe (1981), who has divided the Shilla tombs into six periods based on the structure of the burial chamber and associated grave goods chamber, places the south mound at 350–400 A.D., and the north mound in the 400–450 A.D. group. This would make the buried King Naemul (r. 356–402) and the queen Poban, daughter of King Mich'u. Another possibility is that the King might be Nulchi (r. 417–458), whose queen was Aro, one of Mich'u's granddaughters. Finally, King Soji (r. 479–500) has been suggested (Kim and Pearson, 1977), but that ascription is unlikely, for Soji's queen predeceased him, while the queen's grave in Tomb 98 was considerably later than the king's.

A study by Pearson and others (1989), which clusters Ko-Shilla burials of the tumulus period in an attempt to identify social ranks, has found that a group of artifacts, including gold crowns and belts, delineate one group of probable royal tombs. Exotic imports were also found with this cluster. This finding lends weight to the assumption that gold crowns and belts were symbols of rulership.

It is interesting that Korean archaeologists have commented little on this apparent anomaly. Perhaps it introduces awkward questions, challenging the ancient documents in a basic way, or perhaps the problem is simply considered uninteresting. But in the light of both the attempt of some western archaeologists to engender the archaeological record (Conkey and Spector, 1984; Gero, 1985; Conkey and Gero, 1991), and the interest in the process of state formation (Patterson and Gailey, 1987), the mystery of Tomb 98 presents an important opportunity to probe further, not only to discover what the "facts" of the case might be, but also for whatever light this tomb may shed on the development of gender roles within states.

Although the Shilla kingdom was a secondary state, discovering gender equality in Ko-Shilla would allow another look at the generalization that women's status becomes subordinate in all state level societies, a premise underlying much of the feminist literature on state origins (e.g. Rohrlich, 1980; Lerner, 1986).

Documentary evidence on Shilla includes the *Samguk yusa* written by a Buddhist monk (Ilyon 1972 [1281]), *Samguk sagi* written in 1145 by Kim Pu-shik, a Confucian scholar, some brief notes in Chinese histories, and a fragment of an eighth century census. Of these, the partial census can be considered to be unbiased with regard to gender relations, along with the disapproving Chinese observations. In deference to Chinese attitudes, it is likely that both Buddhist and Confucian authors would suppress or distort gender equality in Shilla in early times, if it existed. Evidence for women's statuses can be teased out of all the documents, however.

Certainly constraints on women existed, but they were the same as those on men—by *kolp'um* bone ranks, rather than by gender. *Kolp'um* are inferred to be kin-based groups stringently enforced with a rule of hypodescent—a child belonged to the *kolp'um* of the lower-ranked parent (Kim C.S., 1977). The highest rank was the *sŏnggol* from which the rulers were selected. Next came the *chin'gol*, true bone, also eligible for high office short of the rulership. Six ranks below the *chin'gol* had decreasing statuses and roles. The ranks were caste-like in being endogamous, and each was composed of one or more kinship groups.

Further information on women's status in Shilla can be inferred from the sumptuary laws, designed to keep each bone rank firmly in place. Some scholars believe that the sumptuary laws date only to Unified Shilla time, but the inclusion of *sŏnggol* by inference place the laws in Old Shilla (after which the *sŏnggol* died out); otherwise no restrictions on the *chin'gol* would be necessary. Different although similar rules were decreed for men and women, suggesting a consciousness of gender distinctions, but not gender hierarchy. For example, women and men of the same rank were allowed similar quality in costume. Male *chin'gol* were not allowed to wear embroidered trousers made of fur, brocade, or silk, while *chin'gol* women were enjoined from wearing hairpins engraved and inlaid with gems and jade. Also interesting are the provisions for the type of saddle that could be used by women of various ranks—demonstrating that women of all ranks rode horses freely, and had their own saddles. This suggests considerable mobility for women, contrasting with the lot of Korean women in later times. The census fragment mentioned above also suggests gender equality. Of course this document cannot be applied directly to Old Shilla, but in terms of gender equality it seems the trend through time was toward increasing domination by men. Therefore while Ko-Shilla might have been more favorable to women than Unified Shilla, it is unlikely to have been less favorable. Thus, the census document has some applicability to understanding earlier times.

The census figures are divided into six age levels. Land was allocated to each adult, male or female (Kim C.S., 1965), rather than being assigned by household, or to a male head of household. This in itself demonstrates that women were considered to be full adult members of the society. According to the census, more women than men inhabited these villages, by a wide margin (194 adult males to 248 adult females in three villages). Although undercounting of males is possible (able-bodied men might have hidden to avoid military service, for example), the discrepancy is so great that it must indicate at a minimum that a preference for sons over daughters had not yet arisen; the social system did not yet favor males. The *Weizhi* relates disapprovingly that the predecessors of Shilla "drew no distinctions of sex and age" (Parker, 1890:209), framing the times both before and after the rise of Ko-Shilla as lacking gender inequality.

More circumstantial evidence of gender equality can be found in folklore and in anecdotes regarding the early rulers. Many local deities, especially mountain spirits at the top of the pantheon, were female. Ano, the sister of King Narnhae, directed the ceremonies in ancestor worship (Kim C.S., 1965: 273). Even today, village ceremonies are performed by women (*mudang*), and the carved village guardians were traditionally a pair, a male and a female. This configuration is congruent with Sacks' (1979) argument that when women's place in the society is defined primarily as part of a kin group, gender equality is more likely than when women are considered primarily as wives.

To return to the royalty, according to the king lists, which include information on the queen's forebears as well as the king's, the succession was unpredictable by any rule of linearity. The only obvious rule is the necessity for the ruler to be *sŏnggol*. Beginning with Naemul, a father-to-son sequence can be extracted, although one of the intervening rulers is an unrelated man. A mother-to-daughter pattern can also be isolated from Sullye's mother to Aro (Figure 5). Cross-cousin marriage, of course, allows both of these patterns to be found at once, but a shift from mother-to-daughter toward father-to-son seems to be occurring during the period of the gold-crown tombs.

Although Shilla was the last of the Korean kingdoms to become Sinicized, some movement in this direction occurred during the era of gold crowns in Shilla. The first Chinese mention of Shilla is in the *Nanshu*, reporting that in Wei times (220–264) there was a state in Korea called Shillu (Parker, 1890:221). Naemul (r. 356–402) was the first named Shilla ruler in Chinese annals. In 375 the custom of posthumous names for kings was instituted (Kim C.S., 1965:80). By 528 Shilla used the Chinese term *wang* for king, adopted the Chinese calendar, and allowed Buddhism to flourish. Thus, a gradual change from gender complementarity to male dominance may have begun about the fifth century, under China's influence, but it took many centuries to complete.

The assumption of the husband/wife double burial appears to be correct for Tomb 98. All other evidence suggests that the gold crowns and belts indeed are markers of rulership status. Thus the third assumption, that the rulers were men, needs to be modified. But there is no need to denigrate these men, who may also have ruled. It may be our unstated assumption of a single ruler which requires modification. Since the crown in the woman's grave suggests rulership, and women rulers would probably have been suppressed where possible by later historians, I conclude that the burials in Tomb 98 may represent a married pair which ruled jointly, the man as the military head and the woman as the secular (and perhaps spiritual and ceremonial) leader. Complementarity of men and women, and of male and female roles, is implied in other evidence regarding Ko-Shilla, making this hypothesis seem all the more likely.

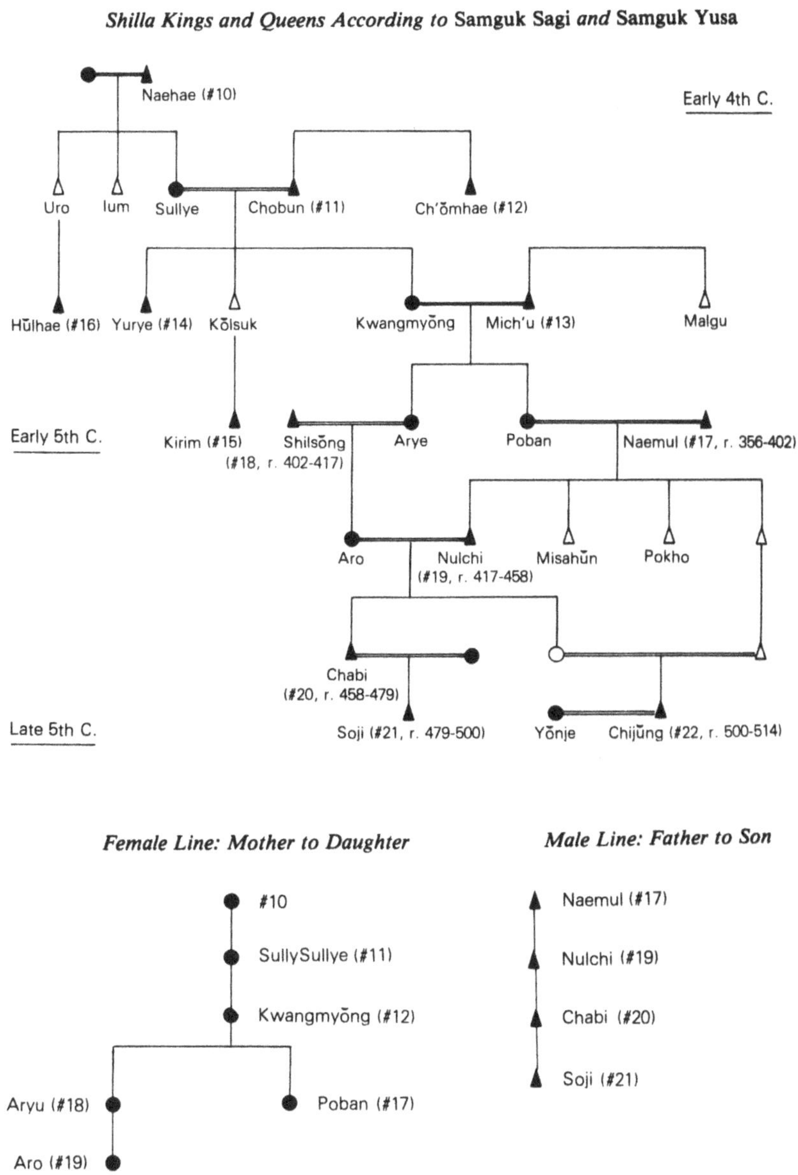

FIGURE 5. Genealogy of Silla Rulers

Chapter 4

Performing Power in Early China: Examples from the Shang Dynasty and the Hongshan Culture

THE WORD *POWER* IN ENGLISH covers a wide range of meanings, from influence to control to implicit force. Autonomy, or "power to," is often contrasted with forms of dominance, or "power over." When archaeologists discuss power, they usually mean "power over," and understanding political power is the goal. Timothy Earle (1997), for example, distinguishes between power and authority, of which the notable difference is that compliance with power is unwilling. Power, for Earle, includes the threat of force. Others have seen the powerful as "thugs" (Gilman 1995) or extortionists (Hayden 1995), following the line of power as compelling compliance. Ames (1995: 179) refers to power as "slippery"—a notion that better fits the kind of power I discuss in this chapter.

Earle examined the routes to political power, through warfare, economics, and ideology. But I suggest that these routes to power result in qualitatively different kinds of power. Power that *controls* a populace through ideology springs from other sources and has different consequences for the unpowerful than power achieved through military might, and neither is the same as power acquired by differential access to valuables or control of the means of production. In each case, the power is "over" different facets of life and has consequences for the non-powerful members of society. The impact of power over crops is not the same as power over lives. It might be useful to consider how chiefs *create* power rather than "come to" it (Earle 1997), an expression that makes it seem as if power is already there, waiting for a claimant or an occupant. The concept of power as a "thing" that a person or group of

Sarah M. Nelson (2002b). In *The Dynamics of Power*, edited by M. O'Donovan, pp. 151–167. Center for Archaeological Investigations, Southern Illinois University, Carbondale. Republished in *Shamans, Queens, and Figurines: The Development of Gender Archaeology*, by Sarah Nelson, pp. 87–102 (Taylor & Francis, 2015).

people can "have" or "come to" could be discarded and replaced with a more flexible view of power as contingent and negotiable, as well as dispersed and intermittent. Absolute power may corrupt absolutely, as Lord Acton famously said (see Janeway 1981), but it is a rare and short-lived phenomenon—the most appalling of tyrants have eventually been overthrown.

Power is most often represented as desirable, either to allow management of one's own destiny or to draw on the strengths of others to accomplish personal goals. The dangerous side of power, whether in the form of manna or electricity, is less often invoked. The Powers may even be personified nature spirits, who are seen as unpredictable and dangerous (Keightley 2000:116). Power surely has its dangers, for the holder as well as for those acted upon. The holder of power is in perpetual fear of potential usurpers. The powerless or the less powerful, on the other hand, may find their lives disrupted by the actions of those with power over them. On the plus side of the power discussions, various models of how groups or individual people within a society gain power have been produced (e.g., Feinman 1995). A nuanced understanding of particular kinds of power—their limitations and their consequences, their pleasures and their dangers—is still needed.

To narrow the immediate quest, I concentrate on some roles and ideologies that may shed some light on the "powers of the weak" (Janeway 1981)—how various categories of people may use power in a given society and under what circumstances. Basically, it is not enough to direct attention to the apparently powerful alone, for power is reciprocal, even if those who are acted upon by the powerful do not willingly comply. It is important to study the "others" in the society—whatever degree of power or powerlessness they may represent. In what ways may they be able to use the power system for their own ends, or at least carve themselves a niche protected from the powers of others? What roles may be temporarily powerful in given societies? What kinds of power are distributed to a number of people? And which kinds are tightly held by the most powerful? What are the sanctions or punishments for usurping power? When questions such as these are asked, we shift to perceiving power as a process rather than as an entity (Janeway 1981; Wylie 1992).

Although there are a number of ways to approach the underside of power, I concentrate on two illustrations of variations on power. One is the power that can accrue to practitioners of ecstatic religions, practitioners who can assert direct connections to otherworldly powers, perhaps confounding persons with secular power. If immediate access to the spirits cannot be denied, people with the ability to call down the spirits can control many situations. Recall the tactic of Repp Tevye's wife in *Fiddler on the Roof*: she was able to frighten her husband into undoing her daughter's marriage contract by claiming to have seen angry spirits in a dream. The other illustration I use is the creation of power by women, even in societies where one or a few men seem to have garnered all the power for themselves and their agnatic kin. This kind of womanpower may stem from women being links between males or having links with males, but the power is nonetheless real. Men cannot produce heirs without women. Time-honored anthropological expressions, such as *exchange of women* or *acquiring women in marriage*, implying that males are the only actors, mask the roles that women play in making marriage alliances, and mute women's voices, as well as their choices.

Although many differences separate shamanism and gender as sources of power, both help to illuminate the limits of "legitimate" power in state-level societies. These two types of power may even be utilized by the same person in different ways when the shaman is a woman.

SHAMANIC POWERS

I use *shamanism* to describe religious practitioners, who claim to have direct contact with spirits, rather than to describe state-sponsored and state-regulated rituals (Kehoe 2000; Thomas and Humphrey 1994). My interest is in their political dimension more than in their practices or beliefs. Since northeast Asia is the source of the word *shaman*, one should not be surprised that shaman-like practitioners are mentioned in the earliest extant Chinese writings. The Chinese graph found on oracle bones, now pronounced *wu*, is most often translated as *shaman*, and the male *xi* and female *wu* were said to have had direct contact with the world of the spirits in ancient times (Ching 1997:14–15). Thus, the practice of shamanism as a claim to power is relevant to early China, even if the word has been extended too far in other circumstances (Kehoe 2000).

Shamans can either be part of the state ideology or be outside it; if outside, they may be either antithetical to state cults or irrelevant to them (Thomas and Humphrey 1994:3). Which route shamanism followed in a given instance was specific to local historical processes. For example, Nicholas Thomas shows that in Polynesian societies, "ritual and political roles were divided between chiefs, shamans, and chiefs' priests" (Thomas and Humphrey 1994:6). This model is similar to the system that can be discerned from a close reading of the Late Shang oracle bones. The king could be the diviner, or a specially designated person could divine. Ancient shamanism may have been co-opted by the state and made to serve its own ends, but in the Shang it rested upon unforgotten predecessors. And balancing this state-level utilization of shamanic practices is the "realization that political power, even in state systems, operates through ideas of fertility, blessing, ancestry, or knowledge of destiny, which are also the domains of inspirational agencies" (Thomas and Humphrey 1994:11). Shamanism and state cults, therefore, are not polar opposites but different recipes for power using the same ingredients.

Shamans are particularly powerful during the times when they are in touch with the spirits. The spirits are frequently perceived to be dangerous, and contact with them is only for the hardy and strong. Partly for this reason, the role of shaman is often rejected by people who accept their fate only under duress (Kendall 1985). Shamans may be called upon to communicate with spirits (or ancestors) simply to inquire about the future or to intercede and change the future. Caroline Humphrey (1996) usefully considers shamans in Mongolia and Manchuria over a long span of time. She shows that in northeast Asia, shamanism has always been a viable alternative to "standard" religions, such as Buddhism and Lamaism, as well as having a place within them.

Powers of Women

The possibility of women having power has been overlooked, I believe, because power is so completely gendered male in our own culture. The idea that chiefs and kings have inherent power is embedded in the language we use about chiefdoms and states. The very words *chief* and *king* appear to be gendered male, although women rulers are known from various early societies (Nelson 1997a, 2002a). Women are thus perceived as powerless *by definition.* In China, where female rule cannot be denied by historians, women rulers were always described as detrimental to the society (Keightley 1999a). Ruling queens were examples of the world run amok (Cutter and Cromwell 1999).

Elizabeth Janeway (1981:4) similarly points out for historians of our own society that "the meaning of female experience has been fed only rarely into the larger reservoir of valued social knowledge." This partial blindness is not applied only to women. It is typical of a general tendency of the rulers to ignore the humanity, and even the presence, of groups whose roles render them weak in that society. Women are often seen as a category with particular functions (e.g., sexuality, fecundity, childcare, home maintenance), but as individual people, they are interchangeable and indistinguishable. Janeway (1981:3) directs attention to the fact that "conventional books on power tell us a lot [about the powerful . . . while the governed . . . are pretty much ignored."

The happy combination of a new focus on agency within both archaeology and feminism (Nelson 1997a), as well as data on individual women in early China, allows me to pursue this theme. However, there is still the dual problem of challenging the power paradigm within the established male-dominant context. Janeway (1981:6) notes that the concept of reality has been "filtered through . . . those who see their role as being in charge . . . of deciding what's important." To begin to remove the filter, the notion that only males can be powerful needs to be destabilized, as does the implication that some form of power belongs to all males. Some males were surely powerful in the Shang, but others belonging to the conscripted labor force were powerless (Keightley 2000:24). Men who were decapitated or chopped into two pieces at the waist in Shang China must have realized in their final moments that they were utterly powerless, whether they were captured soldiers, slaves, peasants, or criminals.

The powers of women stem from a variety of sources. Sexuality is often perceived as a kind of power—a dangerous one that needs to be curbed and controlled, if men are in charge of the society. This is by and large a power only available to young women. In China, the production of sons was often used by women to enhance personal power. Fecundity was not so much the point as the influence over male issue. A woman might, at death, become an ancestor to be worshiped based on her place in the kinship system. On the other hand, a mistreated woman could have the last bitter laugh by throwing herself into a well and becoming a wandering and spiteful spirit, simultaneously spoiling the drinking water. This type of power was clearly a last resort but one that could produce a desired result.

POWER IN EARLY CHINA

Early forms of power are not easy to pin down, even when several kinds of written sources, as well as extensive archaeological material, are present, as they are for the Late Shang dynasty in China. Even more elusive are earlier and more shadowy cultures, such as Hongshan, with its elaborate burials and evidence of extensive ceremonialism but little else on which to build a firm understanding of its power negotiations. The previous discussion of power in early complex society can be used as a guide to what one might seek to understand changes in the power balances of early China. Archaeological evidence throws some light on unauthorized power that might be acquired in Shang and Hongshan—by women and by shamans, who may sometimes be the same person.

Rather than discuss the two sites from China in chronological order, I consider Late Shang first. Some features of the Late Shang period may be distant echoes of their antecedents in the Hongshan culture some 2000 years earlier. Reciprocally, that reflection may shed some backward light on the Hongshan (Nelson 1991a). The juxtaposition of the two cultures, although they are neither contemporaneous nor contiguous, illuminates the power relations of both. However, there are reasons to postulate relationships between the two polities through time, for Lady Hao's tomb from the Shang dynasty contains artifacts that relate her to the region where the Hongshan culture flourished.

Shang Dynasty

The usual view of the Shang dynasty (fifteenth through eleventh centuries B.C.) is that of a highly male-dominant society. The rulers were all kings who practiced polygyny, perhaps for political alliances (Chang, K.-C. 1980a; Chang, ed. 1986; Keightley 1983, 1999b). The Zhou dynasty historians, writing after the fall of the Shang, depict the final Shang king as a lush and a womanizer, wallowing in wine among the ladies of his harem, thus legitimizing the conquest of Shang by Zhou. The implication drawn has been that no women had any power at all—that even queens and certainly consorts were simply pawns of the male royalty. But these later accounts provide no sense of the women in the court. In fact, the distribution of power in general, including any power of men other than the king, is not at all clear. The kings are named, but the nobles are largely unknown, although factions forming around the king's sons are noted (Wu, K.C. 1982:198).

Those who ruled at the final Shang city at present-day Anyang were listed in the succeeding Zhou dynasty chronicles. Although these lists were once thought to be fabrications, oracle-bone inscriptions confirm the names, and vast tombs imply their power. Each king was buried in a large, deep cruciform pit. The largest, possibly that of King Wu Ding himself (Bagley 1999), was almost 18 × 16 m in plan and was 12 m deep (Allan 1991:6). Four long ramps led down from the surface, the south ramp to the bottom of the burial chamber, the other three to its upper ledge (Thorp 1980). Human and animal sacrifices were placed on ledges surrounding the actual coffin pit, presumably to serve as guardians of the tomb. For example, about 400 sacrificed humans were found in Xibeigang Tomb 1001. Some were headless skeletons in rows, while skulls were grouped on the ramps. We can be certain that the kingly tombs were characterized by rich burial goods, but all the kings' tombs in Anyang were looted before professional archaeologists could excavate them. The later kings, beginning with Wu Ding, also appear in oracle-bone inscriptions as the diviner or the one on whose behalf the divination was made.

Human and animal sacrifices occurred on a large scale. The number of human sacrifices enumerated in the oracle bones is more than 13,000 (Allan 1991:8), and one must remember that this record is not complete. Many bones are broken or illegible, and other caches no doubt have yet to come to light. Sacrifices were discovered in the city, as well as in the tombs. In Xiaotun, near the foundations of seven large buildings identified as palaces, 852 sacrificed humans (including children) were found among 15 horses, 10 oxen, 18 sheep, 35 dogs, and 5 chariots. Clearly, the ancestors were bloodthirsty, preferring humans to other sacrifices.

A hierarchy of power has been assumed because under "kings" there should be other nobility and hordes of retainers. But for the Late Shang period, little is known about their lives or even their specific duties. Most individual people, even the other members of the king's clan and men of the court, are shadowy. However, several of the court women are mentioned in the oracle-bone inscriptions often enough to begin to flesh out their lives. In addition, some queens and consorts were provided with tombs of their own, miraculously unlooted. Inscribed bronzes even reveal their names in life and after death, allowing them to be connected to specific oracle-bone divinations.

Later Chinese historiography is notoriously androcentric, not to say gynophobic, as noted above. For example, a text compiled in the third century A.D. from much earlier sources describes a Shang king invoking the spirits to discover the cause of a serious drought. "Is it that the government is not frugal?" the king asks. "That food bribes are common?" And perhaps the worst possibility, "That women's advice is followed?" (Allan 1991:41). Any woman who ruled was seen as illegitimate—even Empress Wu, of the brilliant Tang dynasty, is denigrated in official Chinese history. Whether the Zhou historians would have suppressed women of power who might have existed in the Shang, it is highly likely that any such representations would have been eliminated by later editors. The only dim reflection of a powerful woman in the past is the mythical Nuwa, styled by late chroniclers as the wife of the first sage ruler rather than a sage in her own right (Wu, K.C. 1982:4). But contemporary inscriptions and the archaeology of the Shang give a different sense of gender relations than do official histories. The distribution of power is not as authoritarian, nor as completely top-down, as it might seem.

Contemporary written sources for the Late Shang dynasty allow glimpses into their world. Both inscriptions on bronzes and records of divinations on the oracle bones reveal much about the Shang. Bronze inscriptions, often consisting only of the name of the owner, are limited to vessels placed in graves. Sometimes the inscription is a temple name, showing that this newly deceased person has become an ancestor. The combinations of vessels with the names used in life and death provide insight, but it is only in combination with oracle bones that a wider understanding can be reached.

In the Late Shang or Anyang period, divinations are inscribed on turtle plastrons and cattle scapulae. Some 150,000 oracle-bone fragments have been unearthed and cataloged (Keightley 1994). However, the Shang did not invent scapulimancy. Bovine shoulder blades with holes burned on one side and cracks on the other are found much earlier than the Anyang period. Some, dating to the sixth and seventh millennia B.C., are inscribed with symbols, perhaps protowriting. Other burned bones from the fourth millennium B.C., contemporaneous with and not far from the Hongshan culture, have no engraving at all. Shang oracle-bone inscriptions reveal the preoccupations of the king—prognostications for future events, including childbirth and toothache, as well as auspicious days for battles and the likelihood of rain and destructive wind (Keightley 1978b). The king's power may have been based on his ability to consult the Powers, the spirits that were everywhere in the Shang world (Keightley 2000).

Although (as I discuss below) the difference in mortuary treatment between kings and queens confirms a patrilineal society in which only men could be rulers, it may come as a surprise that elite women also had roles in warfare, the economy, and ideology—all potential sources of or avenues to power, according to Earle (1997). Oracle-bone indications of particular women's roles lead us to examine the burials of elite women.

Shang Royal Women

While kings' graves were the targets of thieves, some of the tombs of royal women have been found undisturbed, providing a concrete and detailed picture of royal tombs and their entire assemblages. Katheryn Linduff (1996, 2002) has examined in detail the excavated burials of three elite women at Anyang. Both the richness of the tombs and the inscribed bronzes included in two of them suggest that these women were in some sense royal. The oracle bones indicate that both women were wives of King Wu Ding (Chang Chen-hsiang 1986; Chang Pin-chuan 1986; Cheng Cheng-lang 1986). Thus there is evidence that women of royalty were in polygynous marriages, as has been previously noted. But the notion that polygyny means powerless women needs to be reexamined. Oracle-bone records show that three of Wu Ding's wives, Lady Jing, Lady Hao, and Lady Zi, were designated as royal ancestors, receiving the ritual title of Mu (mother) and being inserted into the ritual calendar after death. (Other wives named on oracle bones are Ladies Geng, Liang, Fu, and Zhu, but their graves have not been located [Qian 1981:24]). An ancestral temple to Lady Hao was erected above her grave, where royal descendants could go to worship and ask for beneficence. She became after death one of the Powers that could control the future. Her blessings on succeeding generations were important, although they were not patrilineal descendants. The existence of the temple demonstrates her continuing power after death, perhaps for several generations.

Linduff points out that, in writings about women from the legendary period, women are seen to have conducted divination themselves and to have interpreted the results of divination to others (O'Hara 1971:280). While the royal women were alive, they had the power to appeal directly to the ancestors in divination by asking questions about various concerns for the future. They inquired about the crops on land that they managed and about military campaigns that they conducted. They also inquired about the weather, matters of health, and hunting. The oracle bones indicate that Lady Hao "conducted ceremonies in worship of Shang ancestors and the gods. In presiding over these ceremonies, she made offerings of wine, and prisoners of war, slaves, and cattle were sacrificed" (Linduff 2002). Emphasizing their roles in warfare, weapons and armor were abundant in the tombs of both Lady Jing and Lady Hao.

Lady Jing's title was Queen of Wu Ding, a title his other wives did not hold (Linduff 2002). As such, she was interred in the area of the kings' tombs. Hers was a smaller tomb than the king's; and while kings' graves usually had four ramps, Lady Jing's had only one. As Wu Ding's designated queen, Lady Jing was presumably the mother of the crown prince. She is treated as an ancestor on the bronzes deposited in her tomb and, as noted earlier, received the designation Mu, or mother. The wealth of Lady Jing's grave goods is massive. Her tomb held ritual bronzes, jades, and many other precious objects, as well as sacrificial human victims. A bronze *ding* (food vessel) in her grave is the largest known from the royal burial grounds at Anyang. It weighs 875 kg and is 133 cm tall (Ma Cheng yuan 1980:70). Although the kings' tombs were looted long ago, as noted above, their contents, especially the bronzes, have found their way to major museums around the world. It seems unlikely that a larger *ding* was ever made. Wen Fong (1980:xi) suggests that "whether weapons or ritual vessels, bronze objects meant power for those who possessed them." What enormous power, both economic and spiritual, may then be implied by this huge vessel!

Lady Hao also was buried with extraordinary riches, in some ways more impressive than those of Lady Jing. Her grave goods included nearly 7,000 cowrie shells (believed to have been used as currency [K.-C. Chang 1983]), 23 bronze bells, and more than 130 bronze weapons, as well as 27 knives and dozens of other bronze artifacts. Ornaments placed in her tomb included 590 elegantly carved jade objects, in addition to more than 100 beads and disks, 490 bone hairpins, and other artifacts made of precious materials (K.-C. Chang 1980b:42). Sixteen sacrificed humans and six dogs were buried with her. Her tomb produced the first complete set of ritual vessels, consisting of 217 bronze vessels in 21 different shapes (Ma Cheng yuan 1980:7), found together at Anyang. Of these vessels, 40 were food-offering containers, and an amazing 117 held wine. She was designated "Mu Xin" on some of her bronze offering vessels, showing that she became an official ancestor, being granted a temple name.

King Wu Ding inquired of the spirits about the outcome of Lady Hao's pregnancies by means of the oracle bones. It appears that she bore at least two daughters and had one son who did not survive to adulthood. By these prognostications, we learn that the births of daughters were considered to be "inauspicious" and "not good" (Keightley 1997:38). Clearly, Wu Ding was hoping for a son with Lady Hao, who had many characteristics that would have benefited a son. Lady Hao led a busy public life. There is an instance when she was charged with leading 13,000 troops against the Qiang, barbarians on the west, and she also is recorded as having fought enemies from the other directions.

Some unique artifacts link her with the north—the direction of the Hongshan culture (Linduff 1996; Nelson 1991a). These items include jades that seem derivative of those found in Hongshan tombs, although thicker than most of the Hongshan jades and, of course, later in style. Also in her grave were actual antique Hongshan jades and other Neolithic jades (Bagley 1999:202). Four bronze mirrors and several bronze knives of the northern style are particularly interesting because other such mirrors and knives are almost unknown in Anyang. These are objects of the northern cultures (Lin Yun 1986), in the same region as the earlier Hongshan culture. It seems reasonable to hypothesize that Lady Hao married into the Shang from that region and that these are objects she brought with her, perhaps as part of her dowry. It is possible that these northern horse breeders were "pacified" by a marriage alliance. Horse cheek pieces were included in Lady Hao's tomb. It is worth noting that chariots and horses, which came to the Shang from the north, appear in Wu Ding's reign with no antecedents (Bagley 1999:202–208). The mirrors and knives are interesting from another perspective as well—such objects are documented (albeit much later) as shamanic paraphernalia. Music was an important element of shamanism. Musical instruments found in the graves of both Lady Jing and Lady Hao may also link them to shamanic practices. Symbolically, the mythical first queen, Nuwa, was credited with inventing music. Music and dance were a central part of state ritual in early China, as well as in shamanic performance.

These examples of powerful women to some extent counter the interpretation of exclusive patriarchy in Shang. At the very least, they reveal that class or clan status took precedence over gender distinctions.

Shamans in Shang: Wu and Xi

Kwang-Chih Chang (1983, 1994a) has repeatedly argued that shamanism was a characteristic of the Shang and that the king was the head shaman. He based his arguments both on the existence of the character *wu*, meaning shaman, on the oracle bones and on some of the depictions on Shang bronzes. The most striking of the bronzes depict humans with their heads in the mouths of tigers and other fierce animals, which Chang interprets as spirit familiars. Elizabeth Childs-Johnson (1995) points to the use of mask symbols as identifying shamanic rites, but Chang is particularly interested in the manipulation of symbols, especially ritual symbols, by political elites and shamans. He suggests that such manipulation is "for the purpose of acquiring, retaining, and increasing such power" (Chang 1994a:62). Chang and Childs-Johnson agree that shamanism existed at least as far back as the early Neolithic. Childs-Johnson (1995:91) concludes that "Shang art and religion were based on an earlier tradition of shamanism."

More recently, Julia Ching (1997) has connected mysticism with kingship in China, which she interprets as beginning with shaman-kings in the Shang dynasty. While this view has not been universally accepted, it does seem that the Shang strongly believed in several kinds of prognostications and that anticipating the will of heaven was of prime importance to the state. Ching does not seek shamanism earlier than the Shang. Lothar von Falkenhausen (1995) mentions various references to the *wu* from later documents, especially the Zhou Li. As spirit mediums, the *wu* were expected to dance for rain making and to handle ancestor tablets. While Falkenhausen does not conclude that the king must have been a shaman, it is clear that shamans existed and had specific functions.

Since the oracle-bone inscriptions were intended to discern the will of heaven, they were related to shamanic practices, according to Ching's extended view of shamanism (1997). Even observing the movement of heavenly bodies was connected with shamanism. The notion that a given dynasty ruled by the will of heaven is ancient in Chinese thought. The positions of the planets in relation to star clusters were believed to relate to the Mandate of Heaven, the right of the dynasty to rule. The occurrence of the conjunction of all five planets was interpreted as indicating the overthrow of a dynasty and was so important that the Zhou ruler waited to stage the final battle with Shang at the precise moment when the planets were closest together, thus emphasizing the transfer of the Mandate of Heaven to Zhou (Pankenier 1995). (Parenthetically, it is interesting that astronomical phenomena were also used as proof that rule was "decreed by destiny" in the Roman Empire [Thomas and Humphrey 1994:9].)

It is also telling that the graph *wu*, which is translated as "shaman," occurs often in the oracle bones (Zhang Yachu and Liu Yu 1981–1982:49). Shamans, scribes, and milfoil diviners are all mentioned and seem to be equally in touch with spirits in different ways. The *wu* in particular were expected to "call down the spirits" in ceremonies, but scribes who recorded divinations and diviners who could read the yarrow stalks when they were thrown were all powerful and dangerous (Falkenhausen 1995). Thomas and Humphrey have studied later but related shamanism among the Mongols and Manchu. They demonstrate that claiming to communicate with spirits and to divine the will of heaven was a strategy used by military contenders. "Such a merging of religious and political authority seems to be characteristic of . . . early stages of state formation" (Thomas and Humphrey 1994:10). The conclusion arrived at by one who has studied the Shang closely is that "the Shang slave-master elite worshipped the spirits with fanatic zeal, and the consciousness of the society was permeated with reverence for and delusions of the superhuman forces of nature" (Ma Cheng yuan 1980:8).

The Hongshan Culture

The Hongshan culture in northeastern China, which flourished from 6,000 to 4,500 years ago, has several indicators of elites, presumably representing people with "power over" others in the same society. These indicators include large tombs with evidence of elaborate rituals, which would have required coordination of artisans, tomb builders, and ritual specialists (Guo Dashun 1995a; Nelson 1995a, 1996, 1998a).

Hongshan is spread over a large part of western Liaoning province and eastern Inner Mongolia. Most of the sites are simple villages. Stone tools may be chipped or polished, and much of the pottery consists of buff-colored vessels with zigzag impressions. Both are continuations of the far northeastern Neolithic. Hongshan village sites deviate only in one way: the more elaborate pottery is painted black on red, with curvilinear or geometric designs.

Recently discovered ceremonial sites have cast Hongshan in a new light. Two ritual sites, Niuheliang and Dongshanzui, feature female representations, although they are quite different. At Dongshanzui, earth platforms edged by stones have been interpreted as altars. Other stone alignments appear to be oriented to the cardinal directions. The clay female figures are found in both small and medium sizes. One of the small ones is clearly pregnant, and another may be nursing (she holds something missing to her breast). The medium-sized female figures sit with crossed legs, wearing a belt of knotted rope. This site appears to be intended for rituals to fertility and life. In contrast, Niuheliang is a large area of tombs in clusters on hills or, in one case, in a valley. It seems to be focused on death. In the midst of these tombs and visible from most tomb groups is the Goddess Temple, a lobed building in which a life-sized figure of a woman, made of unbaked clay with eyes of green jade, was found. The tombs vary from a single interment under a small mound ringed with stones to elaborate, carefully built stone constructions with thousands of bottomless painted cylinders placed in rows around the circumference. Most of the individual graves are slab lined, and the occupants are accompanied by beautifully worked, highly polished jades; these include bracelets, earrings, and pendants in specific shapes.

Shamans in the Hongshan Culture

Chang (1994a) points to a number of Neolithic discoveries that may reflect shamanic events. The famous burial at Puyang, with a dragon and a tiger created in shells on each side of a male burial oriented to the south, is one such example. Another is a Yangshao painted bowl that appears to show a line of dancing nude males. The astronomer Bella Chu (personal communication 1999) believes that there is evidence that the solstices and equinoxes were known back into the early Neolithic based on later texts, which preserve knowledge about which star clusters occurred at those times. The Puyang burial's tiger and dragon may also be related to the sky, for the Chinese believed that the guardian of the east was the dragon, of the west, the tiger. Chang believes that "the path to power was through shamanism" (Chang 1994a). Other paths to power in slightly later times were warfare and access to sources of jade and copper. But Hongshan has no evidence of warfare and only uncertain indicators of the use of metals. If Chang is correct, power was held by those who could contact the spirits—which, as I have demonstrated, may still have been the case in the Shang dynasty.

That divination by boring holes in cattle scapulae and reading the oracles was practiced by the neighbors of the Hongshan is quite suggestive. Myths also relate this time period to the beginnings of divination by milfoil stalks, which became codified as trigrams and hexagrams in the I Ching (Wu K.C. 1982:51). The legendary Yellow Emperor in the third millennium B.C. is recorded to have conquered his enemy the Flame Emperor at a site within the Hongshan territory. The Flame Emperor may have been the leader of a successor group of the Hongshan, represented archaeologically by the Lower Xiajiadian culture. Lower Xiajiadian, like Shang, used the depth of burials, as well as the richness of grave goods, to differentiate social groups. They made cruciform coffins and side niches, perhaps prefiguring Shang burial customs. The pottery shapes and designs are forms that are used later for Shang bronzes, especially the wine-pouring vessels, which have not been found elsewhere.

Rain making was a particular duty of shamans, as described in oracle bones and in Zhou ritual. This duty has relevance in relation to the Hongshan, who experienced climatic warming and drying (Wagner 1993). An argument I have made about the importance of pigs in the Hongshan ritual relates to desiccation (see Nelson 1998a). Ching (1997:19) notes that, in the Zhou writings, women dancer-shamans were preferred, because yin (the female side of yin and yang) is associated with water and rain. The symbols of Hongshan jades are mostly related to yin and water, suggesting an emphasis on female contacts with the spirits (Nelson 1996).

Gender in the Hongshan Culture

The Hongshan culture in northeastern China has some features that open a discussion of gendered power. The roles of women are far less delineated in Hongshan than in Late Shang, with only female representations as equivocal evidence of women's possible power. Statues and figurines of women, however, suggest that women in general, or a few specific women, were perceived as able to contact the spirits on behalf of the society. The juxtaposition of two very different ceremonial centers about 40 km apart indicates a sophisticated belief system in which life and death were both celebrated. We cannot know whether the face found in the Goddess Temple was a representation of a spirit or a person who could call down the spirits, but in either case, it seems that females were not held in low esteem.

By reading later texts with an eye to ferreting out earlier myths, Sarah Allen has discovered several female gods and ancestors who must predate the Shang and are probably even earlier than Hongshan. Two remote ancestors of Shang are Dong Mu, the Eastern Mother, and Xi Mu, the Western Mother, related respectively to the rising and setting of sun and moon. Spirits of rivers and mountains are also female (Allan 1991:52–53). Another view of Neolithic religion can be found in work by Overmeyer and his colleagues (1995). Without resorting to the idea of matriarchies in the Chinese Neolithic (Pearson 1981; Wang 1984), it seems clear that women were respected within the society. Hongshan has evidence neither of warfare nor of human sacrifice. Without a need for fierce fighters, they concentrated on rituals, whose pomp and color can only be imagined, with the aid of the jades and painted cylinders.

CONCLUSION

Concentrating on the powers of women and shamans throws a different light on state formation. In both Hongshan and Shang, women are important players in the power game. While the lack of writing limits interpretation of the Goddess Temple, at the very least one may infer that some women were credited with spiritual powers. Later textual evidence implies the importance of both sexes, but the use of the term *wu* to apply to both men and women shamans by the time of the Shang may indicate the precedence of women shamans at some point. In later writings, *wu* are women, and *xi* are men performing the same functions.

Leadership in Hongshan was clearly not based on military might, for there is no evidence of warfare. However, even at the time of the Shang, when warfare had become endemic, women could lead armies. Rulership had become gendered male, and the birth of royal daughters was looked upon with dismay, but talented women could expect to take on considerable responsibilities in the military, the economy, and the spirit world.

For the Hongshan, leadership through ceremony and ritual, coupled with differential access to jade sources and elite control of jade working, was the dominant mode (Nelson 1996). In contrast, the Shang dynasty some two millennia later practiced almost continual warfare, and sacrificial victims are ubiquitous in the sites. The scale of power had escalated steeply. Shang power was far more coercive than Hongshan power. On the other hand, while the gender balance is certainly different in the two societies, burials of high-status women and oracle-bone inscriptions show that women were still playing roles in the power game, roles that were similar to those of contemporary men. Shamans too were present and powerful in both times and places. These similarities and contrasts help illuminate the nuances of power in Shang and Hongshan.

PART V
Gender in Archaeology Spreads

A BREAKTHROUGH PAPER that laid the intellectual foundation for gender in archaeology was published in 1984. Meg Conkey and Janet Spector explained in clear academic terms why gender was an important topic for archaeology. The buzz about the article was loud, but not much seemed to happen as an immediate result. In retrospect, the five-year time lag before conferences on gender in archaeology began in earnest and new ideas and papers began to flow freely through various pipelines is surprising. Maybe it was simply time to take a deep breath.

The first open meeting about gender in archaeology in the Americas was the Chacmool conference at the University of Calgary, Canada, in 1989. The gathering was stimulating on a theoretical level and just plain fun as well. I reveled in being in the midst of so many female archaeologists gathered together in one place. It was at the Chacmool meeting that I first met Peggy Nelson—no relation, although we sometimes have called each other "sister" as an inside joke. We are both Nelsons by marriage, and even the Scandinavian ancestors of our husbands came from different countries. This meeting facilitated collaboration on the *Equity Issues* volume, including the joint paper included here as Chapter 2, a summary of problems for women in archaeology and some solutions.

The Chacmool conference proceedings published 72 papers, with a wide range of topics. While it was the first such conference in the Americas, it was not the world's first feminist archaeology meeting. "Were They All Men?" took place in Norway in 1979, although the papers weren't published until 1987. The first feminist journal, *KAN*, came from Scandinavia as well, and a feminist newsletter sprang up in Germany, *Netzwerk Archaeoloigische Arbeitende Frauen*, to which I was an avid early subscriber.

Shamans, Queens, and Figurines: The Development of Gender Archaeology, by Sarah Nelson, 103–112.

Soon after the Chacmool conference, Cheryl Claessen established the Boone Conference, which continued as the Gender in Archaeology conference. It later met at various universities around the US. Another periodic feminist meeting was the Women in Archaeology conference in Australia. Three meetings of the Theoretical Archaeology Group (TAG) in England were dedicated to feminist archaeology (Wylie 2002, notes to Chapter 14:278–281). Edited volumes of provocative papers resulted from most of these meetings. So many pent-up ideas came swirling out into a hurricane of writing activity. Gender in archaeology was an idea whose time had come. Or women in archaeology. Or feminist archaeology. There was no clear consensus about the name or focus of our topic.

GODDESSES

One of the papers I read at the Gender in Archaeology conference concerned a site I had just visited in China, one with a life-sized face that the Chinese called a "goddess" and the place of the find the "Goddess Temple." But goddesses became controversial among women archaeologists, and ways to think about goddesses became a split in the gender in archaeology movement. Goddesses were an important topic in parts of the feminist movement in America, using ancient goddesses as inspiration but rarely producing scholarship about them. The Gender in Archaeology conferences continued to have a group of goddess papers submitted through the final meeting in California. Even though the goddess movement has been ignored by most archaeologists, it is part of the women/gender/feminist story. A complete rift did not occur, but the relation between the goddess movement and archaeology demonstrates one of the first cracks in the feminist notion of sisterhood in the archaeological community. Papers about goddesses were accepted, and their authors welcomed at most meetings, but archaeologists tended to be uneasy about ancient goddesses.

The branch of the women's movement that focused on women's spirituality was large and lively, and there are still multiple, vibrant websites devoted to the topic. In rejecting patriarchy, some groups of women also were eager to overthrow gods with long gray beards, and were delighted to substitute ancient goddesses. There were other revivals of women's spirituality. For example, some women took up Wicca, others focused on shamanism. Some formed circles to worship the moon and celebrated solstices. As an agnostic, I didn't care who the gods were, except that beliefs about deities might shed light on gender as it was lived in various places in the past.

Many goddesses were found that had been anciently worshipped in Europe, Asia, and the rest of the world. Other goddesses still had active temples—in India, for example; others had been supplanted in the past by male gods. But finding goddesses was often a more literary than an archaeological endeavor, although the results of archaeology were often cited. Tours to goddess places became popular—Crete, Malta, and Ireland, for example. The site of Çatalhöyük in Turkey, with its imposing female figures, became a place of pilgrimage. Books on goddesses proliferated—I have an entire bookshelf of them. Each is interesting, but the point was rarely about the lives of women in the past. Ancient goddesses were sources for female spirituality in the present.

Some scholarly attempts to uncover ancient women's lives looked to the classical world. Sarah Pomeroy (1974) discussed women in the classical period as *Goddesses, Whores, Wives and Slaves*. Carol Myers (2001) wrote about women in the Bible, and Joan Connelly (2007) used images of priestesses to analyze women in ancient Greece. But the bottom line is that few archaeologists were active in this search for ancient goddesses or priestesses, even when those being discussed were from ancient cultures where archaeologists were digging. Goddesses were too far out for many anthropological archaeologists. An interesting exception is Ian Hodder's work at Çatalhöyük, where all who are interested in the site are welcome, and the goddess worshippers become part of the story. This interesting experiment is ongoing.

The archaeologist Marija Gimbutas joined the discussion of goddesses with her own archaeological data. She had been at Harvard before she moved to UCLA, where she wrote about the culture of "Old Europe," part of her region of expertise. She hypothesized that an area of the Balkans had been a woman-centered culture, a matriarchy, which was ultimately destroyed by horse-riding invaders, the Indo-Europeans. Her books were lavishly illustrated with drawings of figurines and other artifacts. Her first book received a favorable review in *Antiquity*, and she was lionized by the goddess movement, but archaeologists in general either ignored or criticized her hypotheses (see Elster 2007 for a discussion of Maria Gimbutas's life and work).

The criticism of Gimbutas's later work was that it had become less scholarly. Some wanted to disassociate themselves from her hypotheses (Conkey and Tringham 1995). I didn't hop on either bandwagon, but it seemed worth considering that goddesses in the past might provide an avenue to understanding gender roles. I was encouraged in this perspective by Peggy Sanday's (1981) volume, *Female Power and Male Dominance*, in which she suggested that the traits of gods and goddesses were scripts for gender roles and behavior. Later I invited Peggy to contribute to a book on female rulers and queens. She studied the Minankabau, of Sumatra, Indonesia, the largest matriarchal society in the world. I was surprised to learn that the men of this matriarchy are mostly Moslem (Sanday 2003). It is a fascinating society. I continue to use Sanday's provocative and useful hypothesis.

I envisioned different possibilities for the study of goddesses. I worked on the "Goddess Temple" site of northeastern China for most of a decade, because I was intrigued by what the life-sized female statues might have indicated. My paper at the Chacmool conference, reprinted here (Chapter 5), was mostly descriptive about the site, but it dropped like a stone into a well. Some archaeologists were not comfortable with any arguments that extended spiritual beliefs to social behavior. My position is that beliefs in goddesses are not per se the concern of archaeologists. What we should be attempting to do is to learn about women and gender in the past. Any kind of data that is supported by archaeological discoveries should be admissible in that endeavor.

EQUITY AND GRANTS

In another session at Chacmool, John Yellen of the National Science Foundation presented data showing recipients of NSF grants by gender, comparing the rank of the applicant, the approximate date of the PhD, and gender. He then looked at the ratings given to these applications. The female success rate was 21% compared with 37% for men's proposals. He didn't consider that significant. Judge for yourself. Yellen (1991) admitted that the FY 1978–1981 awards "support Joan Gero's contention" ["that female archaeologists who attempt to lead field projects would tread on male sensibilities and be discriminated against accordingly"] but claims that ten years later, the data did not show such discrimination.

In manipulating the data, he noted that of the "senior" women applicants in 1979–1981, four were deemed to be "inappropriate proposals." My recollection, which admittedly could be inexact, is that in his oral presentation he characterized these as "kook" proposals. He did not use this word in the published version. These senior women, I think he said, hadn't been properly taught the culture of grant writing. One of those senior female kook-proposal writers had to be me, my proposal for the figurine study. I was insulted all over again. A relevant reason for my irritation was that in that time period, NSF did fund a truly kooky proposal by Lew Binford to go to China—a place where he had never been and whose language he could neither speak nor read—and tell the Chinese how to do their archaeology. Or that's how Binford's trip appeared to me and to other archaeologists then working in China. I didn't see how Binford's trip to China was fundamentally less kooky than Nelson's trip to Europe, but there was an obvious gender difference, as well as the element of (Binford's) stature in the field.

In the 1970s, the American Archaeological Association established a Committee on the Status of Women in Anthropology (COSWA). Statistics on the gender balance in anthropology departments were kept, and COSWA even censured three departments for having too few women anthropology professors—or even none at all. A fund was set up to provide legal aid to women who had an academic grievance, and it is still active and, sadly, still needed. Serious problems for women in academe caused the American Association of University Professors to create Committee W, for Women. Women's informal groups were organized in many universities.

Rita Wright, as chair of COSWA, had tried to obtain continuing comparative gender data from NSF, but she was unsuccessful. She passed the task to me as the next chair of COSWA, and I was not successful either. My sense is that the SAA Committee on the Status of Women in Archaeology was not nearly as bold as AAA's COSWA, but we did keep the membership aware of continuing bias against women archaeologists. Rita has been a stalwart friend, always with interesting views on women's careers as well as women in the past. I try to meet with her whenever I'm in New York, which isn't often enough.

At the University of Denver, the Committee for Women on Campus had as one goal of our broad agenda the promotion of women into positions of power. I had been chair of Anthropology by virtue of being its fiercest defender when it was repeatedly under threat of dissolution. I decided to run against two "science guys" for the position of Vice Provost for Research, and to my surprise I was selected for the position. It took awhile before the grant-getters in the science departments were comfortable with my leadership, but eventually they were. For the last five years of my career, I was Vice Provost for Research at DU, and as an administrator I was asked to write a piece for the *SAA Archaeological Record*. My point was that women archaeologists should consider their skills, and apply for positions in administration, in order to change their institutions.

NETWORKING

One of the most effective strategies for women, both in the workplace and within disciplines, has been networking. Whenever I could, I attended archaeology meetings, anthropology meetings, Asian meetings. I almost always go to SAA, as well as international and regional meetings, to meet people, present papers, and keep up with the field. I usually found a roommate to keep expenses down, and a frequent roommate was Susan Kent. Sue exemplified everything the ambitious young archaeologists should do. She had worked with Lew Binford, and, using his ideas about extracting social structure from the locations of objects in sites, she extended the data to gendered spaces. Sue was full of ideas, and the list of books she wrote and edited shows an appetite for almost any archaeological topic.

Sue was a savvy networker. At meetings, she organized dinners with the leading feminists of the day. For one memorable dinner in Washington, DC, seven us waited in the rain for a cab. When we finally crammed into one, it turned out the restaurant Sue had chosen was only two blocks away. We would have been less wet if we had walked in the rain. The point was to chat informally about our work and perhaps find ways we could work together.

Sue had begun to look at hunter-gatherers in Africa for gender inspiration, turning to the Kalahari San for her fieldwork. I especially enjoyed her observation of a man's spear being used by a woman to stir a pot full of food. She organized a gender symposium with papers about African sites, to be held in Cracow, Poland, and urged me to attend as a discussant. I demurred. How could I discuss African sites when I worked in Asia? Sue was persistent and persuasive. Although I didn't attend the meeting, Sue insisted that I write some comments for *Gender in African Prehistory* (Nelson 1998b). My chapter is a measure of the various ways gender was approached in those days. I show that the study of African prehistory was ahead of East Asia in appreciating the value of studying gender in archaeology, but the approaches in this book were varied in both the types of data and ways of assessing the data. Gender in archaeology had multiple meanings; gender in past times and places had multiple expressions.

Laurel Kendall was my main entry into Korean social anthropology, as I often saw her when we were both in Korea. I had found Laurel's work on the shamans of Korea inspirational and have always relied on her for pithy insights. Eventually I asked her to comment on the novel about Korea that included a Korean shaman as an important character (see Part VIII). She was kind enough to read it and keep me from cultural gaffes, although she is not responsible for any that are left.

At a meeting of the Pacific Science Conference (PSC) in Seoul, I came to know Fumiko Ikawa-Smith and learned from her about the Indo-Pacific Prehistory Association (IPPA). Fumiko was headed to Japan for the IPPA meeting right after the PSC. I couldn't stay in Asia for IPPA, but I did join, and went to exciting meetings every four years thereafter, beginning in 1990 at Jogjakarta, Indonesia, followed by Chiang Mai, Thailand, Melaka in Malaysia, Taiwan, and Hanoi. Eventually I persuaded Fumiko to look at gender by writing about Jomon figurines, a paper she gave at the Bellagio conference.

I had met Gina Barnes when I returned to Ann Arbor to defend my dissertation. She was then a new graduate student, and Henry Wright made sure we connected. Our paths crossed occasionally, since her family lived in Colorado, but Gina lived in England and we rarely had any sustained time to compare notes on East Asian archaeology.

When Gina created a newsletter, the *EAANouncements*, for those interested in East Asian archaeology, I was delighted and impressed. This networking linked the few and far-flung Asian archaeologists who were just beginning to find one another. She asked me to be the North American treasurer, which meant collecting dues from archaeologists scattered in the US and Canada.

By 1996, we were ready for a real organization and held the first meeting of the Society for East Asian Archaeology in Hawaii, in connection with the Association for Asian Studies. Gina served as president, I became vice president, Simon Kaner was treasurer, and Yangjin Pak was secretary. Before the meeting, the four of us hammered out a constitution for the new organization. About 50 people attended the first SEAA meeting in Honolulu.

Following the pattern established by IPPA, SEAA met every four years, in the even years between IPPA meetings. The 2000 SEAA meeting took place at Durham University, England, where Gina was employed, followed by Daejon University, Korea, Yangjin's academic address, in 2004; Beijing, China, in 2008, organized by Wang Wei at the Chinese Archaeological Research Institute, and Kyushu, Japan, in 2012, arranged by Koji Mizoguchi. Attendees voted to meet every two years from then on, and we gathered in Ulaan Bataar, Mongolia, in 2014. This was a network of East Asianists, not necessarily feminists, but the connections were important in introducing gender in archaeology to many parts of East Asia. Even Gina, who would probably not call herself a feminist, found all the women mentioned in an important Japanese text (Barnes 2007).

GENDER IN ARCHAEOLOGY SPREADS FURTHER

The Gender in Archaeology series for AltaMira Press was an important outlet for young scholars writing about gender. Several innovative approaches based on dissertations were published in the series. I was particularly pleased with Kelley Hays-Gilpin's *Ambiguous Images* (2004), with its foundational approach to gender in rock art around the world. Other comparative work is found in the *Handbook of Gender in Archaeology* (Nelson, ed. 2006) and, more recently, *Companion to Gender in Prehistory*, edited by Diane Bolger (2013).

And is there gender in Asian archaeology? Slowly, the word is spreading and finding enthusiasts. Lis Bacus, who works in the Philippines, and Rasmi Shoocongdej, from Thailand, both have PhDs from the University of Michigan, and both have written innovative gender papers. Edited volumes about gender in Asia include *Gender in Chinese Archaeology* (Linduff and Sun 2004) and *Are All Warriors Male?* (Linduff and Rubinson 2008), with archaeological papers from Central Asia. Both made big splashes in Asian archaeology circles. The China volume has been translated into Chinese.

I was invited to a gender symposium at Jilin University in northeast China, with Kathy Linduff, who has made converts to gender archaeology in China. In 2010, I was asked to give the keynote address for a gender symposium in Korea, organized by Yangjin Pak. Several of the speakers were women archaeologists from Korea and Japan, which I considered a great triumph for women in East Asian archaeology.

I have been asked how the network of women archaeologists differs from the networks that we dismissed as the "Old Boys." The answer has appeared in various places in this book, but perhaps it is worth repeating and emphasizing that power differentials make the difference: power to influence who gets grants for what kinds of projects, power to prevent publication of topics that are disagreed with, power to give preference to certain students, power to decide which symposia are placed in the most desirable spots in conference programs—the list is endless. It's true that more women are now found in the ranks of full professors, but it is also true that many brilliant and creative women archaeologists are employed in small colleges, where they tend to have heavier teaching loads and less time to be influential in the field. Granted that they are influencing students and many are doing first-rate research and writing, but they have scant access to grants because their college or small university may have lesser facilities than a research university.

Women are increasingly being elected as presidents of major organizations, which has the effect of slowly changing the way that business is done. It is important also to note that not all male archaeologists are "Old Boys" in the sense the expression is used above. Some have written gendered archaeology papers. The next chapter looks at women and gender in the past, and how finding them makes a difference to women in the present.

Chapter 5

The "Goddess Temple" and the Status of Women at Niuheliang, China

Niuheliang is a recently discovered Chinese site with several unexpected features, including life-sized female statues, an irregularly shaped building which is interpreted as a ceremonial center, a group of high-status burials, and a large number of finely worked jade ornaments. The site lacks domestic architecture, at least so far, but a number of refuse pits have been excavated. The most parsimonious explanation of the site is that it is a ceremonial center with intermittent use. The female iconography might be interpreted as indicating a previously unsuspected high status for women in the beginning of complex society in China, but such an interpretation needs to be made with care.

Radiocarbon dated to 3500–3000 B.C., the site of Niuheliang is a late manifestation of the Hongshan culture, showing clear signs of social stratification and other complexity. The site contains typical ceramics of the Hongshan culture of Liaoning province in northeastern China. The Hongshan culture appears to be an outgrowth of much earlier Manchurian cultures, rather than being derived from the Yangshao Neolithic of the Yellow River region, as was previously thought. The two Neolithic manifestations are now known to be of equivalent age. As early as about 7000 B.C. the site of Chahai near Fuxin has pottery with rocker-stamping, a trait which can be traced without a hiatus to the site of Niuheliang. In general these earlier sites (including Houwa and Xinle) contain pottery with impressed and incised designs. They are also characterized by jade working, in continuity with the Hongshan culture.

Sarah M. Nelson (1991a). In *The Archaeology of Gender, Proceedings of the 22nd Annual Chacmool Conference, Calgary*, edited by Dale Walde and Noreen Willows, pp. 302–308. Department of Archaeology, University of Calgary. Republished in *Shamans, Queens, and Figurines: The De-velopment of Gender Archaeology*, by Sarah Nelson, 113–119 (Taylor & Francis, 2015).

Hongshan sites, however, are notable for the addition of black-on-red painted pottery. The designs are similar to those of Yangshao, but they also have their characteristic differences. Contact with the Yellow River sites is now postulated to explain this phenomenon. Perhaps long distance trade was carried on between these regions, but it has not been sufficiently studied.

The subsistence base of Hongshan consisted of both grain agriculture and domesticated animals. The mix of animals is an odd one, with sheep as the major sacrificial animal, pigs represented in the iconography, and cattle appearing as grave offerings. The sites are located in the hilly region between the grasslands of Mongolia, which are suitable for range animals, and the wide, flat Manchurian plain, where millet cultivation and pig raising had been established for millennia Perhaps it was the conjunction of these ecological zones that gave the impetus for the florescence of the Hongshan culture.

Before describing the site of Niuheliang and its "Goddess Temple" in some detail, it will be useful to frame the discussion with some theoretical issues. The important question for this paper is, what is the meaning of the female statues? Can we infer anything about women's status from them? Can we learn anything fresh about the relationship between presumed goddess worship and women's place in the society from this archaeological example?

Peggy Sanday (1981) refers to myths about origins as "scripts" for interpreting the relationship between males and females; for female power or male dominance. She used creation stories, not the gender of the deities *per se*, but perhaps we may be permitted to consider goddess representations as a related phenomenon. The script for female power lies in the importance of women in the origin myths, linking the "symbolic template" with the sex role plan selected by that culture. Sanday's data indicate that the presence of female origin myths does not necessarily predict high status for women (Sanday 1981: 132). Thus archaeological interpretations must be made cautiously. In general, though, there is a tendency for these traits to occur together. Ian Hodder (1991) demonstrated that it is not possible to go directly from iconography to conclusions about gender, but it may still be an indication that can be followed up with other evidence.

Marija Gimbutas (1982) does read her sample of figurines from Old Europe as a script that tells us about gender relationships, although there is little discussion of the issue:

> The pantheon reflects a society dominated by the mother. The role of woman was not subject to that of a man, and much that was created between the inception of the Neolithic and the blossoming of the Minoan civilization

> was a result of that structure in which all resources of human nature, feminine and masculine, were utilized to the full as a creative force (Gimbutas 1982:237–238).

Gimbutas' line of argument is plausible but not compelling. In the case of Niuheliang, if we can consider the female figures as a script from which we can hypothesize female power, status, or autonomy, independent supporting data are required. I will consider two lines of evidence: continuous threads in Chinese culture which could be followed back to women of power, and skeletal evidence from the site itself.

One difficulty of approaching this question is that Chinese archaeologists see matriarchies in all the Neolithic sites of China, and so report them. This amounts to Marxist dogma, and is not necessarily supported by the data they adduce (Pearson 1988). While matrilineages cannot be ruled out, they are not conclusively demonstrated either. There is a delightful mural in the museum at the site of Xinle which illustrates this point. It depicts the matriarch holding her emblem of power—a wand with an elaborately carved bird. You will note that this society was remarkable in another way—none of the women seem to be much over the age of 20.

With the quantity of writing that has been preserved from ancient China, one might expect that the question of the meaning of the statues would be easily solved with reference to Chinese documents. However, Chinese written history is peculiarly, perhaps even uniquely, misogynist. Chinese historians have had little use for females. Women who ruled were inevitably portrayed as inept rulers, and were held up as examples of the pernicious influence of women. Even the Empress Wu, who ruled in the brilliant Tang dynasty, has gone down in Chinese history as a terrible tyrant. Perhaps one should say especially the Empress Wu, because successful women are particularly unforgivable. In the 6th century B.C., Confucius codified the inferiority of women, but it took many centuries after him to teach women their proper place, judging from the ferocity of the historians' attacks.

But China did have female deities, inexpungible from the folklore and literary writings of China. Most notable of these is the Queen Mother of the West, whose powers were fearful. Does she reflect a pre-Confucian time, a time when women did not have to obey their husbands? This question is unanswerable with written documents, but perhaps the forebears of the Queen Mother of the West are portrayed at Niuheliang.

The earliest writing in China comes from the Shang dynasty, in the 16th to 10th centuries B.C., 14 centuries and more after Niuheliang. It consists of inscriptions on oracle bones, relating largely to warfare and the weather, but also to health and childbirth. The rulers named on the oracle bones and in later histories are all men. The accuracy of the king lists has been confirmed by the oracle bone inscriptions, and the royal graves provide additional evidence of their historicity (Chang, K.-C. 1980b). Yet a 1976 discovery at the capital of Anyang contains a surprise. It is not a royal grave, but it is the richest grave that has ever been found with all the burial goods intact. The Tomb of Fu Hao is the burial of a woman. Her name (or rank or title, there is some dispute about this which is not relevant here [Chang C. L. 1986]) is inscribed on the bronze vessels which constitute part of her burial suite. One of the bronzes is the largest known from the Shang dynasty (Qian 1981). Fu Hao is named on some oracle bones as a king's consort, on others as a leader of armies (Chang P. -C. 1986). Without doubt the grave is that of a person of importance, not mentioned in the later histories. This is enough to emphasize the autonomy and power of at least upper class women of the Shang dynasty, suggesting that women's power may have persisted even to the origin of the state in China. But there is another salient feature of Fu Hao's grave. She was buried with three bronze mirrors—not only the earliest mirrors in Shang, but also mirrors in the style of the "Northern Bronzes", from the same region as Niuheliang (Lin 1986). The northern connection of Fu Hao, an important woman of Shang, strengthens the possibility of a persistent tradition of female power in the hills between Mongolia and Manchuria.

And what of the North? Does Niuheliang provide the missing link between the possible "matriarchies" of the Neolithic and the enigmatic grave of Fu Hao?

Let's turn to the site of Niuheliang, which is spread over the tops of several adjacent hills. It appears to be purely a ceremonial center with several areas of tombs. Test pits at Niuheliang were made in seven areas, six of which are burial clusters (Fang and Wei 1986a).

At the highest elevation there are two features: a "platform" and the "goddess temple". The platform is an enormous rectangle, 175 × 159 meters. It was made of earth, edged all around with stone walls which are still intact in several places. The longest consecutive stretch remaining is 85 meters. Surface scatter includes sherds of red pottery and globs of burnt clay. An interpretation as a gathering place for outdoor ceremonies seems possible. To the north of the platform there is an area of burnt clay 13 meters long by 5 meters wide. Red potsherds and a piece of an unbaked statue—a larger than life-size human ear—were found in a test excavation. Perhaps this is a pottery firing area, and/or the place where statues were constructed.

Three pits were discovered in the vicinity of the platform. One, an ashpit, is 12 meters south of the platform, and the other is 61 meters to the east. The latter pit, which is very long and narrow (7.2 × 1.7 m.), is full of potsherds of cylindrical painted vessels. These vessels seem to have only a ceremonial function since, having no base, they could not have been used as containers. Yet another small (1.74 × 1.64 m.) rectangular pit was found. Six layers of fine clay had been applied to the walls and burned to harden them. These enigmatic pits may be simply disposal places for ritually dangerous broken materials.

The "goddess temple", located below the platform and 18 meters to the south, is an irregularly shaped building containing several rooms with curved walls. Overall it measures 18.4 × 6.9 meters. A test trench in the main room located a number of pieces of painted clay statues representing women in the main room—a head, shoulder, arms, breasts, and hands, belonging to several different statues. Although the clay was not baked, very fine clay was applied to the exterior and then painted, so that some of the pieces did not entirely disintegrate. The face of a life-sized statue is quite striking. It is painted pink, and has blue jade disks set in to represent eyeballs.

Traces of red, yellow, and white paint in geometric patterns, most commonly triangles and hook shapes, were found on the small footing of the remaining wall. In other rooms there were parts of a "pig-dragon" and the claws of a large clay bird statue. A vessel lid with rocker-stamped designs and a whole round-based bowl were also found. A very large example of the cylindrical red-painted pottery was excavated from the temple as well. A small pointed tool of dark red flint and a grinding stone were the only tools unearthed in the ceremonial center. Another smaller building is located to the south of the main ceremonial center.

An ashpit 12 meters to the south of the temple was excavated. This pit is just under three meters in diameter and 1.5 meters deep. Mixed with the white ash are potsherds, stone tools, and animal bones, mainly sheep long bones which have been chopped up and burned. The pottery is mostly brown and black utilitarian pottery, suggesting refuse from the daily lives of the temple personnel while the site was active.

Down the slope from the temple the most impressive of the tombs are located. There are four large stone tombs in a line from east to west. The earth which covered the tombs appears to have accumulated later, although the innermost layer is a dark humus soil with sherds of the red-painted cylinders, which might have been deliberately placed over the stones. All the tombs have been robbed, so there has been some displacement of the stones, but it is possible to discern the original shapes of the tombs. The grave robbers left the elaborately carved jades; we don't know what they took. Grave Z-1, for example, is rectangular, 26.8 × 19.5 meters. It is composed of an inner wall and an outer wall, with earth between containing sherds of red cylindrical vessels. On the less disturbed side a row of 24 of these vessels was discovered in place, with the painted sides facing outward. In the inner space there were 15 small graves, many sharing a wall with another grave pit. Each pit was outlined with stone slabs or piles of rocks, and stone slabs covered the pit. Contents of the graves differed remarkably.

For example grave M-4 was long and narrow, 1.98 meters × 0.4 wide. The body was buried on its back with ankles crossed, left leg on top. A polished tubular jade ornament was placed at the back of the skull, and two jade rings in the shape of "pig-dragons", one white and one light green, were placed back to back on the chest. This grave also contained sherds of a large cylindrical vessel. M-6 adjoins M-4, and has many similarities. However, the bones of the single burial were piled together in the center of the grave, and there were no grave goods. M-7 contains three bodies, also secondary burials. Two jade rings and two round flat jade pieces (*bi*) were buried with them and placed on top of the piles of bones. M-11 contained scattered bones of a secondary burial and three jade pieces—a ring, a square-shaped ornament, and a bar-shaped ornament. M-14 contains an extended burial with its hands across the abdomen. Two jade bracelets were on the wrists, and a finely carved white jade piece lay on the chest. M-15 also has an extended burial. There are five jades—a cylinder under the head, a *bi* and a ring at the waist, and a bracelet on each wrist.

The next large stone tomb, Z-2, is almost square, 18.7 × 17.5 meters. There is a square stone construction in the middle, 3.6 meters on each side, which the excavators call the outer coffm. On the inside there is a space 2.21 × .85 meters. The grave had been looted, leaving only one human bone, along with a few red potsherds and pig and cow bones. Outside the inner coffin on the south side there were abundant red sherds. No additional burials are noted.

In contrast to the other graves, Z-3 is round. There are three circles of pink granite on the ground under the mound. The inner ring is made of the smallest stones, with increasingly bigger circles toward the outside while the height of each ring increases toward the center. The outer ring has a diameter of 22 meters, the innermost about 11 meters. There are many sherds of the red cylindrical pottery. Three skeletons were found, but no burial objects.

Two other pits were excavated between the ceremonial center and the tombs. H-2 is an oval pit, 1.8 meters in length. The earth in the pit was fine, and contained sherds of plain red and painted bowls, and black pottery with rocker-stamping. There were also animal bones and lumps of red burnt clay. H-3 is a larger pit, about 3 meters in diameter. It is quite shallow, only 0.45 meters. Vessels for daily use were found on the bottom of this pit, including a jar with two ears on the sides, a wide-mouthed shouldered jar, and two bowls. There are also sherds painted black-on-red. A small human head modeled from brown clay, and a crude, broken human torso, were also found. Two chipped stone tools complete the artifact inventory. This may have been a cache for reusable items, if the site were only visited intermittently.

Although not all the features of Niuheliang are easily explained, and some of my guesses may prove to be wrong, its designation as a ceremonial center seems appropriate. The authors of the report conclude that the statues represent "some powerful people and ancestors," and that there is a "sacred system" of stratification. Not only the complexities of the site, but also the creation of a mythical animal, the pig-dragon, signals a highly complex culture. But the excavators make no specific comment on the gender meaning inherent in their finds.

If we take the Sanday and Gimbutas models as hypotheses, it would be possible to test them at this site. Most obviously, we need to know the sex of the skeletons. If they are all female, we are probably safe in concluding that women were the priestesses and perhaps secular rulers as well as the goddesses, given the thread of continuity to later times. If they are mixed, then we need to know which burials are women. Depending on which they are and how they are treated, women could have high status as well as men. However, if the burials are all male, that would suggest that the high status of women as deities did not extend to social stratification. It is clearly crucial to any gender interpretation to know the sex of the skeletons, a task that has not yet been accomplished.

It would also be useful to learn the contents of the other groups of burials on the hillside of Niuheliang. Are they lower status burials? Was everyone in the society buried in this sacred spot? What size population do the burials imply, over what range of territory? The site is intriguing, and perhaps eventually may be able to answer some of the questions regarding early gender hierarchies in northern China.

Chapter 6
Feminist Theory, Leadership, and the Spirits of States in East Asia

> One thing about the shamans involving a condition alien to healthy individuals has always impressed observers: the incoherent exclamations and movements, the foaming at the mouth, vacant stare, and total loss of consciousness at one of the most critical moments of the ritual (Basilov 1997:3).

> Anciently, human beings and spirits did not mix. But certain persons who were so perspicacious, single-minded, reverential and correct that their intelligence could understand what lies above and below, their sagely wisdom could illumine what is distant and profound, their vision was bright and clear, and their hearing was penetrating. Therefore the spirits would descend upon them. The possessors of such power were, if men, called xi, and if women, wu. They supervised the positions of the spirits at ceremonies, took care of sacrificial victims and vessels as well as of the seasonal robes.
>
> Guo-yu, Chu-yu, part 2, 18:1a. Translated by Ching (1997:14–15).

These two contradictory views of shamans (minimally defined for this paper as people who have the ability to interact with spirits) illuminate several difficulties with discussing shamanism, leadership and gender in East Asia. An obvious place to begin is the contrast between the disdain of shamans shown by Basilov, the Soviet ethnologist in the first quote, and the admiration of the author of the Guo-yu. The latter shamans are seen to achieve their positions by exhibiting high intelligence and many other virtues. Basilov's shamans are abnormal and sick.

Sarah M. Nelson (2011). From *Archaeologies, Journal of the World Archaeological Congress*, Vol. 7, No. 1 (April): 34–55. Republished in *Shamans, Queens, and Figurines: The Development of Gen-der Archaeology*, by Sarah Nelson, pp. 121–136 (Taylor & Francis, 2015).

The way Anglo-American scholars have learned to think of shamans is more like Basilov's version than that of the Guo-yu. This has arisen from dependence on the foundational work of Eliade (1964), who insisted on ecstasy as the core of shamanism. Not only does focusing on ecstasy lead to the perception of abnormality, but much of the data for Eliade's book came from people who had been persecuted by the Soviets, while the wu and xi of the Guo-yu were serving the state. In addition, the two observations are roughly 22 centuries apart in time.

Eliade's work has been criticized by cultural anthropologists (eg. Kehoe 2000) and historians who study shamans in East and Central Asia (eg. Humphrey 1996). The insistence on ecstasy and its concomitants "has made some forms of shamanism peculiarly attractive as forms of scholarly investigation and has made others appear derivative, impure, or secondary" (Thomas and Humphrey 1996:2). Thomas and Humphrey (1996:4) focus on the political dimension of shamanism. They write of "dynamics of state formation in which charismatic power may be appropriated and incorporated at the center or rendered peripheral and persecuted." In much of East Asia, charismatic power was appropriated by the leadership of the state, especially at the beginning of state formation.

As Humphrey (1996:195) points out, "many of the tribal peoples of Eliade's time had been imperial rulers some centuries before." Humphrey specifically examines the issue of states and shamanism in North Asia, including the Manchu Empire which ruled China as the Qing dynasty from 1644 to 1911, as well as its northern predecessors, the [Khitan] Liao Empire (946–1125), the [Jurchen] Jin Empire (1115–1234), and the [Mongol] Yuan Empire (1206–1368). Although Humphrey is looking at later times, there are strong elements of northern influence in the Shang dynasty [1550–1050 BCE] (eg. horses, chariots, divination by cracking bones in fire, mirrors, types of knives and weapons, and of course shamanism) which make it analogous to these later northern overlords of China. A concern with "kinship, ancestry and geography" (Humphrey 1996:194) also characterizes the Late Shang.

The opinion of the Guo-yu is likely to be more relevant to the even earlier Shang dynasty than Eliade's compendium of "archaic techniques of ecstasy." Basilov's shamans were reindeer herders and hunters living in the forests of Siberia, whose religion and customs had been under attack by Soviet Russia (Reid 2002:157–166). The Chu State was one of the Warring States of China (450–221 BCE), with a bureaucracy and an army. A poem describing the shaman's ability to woo a spirit speaks of silks and chariots (Waley 1955). The two worlds are far apart.

The East Asian view is that the ability to "interact with spirits" is at the heart of shamanism, no matter how the interaction may be accomplished. Ecstasy is one of the ways to contact spirits, but spirits can be called down with ritual, songs, dancing or other means. Thinking about shamanism in this way, shamanism and gender are both relevant to discussions about leadership in East Asia, especially China, Korea and Japan.

GOALS OF THIS PAPER

In this paper I challenge several deeply entrenched ideas in archaeology with reference to feminist and other theory. These involve prevailing views of gender, religion, power and leadership in state-level societies. I argue that in East Asia, power in early states was derived from religion, that shamanism was that form of religion, that shamans were leaders, and that shaman leaders could be (and often were) women. While this position goes against the received wisdom, the archaeological, historical and ethnographic data demand that it be taken seriously.

RELEVANT THEORIES

To discuss the relevance of gender and spirits to the formation of states in East Asia requires an excursion into theories of several kinds. A new emphasis on the interrelation of religion and politics is a useful entry into these topics. Current studies of religion and politics in Asia provide a number of examples. Scholars who work in Asia have begun to critique Hegelian and Weberian ideas that saw religion as apolitical. For example, Paramore (2010: 18) notes that, "religion [was] allocated a certain passivity by having been defined apart from the political realm in a specialized sociological category." Van der Veer (2010:19) states the current view from Asia: "religion is always political, always concerns power, including the definition of power."

At least beginning in the Shang dynasty contemporary texts show that power was derived from nature spirits and an ultimate deity called Shang Di through deceased ancestors of the ruler. The ruler had access to his ancestors by means of divination and sacrifice (Keightley 2000). In contrast, early rulers of Korea and Japan claimed access to the Spirits directly, based on their personal links to Spirits of Mountains (especially Korea), Sun (especially Japan), and other Spirits (Nelson 1995b).

As can be seen in the quote above from the Guo-yu, gender is highly relevant to the discussion of Spirits and ancient Asian states. In ancient China shamans were called *wu* if women and *xi* if men, but the generic word for shaman is *wu*, suggesting that women comprised most of the shamans. Thus it is important to survey feminist theories. Feminist theory provides alternative perspectives on leadership, leaders and the processes of state formation.

While awareness of the potential roles of women in specific past societies is a big step in the right direction, simply recognizing the existence of women, or even giving the nod to socially constructed gender, is not enough. The archaeology of gender is grounded in theory, not merely the addition of women and/or gender. This lack of attention to feminist theory has been all too obvious in some of the less nuanced ways that women have been "added" to the archaeological record. Responding to this need, I concentrate on women and leadership, focusing on a particular path to power in a particular place—shamanism in East Asia.

The inability to perceive women rulers is related to theories of the origin of states which have assumed, implicitly or explicitly, men as leaders. The terms of leadership are masculine: chiefs, kings, emperors. In this context it becomes obvious that it makes a difference whether gender is theorized or merely acknowledged. The study of religion as a powerful mover in East Asian archaeology is an example of the way gender theory can lead in new directions, going well beyond simply acknowledging women in the archaeological record.

Spencer-Wood (1998) aptly describes feminist theory as "peeling the androcentric onion," because feminists are continually probing more deeply into standard archaeological theory, and finding previously unnoticed ways that women have been trivialized or erased from the past. Confronting the taken-for-granteds of archaeology is getting close to the center of the "androcentric onion."

Thus while the general awareness that women were present in the past has penetrated the archaeological consciousness, feminist theory so far has rarely challenged concepts of political development. An important exception is *Ungendering Civilization* (Pyburn, ed. 2000), in which the authors challenge the much cited view of Engels about women having lost power with the origin of the state, discussed below.

But for most discussions of the origin of states, the very words we use imply male leadership. As I have shown previously (Nelson [1997a] 2004), feminist theories improve archaeological interpretations, and therefore need more attention in archaeology, in spite of the many feminist ground-breaking studies that have already been accomplished. An excellent approach to well-known and well-worn archaeological/anthropological theory by examining both the theory and specific data is discussed by Pyburn (2000:5). Pyburn explains the purpose of the book: "to engage with assumptions about gender that underlie research on ancient civilizations." She goes on to show that "the old arguments and categories of cultural evolution" need to be dismantled. This is truly getting to the core of the androcentric onion.

My study is less ambitious, but related. In terms of gender theory I propose to challenge the prevailing notion that leadership at a state level is necessarily male. Even though at present few studies fail to notice that women existed in the past, the starring roles are still presumed to belong to men. Women leaders are especially understudied, since the very terminology used is male-biased, and tends to preclude considering any women as forces in the formation of states. As Pyburn (2000:31) notes, "invariably, the stronger the public role of women, the less likely archaeologists are to characterize a culture as a civilization."

I have been interested in understanding women as leaders from the perspective of anthropological archaeology for several years (Nelson 1991b, 1993b, 1997a [2004], 2003b, 2008a). Although much current scholarship acknowledges occasional women rulers but considers them as anomalies, there have been a number of state-level polities in which rulership by women was acceptable or even preferred. While many women rulers are visible archaeologically, often these rulers have been unacknowledged, understudied, or even denied (Arwill-Nordbladh 2003; Bell 2003; Linduff 1996, 2002, 2003; McCafferty and McCafferty 2003; Troy 2003; Vogel 2003). The same may be true of early historic women rulers, such as those acknowledged in the early history of Japan (Piggott 1997, 1999).

But how can women as leaders be recognized in archaeology? Wylie (2002:186) shows that while some archaeologists perceived that the early development of feminist archaeology may have been hampered by a lack of relevant data, data become relevant because they are constituents of a theoretical paradigm. As Wylie (2002:xiv) shows, "what you find archaeologically has everything to do with what is looked for, the questions asked and the conceptual resources brought to bear in attempting to answer them." A feminist archaeologist must be creative in finding ways to select data relevant to a particular question.

Two important trends in feminist archaeology are noted by Brumfiel (2006), trends which are important for uncovering and recognizing relevant data. These trends are an emphasis on variability rather than central tendencies, and analyses of single sites or regions to further sharpen the analysis. Stressing variability requires that categories such as "women" or "men" be broken into a number of subgroups, which are not necessarily exclusive. An individual may have competing or complementary identities, being simultaneously defined by age, class, possibly ethnicity, and other factors in addition to gender. Feminist theory highlights the fact that archaeological categories are rarely refined enough to understand societies and their constituent parts. In some archaeological analyses, men are seen as having varied roles by age, status, and so forth, while variations in women's lives, ages and stages are not examined. Including women as actors makes for more complicated analyses, but the analyses are more likely to go beyond simple platitudes. My recent work on shamanism in East Asian archaeology is an example of how feminist theories can be used to explore questions of women and state formation, and how new questions arise when feminist theory is part of the equation.

Shamanism in East Asian Archaeology

This study did not begin with a focus on either gender or shamanism. My original intention was to revisit state formation in East Asia because it failed to conform to any previously discussed theory. The eminent Chinese archaeologist Chang (1983, 2005) perceived that the forces at work in the origin of the Chinese state differ profoundly from other "pristine" states. He believed that shamanism played a large part, especially in the Shang dynasty (1500–1050 BCE), the first dynasty in China in which contemporaneous writing has been preserved. Chang's arguments include "art, myth, and ritual" and are based on Chinese texts, depictions on Chinese bronzes, and remnants of myths deduced from poetry and other later writings in addition to archaeological data. Childs-Johnson (1995) has also seen shamanism in Chinese Neolithic and Shang art.

While I was pondering alternative ways to think about state formation in East Asia, a summary of recent archaeological excavations in China was published, which concerns the formation of Chinese civilization (Chang and Xu 2005). Chapters are written by Chinese archaeologists, who describe Neolithic and Shang sites of which many are described as having shaman leaders. A variety of manifestations of ritual that could be shamanistic are highlighted: a burial with a possible shaman's costume (a bell at the waist), persons buried with drums or flutes, raised round and square platforms glossed as "altars" that are seen as the prototypes of later temples to Heaven and Earth as non-anthropomorphic deities, and sites that seem to reflect Chinese asterisms and the associated beliefs. The book is rich in data, and interprets the Neolithic period as leading to shaman kings in the Shang dynasty. Evidence for shamans in the Shang period includes the use of the word "wu" (translated as "shaman") on oracle bones, descriptions on the oracle bones of activities of wu, and art that is purported to depict shamans and their animal familiars, especially several that show a human head in the jaws of a tiger (Chang 1983).

No further work might have been needed on the topic, but Chang (2005: 129) adamantly insisted that the shamans were all male because "the extant evidence indicates that shamans were males, but sometimes they enacted both male and female roles." I have long been interested in the shamans of East Asia, and knew how much evidence this statement ignores, especially when the perspective is wider than China, to include all of East Asia, and encompasses East Asia up to the present.

Chang's argument was framed to exclude most evidence of women shamans, archaeological, historical, and ethnographic. But by reframing the issue to include the rest of East Asia and a longer span of time, the insistence on male shamans can be seen as a poor fit. The current shamans of Okinawa, Kyushu, Hokkaido, Korea and Manchuria are all or mostly women. Tedlock (2005) has pointed out that even in Siberia, the supposed region of shamanist origins, most shamans in the historic and ethnographic record are women, as they are in the present. Thus even the reputed homeland of shamanism was known for women who approached the spirits, who were knowledgeable, and who were leaders.

Historic records show that women were shamans during the time that states were forming in Korea and Japan as well as China. It would be an odd and unexplained reversal of gender roles if most shamans of the Neolithic and early states had been male. One explanation that is often given by those who insist on male shamans is that shamanism lost its prestige through time, and therefore its practitioners became female. The problem with this twist is that it begs the question of why shamanism would lose prestige. If the answer is because women are the shamans, then the explanation is circular. Archaeology, history, and ethnology together provide better answers.

But before detailing the gender issues, two other questions have to be considered. Does the archaeological record suggest shamanism before the Shang dynasty? If so, is there evidence for shamans as leaders?

Archaeological sites produce many kinds of possible evidence for shamans in Neolithic China, as detailed in Chang and Xu (2005), but the lack of a pattern is troublesome. The evidence implies a variety of rituals, but each site is an individual event, unreplicated at any other site. There is nothing to suggest widespread closely related shamanisms.

The sites show a number of traits that are consistent with shamanism. Certainly music, which is important in shamanism, is evident early—flutes are the earliest, by 7,000 BCE (Zhang et al. 1999) but chime stones, drums and bells are all found in Neolithic contexts. Music of course can be used for entertainment as well as ritual, but the two are intertwined in shamanism. The presence of so many musical instruments can be reasonably interpreted as a way to seek or call spirits.

Astronomical beliefs about the sky can be related to shamanism. "Soul flight" implies passage through the sky, and there is no doubt that early peoples of Asia observed sky phenomena closely. Chinese beliefs about large asterisms, such as the dragon and tiger of the east and west, do seem to have been present in Neolithic China (Zhang 2005). The concept of the earth as square and the sky as round could underlie the shapes of early "altars" such as were found at Niuheliang (Guo 1995a). The Puyang burial is particularly suggestive of later beliefs, with shell figures as large as the skeleton ranged on each side—a dragon on the east and a tiger on the west. But while the shell figures seem to reflect later Chinese beliefs about directional animals, they are not necessarily related to shamanism. Thus while it is not beyond question that such sites demonstrate shamanism, it is a reasonable possibility that they are related to religious beliefs and practices, given later texts.

Burials that are interpreted as those of shamans are usually found with more grave goods than other contemporary burials. They are, of course, also interpreted as members of the elite. Whether or not these burials are appropriately identified as shamans, they are clearly leaders. Such burials are usually ascribed to males, unless there are artifacts such as hairpins that demand the interpretation of females in Chinese contexts.

The gender issue is complicated by perceiving women of the Neolithic and Bronze Age through the texts of much later historians. An attempt must be made to understand the early societies without the filter of later histories. Von Falkenhausen (2006) suggests that as clans became the social glue of Chinese society, males became the social players, because only male ancestors counted. Because of this bias it is likely that later historians therefore erased much about women, although some information about queens and goddesses can be teased out of even that literature (Paper 1995; Schafer 1973). A goddess known as the Queen Mother of the West is mentioned in an oracle bone of the Shang period (Cahill 1993). A belief in Nu Wa, a creator goddess called Changing woman, is found in a number of contexts, including her appearance on a banner covering a woman's coffin at Mawangdui, from the Chu dynasty (Major 1999).

Ancient Chinese historians, who had a gendered axe to grind, looked down upon the state of Chu, which still included shamans (female as well as male) and worshipped goddesses as well as gods (Cook and Major 1999). If Chinese archaeologists had been grounded in feminist theory, they would have been able to balance the biases of ancient historians with the archaeological discoveries, allowing them to consider their data from additional perspectives, such as myths as scripts for gender roles (Sanday 1981).

In ancient East Asia beyond China the rulers themselves often performed as shamans. This is the case in Korea and Japan, where written records note women who were shamans and leaders (Barnes 2007), and depictions of shamans are often female.

Leadership and shamanism thus were intertwined in the era of state formation on the north and east of China, from the Russian Far East, through the Korean peninsula, and all through the adjacent islands as far south as Taiwan. This circumstance shows a widespread practice of shamanism, and suggests historical continuity. It also implies that these cultures did not share in the derogation of women that took place in China. Left to their own devices, these regions made no gender distinctions in leadership. The gender disparities of the present are the result of late influence from China, the prevalence of warfare, and perhaps other factors as well.

TIME, TRENDS, AND GENDER

Early Agriculture

The distribution of artifacts in male and female graves suggests to many Chinese archaeologists that the division of labor by gender began as early as the Sixth Millennium BCE. Indeed, if the attributions of the invention of pottery, weaving and tailoring to women are correct, the gendered division of labor arose even earlier. Evidence for males as planters and women as textile creators and food processors is said to be present in the Peiligang culture of north central Henan province, China, where grinding equipment is "never in same grave with stone axes, sickles or spades" (Zhang 2005). Spindle whorls and needles were placed only in female burials, thus suggesting the creation of clothing as another of the transformations wrought by women.

While it is important to be somewhat reserved with such attributions, since the division of labor is rarely absolute, the artifacts may mark a general trend in men's work and women's work. If these burials do indicate a gendered division of labor, and we can confidently associate needles with women, then it becomes possible to interpret the bone needles in jade turtle-shaped boxes at Jiahu (Zhang 2005) as belonging to women. Turtles were (and are) associated with Spirits (Allan 1991). Thus these burials can be reasonably interpreted as women shamans who were buried with costly artifacts implying elite status. Jade is associated with elites and turtles with Spirits in East Asia.

At sites of the northeastern Xinglongwa culture (8000–6000 BCE), crude female statues less than a meter high foreshadow both the life-sized statues of the Hongshan period (4000–2500 BCE) Goddess Temple at Niuheliang and the smaller figures at the ritual site of Dongshanzui. Whether spirits of ancestors or spirits of nature, they were gendered female.

The social structure of Neolithic China as it might be reflected in burials has been widely discussed. One particularly intriguing idea is that cultural elements from the Shandong region were introduced into the Central Plains in the Late Neolithic by females, understood as wives who had come from Dawenkou sites to Dahecun, a site near Zhengzhou (Shao 2005). Female burials include eastern pottery shapes such as *ding* cooking vessels raised on legs, and *dou*, serving dishes on pedestals. This interpretation suggests that women as marriage partners were cementing the links between regions long before the Shang and Zhou periods. Such wives might also have brought shamanism from the northern and coastal regions to the Yellow River valley. *Dou* in particular often are found in ritual contexts, and even today are used on shamans' altars in Korea.

Not only gender but age differentiation is evident at the site of Sanlihe in eastern Shandong. Elderly women were given special burial treatment, including extremely thin pottery vessels, jade, and turquoise (Underhill 2002: 192). One interpretation of this phenomenon could be that these women lived to old age because they were privileged with enough food and perhaps servants to make life easy throughout their lives. Another possible interpretation is that those who managed to live to a great age implied greater wisdom which afforded them status. A third possibility is that they were shamans and/or leaders. In any case, the privilege is marked by gender associated with age. Old men are not given the same treatment in death at this site.

Late Neolithic gender distinction also occurs in the placement of bodies by sex at Dadianzi, Inner Mongolia about 1600 BCE. Women were buried facing east, away from the site, while men faced toward the site. The direction of burial is not a status marker. Burials of women and men displayed ranking in the depth of burials and the amount and kind of burial goods. It is possible that the direction of the body indicated that women married into the village from elsewhere. Of the bodies that were well preserved enough to be sexed the number of males (297) and females (286) is approximately the same. Slightly more women than men reached old age, which suggests equal nutrition and equal hardships (or lack of them). Social status was expressed by the size and depth of the burial, the number of niches, and the number and quality of grave goods (Wagner 2006).

The Shang Dynasty

An important royal woman who served the spirits, in addition to leading armies and owning land, was Lady Hao, a wife of King Wu Ding of the Late Shang. Hers is the only unlooted royal burial unearthed so far in the Shang capital at Anyang. Both oracle bone inscriptions and the splendor of her burial offerings demonstrate her impressive accomplishments. David Keightley summarized the meaning of Lady Hao's life for elite women of her time:

> Inscriptions and archaeological finds, such as the richly furnished tomb of the royal consort Fu Hao . . . show that women wielded considerable power in the Shang state—some of them even commanded armies. They may also have influenced the succession. In general, the throne passed from brother to brother, but at certain points it shifted to the next generation, at times that may have been determined by the status of the candidates' mother. This may have occurred when the king's wife was deemed of higher status than the next brother (the heir), in which case the succession would pass to her son by the king. The succeeding Zhou state used primogeniture and denied such importance to women—Zhou propaganda denounced the Shang kings for being female-dominated (Keightley 1999a:25).

The possible influences of elder women did not escape Keightley's (1999a:31) attention, as well as the potential power of wives who brought their own entourage to the Shang court. Shang oracle bones have preserved the names of three women shamans: Lady Yang, Lady Fang, and Lady Fan. Later legends memorialized two of them as Wu Yang and Wu Fan.

China in the Warring States and Beyond

In some of the states of the Late Eastern Zhou period shamanism was alive and well. The state of Chu, for example, is generally agreed to have included practicing shamans, the poetry indicating both women and men (Cook and Major 1999). Shamans, leaders, and gods could all be female in this civilization. Women's influence remained in China throughout the dynasties, and women continued to be knowledgeable about many things. Superstitious rulers turned to women to tell the future, for example female astrologers in the court of the second emperor of Later Chao (AD 334–349) (Paper 1995:fn 20). In order to end a drought in AD 773, the mayor of the capital city constructed an earthen dragon, and personally performed a contradance with the *wuxi*, female and male shamans.

Women Shamans in the Korean Peninsula

The presence of women shamans in Korea from early historic periods until the present is indisputable. At least one queen of the Silla kingdom was buried with the trappings of leadership, including a crown and belt made of sheet gold with shamanistic symbols (Nelson 1991b, 1993b, 2003b). Women continued to share in family inheritance and influence the family through the succeeding Koryo dynasty. It was only with the Yi dynasty (1392–1910), when Confucianism became central to the state, that women began to lose status in Korea (Deuchler 1992).

Female shamans appear regularly in the histories of the Korean dynasties up to the Yi dynasty (Kim Y.-C., ed. 1977). They are still present in large numbers in South Korea (Howard 1998). Current Korean shamans are colorful and forceful. They are not considered to have high status, but they make a good living and have a great deal of autonomy (Kendall 1985).

Shamans in Japan

On the main islands of Japan, ritual is evident as early as 13,000 BCE. Increasingly complex objects with likely ritual uses, such as artifacts made of lacquer and pottery, are found throughout the Jomon period (Ikawa-Smith 1992). A burial of a woman shaman is particularly impressive (Pearson 2007). Women shamans were noted as leaders by Chinese observers during the Yayoi period, and are described in the early histories (Seyock 2004). The Kofun period included reigning queens as well as kings, and sometimes a male and female pair ruled jointly (Piggott 1997, 1999). Barnes (2007) points out the many roles of women, including shamans. Female shamans called *miko* still exist in Japan (Blacker 1975). Women were and remain both ritual and secular leaders in Okinawa. The system of women ritual leaders has continued in spite of invaders, trade, and other religious systems (Rokkum 1998). The tradition of women as shamans is exceptionally strong throughout East Asia outside of China.

The culture of China is not monolithic, but is like a mosaic of interlocking cultures (Triestman 1972). Is shamanism part of the cultural mosaic? Certainly different Neolithic sites have different alleged manifestations of shamanism. But there is also attention to the ancestors. By the Late Neolithic, many sites indicate graveside feasting, which has been taken to imply ancestor worship (Fung 2000; Liu 2003; Nelson 2003b; Underhill 2002). The belief in spirits may be the thread upon which East Asian shamanisms hang, but each region seems to have maintained its own paraphernalia and its own rituals. Shamanisms are not static, but have been modified, and even have disappeared (and perhaps reappeared) in some areas.

Scapulimancy is found earliest in the northeast and northwest. Bronze mirrors also are derived from the west (Juliano 1985; Linduff 1996, 1997; Rubinson 2002). The tomb of Lady Hao of the Shang contained northern style bronze mirrors in her grave, along with jades that could have been used in shamanistic rites. Lady Hao is mentioned in the oracle bones as a preparer of the bones for addressing the spirits.

Shamans were typical among the Yue coastal culture of Shandong. Chinese recorded the Yueshi as non-Chinese (Cohen 2001), but they nevertheless influenced the culture of the plains, and may have been more "cultured" than the central groups (Keightley 1986). Comparing archaeological materials and texts, Keightley came to the conclusion that a relationship between Shang and the Yueshi was likely. This notion founders on the probability that the language of the oracle bones was a form of Chinese, but allows one to wonder if Shang was a hybrid culture. Close connections between Shang and Chu have strong advocates (Chang, K.-C. 1983). Either scenario would suggest a heritage of shamanism from the east coast Shandong area, derived ultimately from Inner Mongolia and Liaoning. Connection between Dadianzi, Yueshi and Erlitou is implied by similar painted designs (Fitzgerald-Huber 1995:22). While the Shang themselves may have been related to the Dong Yi, another way to interpret the sudden appearance of horse-drawn chariots along with writing on oracle bones at the time of King Wu Ding is to attribute the horses and religious writing to one of Wu Ding's wives from a distant land. The most likely candidate is Lady Hao, with Northern Bronzes in her burial (Linduff 2003). This observation is important in terms of weighing evidence of the Shang kings as shaman leaders. Perhaps King Wu Ding did not have shamanism in his tradition, but Lady Hao very likely did. We know from oracle bone inscriptions that she performed duties relating to spirits.

Influences from the west (and vice versa) continued through time. By the Zhou dynasty these influences west are more obvious than those from other directions. Especially in Late Zhou, the Warring States Period, variability in the states was visible in their artifacts. For example, the Zhongshan state, with its shamanistic symbolism, can be seen to have a number of stylistic patterns related to the "steppe silk road" (Wu, X. 2004:7).

In Korea and Japan, successors of early shamans built upon the leadership of small polities to become leaders of larger polities and eventually states, with the power to conduct long-distance trade, organize artisans, garner the most costly and desirable possessions, wage war, and claim additional political and economic powers. Shamans were able to accomplish the integration of larger polities by basing the right to rulership on a claim of access to several kinds of spirits—both ancestors and nature Powers, whose benevolence was believed to be required for human life and society to continue and prosper. Furthermore, those endowed with the knowledge and ability to reach the spirits were credited with the ability to affect the future. They accomplished this feat by discovering the intent of the spirits through divination, and making the proper sacrifices to produce the desired outcome. The well-being of the community and eventually the continuation of the state itself depended on the knowledge of shaman-leaders.

The stage of shaman rulers was followed by the bureaucratization of ritual, but even under that circumstance shamans continued to perform important activities for society, and to hold the popular imagination. In spite of attempts by later bureaucratic states to suppress shamanism, forms of shamanism have survived in Korea (Howard 1998; Kendall 1985), central Japan (Blacker 1975), and Okinawa (Lebra 1964; Rokkum 1998; Sered 1999). Even Daoism in China, which often seems staid and more philosophical than religious, has permitted some shamanistic branches (Ching 1997:xiv; Major 1999:138). The "non-Chinese" rulers of the Chu state in the late Warring States period continued to function as shamans (Cook and Major 1999), and folk religions in China often retain shamanistic elements (Paper 1995:140). Both elite and popular religion found the ecstatic experience important (Paper 1995:81), perhaps as "evidence" of the ability to contact the multiple dangerous Powers. Shamanism remained potent in many East Asian states, in spite of Confucian disdain.

THE GENDER OF THE POWERS

Sanday (1981) argues that origin myths and deities describe the gender template of a culture. In this light, it is interesting to consider the female deities of East Asia. Some Chinese deities are not anthropomorphized, especially those of the sky, but East Asian deities which are specifically female are particularly worshipped. Humphrey and Onon (1996) describe shrines containing female figures among the Daur of Manchuria. In Central Asia, where shamanism may have first been practiced, belief in a female divinity was commonplace, in addition to a god of the sky. We are told that the female deity was beloved and benign. Even when the Manchu ruled China as the Qing dynasty, the culture retained some of its matrifocal aspects (Paper 1995:234). In Korea pairs of village guardians made of wood or stone were inscribed "Earth Grandmother" and "Sky Grandfather," and they both are necessary for protection from wandering spirits.

Although the earliest evidence of the Chinese creator goddess Nuwa in art and literature is found in the Chu and Han periods, she was attributed to much earlier times. As a Creator, she amassed the earth, created heaven, and patched the sky. Chen Mengjia, who was the first to point out female aspects in early China, believed that Nuwa was a deified shamaness, who possibly could be identified with a woman named E on the oracle bones (Paper 1995:156).

A mountain known as Wu Shan, Shaman Mountain, was ruled by a goddess who controlled the rain. In one tradition she was the daughter of the Fire God, Yan Di (Paper 1995:142). Paper suggests that Wu Mountain was named for the shamanesses who practiced there, and was also identified with the goddess. Schafer (1973) finds evidence from Tang dynasty poetry of early goddesses worshipped in China.

Present Shamanism in East Asia

As has been previously noted, present shamans in East Asia are preponderantly women. Shamanism exists in South Korea alongside Christianity and Buddhism, and the Confucian tendencies of the elite; nevertheless, the *mudang* flourish, patronized by businessmen as well as housewives. The blessings from the spirits they alone can reach are highly valued (Kendall 1996).

The shrine princesses of Okinawa have maintained their position in society, in spite of foreign influences of many kinds, and the senior woman in each lineage is the spiritual leader. While Shinto in Japan has the status of a state-sponsored religion, it nevertheless could have disappeared under a number of imported beliefs, including Buddhism, Confucianism, and Christianity. Instead Shinto worships the Sun Goddess as the principal divinity and features shrine princesses, and even the ecstatic practitioners called *miko* dance at Shinto shrines with their hair awhirl (Blacker 1975). The belief that women have better access to the spirit world is strong. It seems that the farther from China, the more the ancient female shamanism flourishes still.

CONCLUSION

The original problem that my exploration of shamanism in ancient East Asia intended to investigate was whether leadership of polities we might call states could and did develop from shamanism. The archaeological, and to some extent textual, data from East Asia show that in some cases leadership in East Asia could arise from shamanism. Shamans were knowledgeable people and leaders, and as polities grew larger, shamans used their ability to reach spirits to gain credibility for mobilizing people on behalf of the polity in various ways.

To understand shamanism and leadership it is necessary to explore gender. A link between the stature of women in the Ryukyu Islands, their continuation in local and larger governments, and their perceived efficacy in reaching powers outside of humans is notable. The power of women has remained in spite of a variety of outside influences. The persistence suggests that the system works well for the participants in it. It can also be seen as a model that includes both shamanism and a balance between men and women.

Women in Japan and South Korea seem to be unequal in the current social structure, although women as spiritual leaders still exist in both nations. Women shamans are known to have been leaders in the formation of the state in both Korea and Japan. Manchu shamanism featured women, and as the Qing dynasty the Manchu never quite assimilated to Chinese culture. A gendered example is that Manchu women did not bind their feet, but wore a kind of clog shoe that simulated the walk of bound feet. The Mongols, who ruled China as the Yuan dynasty, consulted shamans. Mongol *katuns*—queens—sometimes ruled vast territories (Davis-Kimball 2003).

Shamans were thus leaders in many parts of East Asia while states were being formed. At that time, women were often shamans, and often leaders. Men may have achieved and maintained control in China through the lineage system, which, being patrilineal, crowded women out of legitimate power in human affairs. In parts of China, ancestor worship replaced shamanism as the spiritual center, and transferred power to the male lineage. Elsewhere in East Asia, women retained their connections with the spirits, and with power. Feminist theory thus illuminates the East Asian past in a new and more nuanced way.

PART VI
PERSPECTIVES FROM CHINA

WORKING IN CHINA REQUIRED YEARS of preparation and some luck on top of it. But when I was taken to visit Niuheliang, the "Goddess Temple" site, by the lead archaeologists of Liaoning province, it was worth all the previous effort. This is the central site of the Hongshan culture, and it was surprising in the Neolithic in many ways, not least because of its female figures, heretofore unknown in China. The long winding road to the Hongshan culture culminated in an entire book discussing various facets of the Hongshan polity (Nelson et al. 2014). The paper in Chapter 5 was my first venture into describing this remarkable site. The Hongshan culture led me to shamans and queens through its figurines, but of course there were prior influences.

After researching in Korea, Chinese archaeology had almost a magnetic attraction for me, partly due to archaeological similarities between the Korean peninsula and the former Manchu homeland. Sixteen years elapsed before I was allowed to travel in northeastern China, since it was not yet open for Americans to travel, and Chinese archaeological reports were not available to me. In 1970, I stood in the New Territories near Hong Kong, looking across at the People's Republic of China, and thought, "I'll never be allowed to go there." But geopolitics changes possibilities. In 1987, I was introduced to the site of Niuheliang, the "Goddess Temple" site, where I worked many years thereafter until 2007.

From my first adventures in Taiwan and Hong Kong in 1970 and 1971, it was a decade before China was selectively open to American tourists at all, although after the death of Chairman Mao, Americans could travel as controlled interest groups. I was jealous when my mother, Sally Milledge, was selected to go with Ruth Sidel to China in 1977 with a group of women from Wellesley College. They visited schools, factories, hospitals, and communes. I

Shamans, Queens, and Figurines: The Development of Gender Archaeology, by Sarah Nelson, 137–146.

was impressed by how much my mother saw and learned, but those institutions weren't what I wanted to see in China. I wanted to design my own trip, specifically to see archaeological sites.

China opened to the West slowly, a few regions and a few cities at a time, but finally it was possible to travel as a tourist to limited cities and places of archaeological interest. In the fall of 1980, when I returned from my first sabbatical, my opportunity appeared. In my accumulated mail was a flyer from a company called Passages, which offered trips that seemed too good to be real. Professors could earn trips by recruiting students on educational tours. China was one of the places they went. I could teach students as a summer school class and earn my own travel costs. Put that way, it sounded affordable.

"Want to go to China next summer?" I asked Hal.

"Why not?" he said. *Why not?* is the family motto, especially if the question has "go" in it.

I signed up with the tour company immediately and began soliciting students. To prepare for this China experience, I joined the Introduction to Chinese class at the beginning of winter quarter, in 1981. It was only the second year the Chinese language had been offered at DU and, of course, I had missed the first class offered in the fall while on sabbatical in Europe. I boldly figured I could make up for missing the fall class because, in terms of the written language, I already knew quite a few Chinese characters from studying Korean, and because I expected that the many Chinese loan words in the Korean language should be helpful in acquiring a vocabulary.

I was wrong on both counts. South Korea used the classical characters, but New China had created simplified characters, some of which were very different from the original. Effectively, I had to start afresh to learn Chinese characters. Furthermore, the loan words were often pronounced so differently in the two languages that they could be more hindrance than help. I had to study diligently, but by the time I took a group of students to China in the summer of 1981, I could speak Chinese—with a bad accent and a miniscule vocabulary.

I took students who registered for summer school, and interested adults were added to fill out the numbers, in the summers of 1981, 1982, and 1985. Each visit was a different experience, as China began to inch toward a market economy.

The first trip was a standard tour planned by the tour company, but I managed to talk guides into taking us to a few archaeological sites—especially the Zhoukoutian Paleolithic site south of Beijing, and Ban Po, a Neolithic site near Xian.

While Hal took the group to tourist sites in Beijing, I reconnected with Gai Pei from the Institute of Vertebrate Paleontology and Paleoarchaeology (IVPP). I had met him the previous summer when he excavated with Dennis Stanford at Lamb Spring, south of Denver. Hal and I had dared to invite them for Peking duck, barbecued on the grill. They declared it to be delicious. In Beijing, Gai Pei graciously showed me around the IVPP.

My Chinese teacher at DU, Zou Deci, very kindly made an arrangement for me to visit the Kaoguxuo, the Archaeological Research Institute in Beijing. I had a very pleasant conversation with An Jimin and Xia Nai, both of whom had been educated before the Mao era, and spoke English. It was a special thrill for me, although they seemed mystified by my visit.

After Beijing and all its sights, our tour went by rail to Taiyuan, where we saw Buddhist caves, some with enormous sculptures carved into the rocks. A bumpy flight to Xian was redeemed by the sight of the pottery army of the megalomaniac Qin Shiwangdi, as well as the Neolithic site of Banpo and a Zhou-era chariot burial. I sometimes injected a bit of gender into my summer school lectures, but mostly I stuck to the "old" archaeology, placing the sites in time and space. I had learned what China looked like, experienced the vastness of the country, and visited some archaeological sites, but best of all I had met some Chinese archaeologists who might facilitate archaeological work in China.

The next year, I organized a student tour that followed the trail of a group of English-speaking archaeological celebrities (Howells and Tsuchitani 1977). The sites had all been spruced up for their distinguished visitors. In Denver, I had sat at the feet of Marie Wormington, the only woman archaeologist who was famous enough to be included on the tour, to learn exactly where they went and what they saw. I sent the archaeological itinerary to the tour company and asked if they could duplicate it. They did.

This time, my group entered China through Hong Kong, followed by a scenic boat ride on the lovely Li River with its karst hills covered with greenery, to Guilin. From there we visited Xianbi, a Neolithic site with very early domesticated pigs and human burials in a mossy cave. Next was Changsha, with the obligatory trip to Mao's birthplace, but the real goal was the site of Mawangdui, with its remarkably preserved burial of Lady Dai. I had read about this site, but still I was astonished. Lady Dai's body, her clothes, her books—everything usually perishable—had been perfectly preserved, even the squash seeds that were part of her last meal.

Near Xian we visited the pottery army and Banpo again, then made a stop at Zhengzhou, the site of Erlitou, and walked around its wall, still standing head high in some places. A visit to Anyang, the final city of the Shang dynasty, was nearly as exciting to my captive audience as it was to me. A museum about the Yellow River and its flows and changes provided a lesson about the local archaeology as well as geography and geology. Archaeologists showed us around the site and we listened to site explanations in a small lecture area that also housed some artifacts.

For the 1985 China adventure, taking a ship down the Three Gorges was the highlight, but the real topic of the trip was China itself. The progression from a country of peasants in Mao suits who had never seen a Westerner before to the stirrings of entrepreneurship left me breathless. I was especially enchanted by a tiny library on a street corner, where for a few pennies one could sit and read a book, grimy from many previous readers' hands. How had these books escaped the raging Red Guard in the Cultural Revolution? On this tour, we explored Shao Lin Temple where the martial arts were born, and ran across a family burning yellow silk for a funeral—an activity that had been banned for at least thirty years. The boat trip down the Three Gorges was scenic, but the topic of building a giant dam consumed much of the conversation.

By 1987, the northeastern part of China—the Dongbei provinces of Liaoning, Jilin, and Heilongjiang—had been made available to American tourists. Helen Pustmueller, a volunteer in the Anthropology Department, had been to Liaoning province the previous year and had helped a Liaoning University student in Shenyang enroll at DU. "Jimmy" became a student assistant in the Anthropology Department, and since I was department chair, I saw him daily.

Conversations with Jimmy led to my determination to travel in the northeastern part of China, at last open to Americans. Koreans believe that their Bronze Age had antecedents in the Dongbei, the homeland of the Manchus who ruled China as the Qing dynasty, the last before the Republic. I could visit sites and museums to make comparisons with Korea with my own eyes.

Jimmy was a marvel of helpfulness. He found the names of the head archaeologists in Shenyang, Jilin, and Harbin, capitals of three provinces of the northeast, and wrote them letters on my behalf. He also suggested that his classmate, MingMing Shan, would be a good interpreter for me. MingMing proved to have impeccable English and was a delightful companion on our journey. Ardith Hunter, a graduate student in the DU Geography Department, volunteered to go to the Dongbei with me. I was delighted to have a companion. We used my accumulated miles on United Airlines, and Ardith generously shared the land costs not funded by our archaeological hosts.

In retrospect, my timing was perfect. Dongbei archaeologists hadn't had many visitors from America, and we were treated royally. They hosted banquets such as Chinese are famous for, and provided accommodations for Ardith and me in universities. They showed us one amazing site after another, sites I had never heard of. Some of our hosts had tales of a famous archaeologist who had preceded us in the northeast—Lew Binford, who made his impression on them by requesting feasts of roast dog, bears' paws, and any other unusual food they might provide.

Niuheliang, the site that suggested a gendered project to me on my first trip to the Dongbei, is known in China as Nu Shen Miao, the Goddess Temple. A life-sized head made of unbaked clay was an astonishing discovery, part of one of the earliest life-sized human statues in the world. The Chinese archaeologists were just as intrigued with Ardith, who with her green eyes and wide smile looked much like the face of the female spirit, the *nüshen*. A joint project was proposed. The archaeologists, Sun Shoudao and Guo Dashun, made copies for me of everything they had written in Chinese, and MingMing translated the papers about the site when she came to DU as my student a year or so later.

After Shenyang, Ardith, MingMing, and I took the sleeper train to Jilin and Harbin. From Jilin, we saw sites of the Xituanshan culture, with slab burials and pottery that reminded me of sites in North Korea I had read about. In Harbin, we were running out of time, but we did have time for the museum, the old Russian buildings in Harbin, and the wide and impressive Heilongjiang River (alias the Amur River),

Back in Beijing, Ardith and I made notes on the museum exhibit, but in our last few hours we prowled the shops on Wangfujin, Beijing's main shopping street. Just for a lark, we tried on fur coats. "This is a fun fur," said Ardith, twirling around in the coat with patches of different furs that she was trying on. "I wonder what fur it is." We looked at the label, laughed hysterically, and put the coat right back on the rack. "House Cat," the label said.

The following year, I was awarded a six-week fellowship in northeast China by the newly formed Committee on Scholarly Relations with the People's Republic of China (CSCPRC) and later was invited to be an advisor to that committee. I stayed at Liaoning University for the first weeks, discussing further a joint project with Sun and Guo at Niuheliang.

For the last couple of weeks, I pursued my Korea interest, with a trip through Jilin province, accompanied by MingMing and Jiang Peng from Jilin University. Highlights of this journey included a trip through Yanbian, the Korean Autonomous Zone, views of Tianji (Chinese) or Chonji (Korean), the crater lake on the border between China and North Korea, and time to explore Jian, an early capital of the Korean kingdom of Koguryo.

The crater lake is indeed heavenly, its name in both Chinese and Korean, and I used it as a setting for a scene in *Spirit Bird Journey*. I tried to imagine I could see North Korea on the south side of the lake, but it is much too vast for any such view. In Yanbian, I was taken to a small folklore museum. The old man in traditional Korean dress had tears in his eyes when I signed the visitor book in Hangul, and gave him my card with my name in Korean/Chinese characters.

Jian was then a small provincial city that was not on any major route. We had to change trains in the middle of the night to catch the infrequent train to Jian. At that dreadful place, MingMing and I had to spread out our raincoats to sleep on top of our beds. We didn't want to be the Princesses Who Slept in the Pee.

The old city of Jian was worth the trouble, in spite of being rather neglected. Its surrounding stone wall was intact, but the stone cobble ancient tombs were derelict, with houses built on top of them. The hill fort was enmeshed in weeds too high to see much or even to allow walking around. It took quite a while to find the keeper of the keys to the painted tombs, and when he was finally found, I was only admitted to two of them.

The contrast when I was in Jian again in 2008 was astounding. China had discovered the Korean Koguryo kingdom (Kaoguli in Chinese) and, since there are many Koguryo sites in the Dongbei, determined to describe the kingdom as Chinese. The houses on the tombs were gone, with the tomb mounds densely covered in grass. Several of the painted tombs were open for viewing. Walkways edged in stone led to the hill fort, now likewise cleared of weeds and debris. Pamphlets were available in English, and teenage girls in uniforms gave tours through the sites. Needless to say, the Chinese interpretation of Kaoguli is not agreeable to Koreans.

One result of my two early trips to the Dongbei was a book that became an important early resource for studying the archaeology of the Dongbei. I asked archaeologists from each of the three Dongbei provinces to write summaries of the archaeology in their province, so that I could publish them in English. It wasn't an easy task, since the chapters came to us written in Chinese characters and had to be rendered into readable English. My two Chinese students, MingMing Shan and Ke Peng, made rough translations, after which the three of us sat down with the originals and the translations, going back and forth to smooth out the translations and find the best words for unfamiliar artifacts and sites. We three worked on the translation project for most of a year. *The Archaeology of Northeast China*, published by Routledge (Nelson, ed. 1995), was the first book about Chinese regional archaeology in English, and I am still astonished that it came to fruition. In the course of reading the papers so closely, I began to feel like an expert in Dongbei archaeology, and hoped to have a chance to extend my knowledge. I wrote an extensive introduction to the book to situate Chinese archaeology for English-speaking readers.

The Dongbei archaeologists organized several meetings on the archaeology around the Bohai Sea, inviting some Japanese and Russian scholars as well as, on the first occasion in Dalian, David Goodrich, who had been a student at Beijing University, and me. These meetings opened Chinese archaeology for me in a way no amount of reading could have accomplished. I met Miyamoto Kazuo for the first time, whom I believe I have met again at every meeting in Asia since. From Kyushu University, Miyamoto has done much productive work on the relationships among East Asian archaeological sites. Happily, MingMing was also invited to the meeting to translate for me. These meetings occurred every two or three years and were always stimulating.

In 1992, Emmy Bunker organized a meeting in Hohhot, Inner Mongolia. I was very keen to go and invited myself along. The day of arrival in Beijing, I met Karen Rubinson, and we had a long hike through the city and great conversation. Her work in Turkey in some ways parallels mine in Korea. Yangjin Pak was also at the meeting, bringing me news of Korean archaeology. I met many art historians and historians of China who were interested in the early steppe people, and broadened my horizons considerably. Kathy Linduff was a new acquaintance and became an enduring friend.

Other travels with Karen and Kathy expanded my archaeological horizons into the steppes of Central Asia. A meeting at Petropavlovsk in Kazakhstan, organized by David Anthony, focused on early horse domestication and also had a cast of luminaries.

In 1994, I attended a meeting in Vladivostok, in the Russian Far East, and traveled solo in Liaoning and Inner Mongolia on the way. In Chifeng, Inner Mongolia, I was allowed to visit several sites, including the eponymous Hongshan site, which is in the city of Chifeng. My hosts showed me other sites nearby, of which Xiajiadian, an impressive stone-built site on the Yin River, was the most interesting. Later I tried to get funding for a project to photograph such sites from the air and map them, but it was not a practical idea, because there were no small airplanes to rent in that region.

The Russian Far East at the time, after the break-up of the Soviet Union, was desperate for goods of all kinds. The plane I flew to Khabarovsk was full of Russian women with giant bundles of clothing for resale. At the Vladivostok meeting, Irina Zhuschikovskaya had her father drive me to several of the Neolithic sites she had excavated. Since the distribution system in Russia had broken down, second-hand Japanese cars with right-hand drive were flooding into Vladivostok, which made being on the road an exciting adventure.

Yuri Vostretsov and Nina Kononenko from the Research Institute shared pictures of their dig in North Korea, and David Brodianski from the University of Vladivostok was also cordial. A few years later, I had another chance to pick David's brain about the archaeology of the Russian Far East at an invitational meeting in Seoul.

I was contacted by Geoff Read of the World Bank when that institution became interested in a project to clean up the polluted air of Liaoning province. He asked me to recommend archaeological sites for the World Bank to sponsor as a small part of the clean-up project. The Liaoning archaeologists created a brochure on their three favorite sites: the end of the Great Wall at Shan Hai Jing, a Paleolithic site with human remains, and Niuheliang. I discussed this brochure with the Liaoning province archaeologists at the first Hwan Bohai meeting, but in the end, the World Bank gave the project to a firm in England, and they invited Gina Barnes to evaluate the archaeology of Niuheliang.

Gina and I tried to create a project at Niuhelaing, but too many logistical problems foiled the attempt. Later, a project at Niuheliang organized with Yangjin Pak and Hungjen Niu was funded by the National Geographic Fund for Exploration and the Wenner Gren Foundation for Anthropological Research. Each year that we could go to China, a small part of our project was accomplished. Among other projects, we explored ground-penetrating radar, landscape archaeology, and measurements for archaeoastronomy, and donated computers to the Liaoning Institue of Archaeology so we could keep the same records.

Hungjen Niu worked tirelessly to obtain a permit for us to survey between Niuhliang and another ceremonial site called Dongshanzui. However, by the time we finally had the permit in hand, our funding had run out. We were unable to obtain renewals, and in the meantime, our three leaders had other commitments: Yangjin Pak became a dean at his university, and Hungjen Niu remarried and had a baby to look after. I couldn't lead the project alone. Thus, our project at Niuheliang came to an end. We had learned a great deal from the Hongshan culture, however, and perhaps one of us, or all three, will return for further work.

I had ventured to write about Hongshan much earlier. In 1993, at the 13th International Congress of Anthropological and Ethnographic Sciences in Mexico City, I was pleased to be able to offer a paper in the session on early states and ideology, organized by Henri Claessen, who co-edited a series of books about the development of early states. In that session I enjoyed going out on a shaky limb, suggesting that non-patriarchal models were more useful for understanding the Hongshan incipient state than the models typically used in state-origin literature. Some negative comments from the audience were responded to by Liz Brumfiel, who had read the literature I cited, whereas my critics had not. This was a nice example of the sisterhood of feminism.

I don't remember the exact questions, but my critics attacked the suggestion that symbols in the Hongshan culture may have been gendered. I pointed out that the objects carved in jades were associated with yin, the female principle in China. This included pigs as the most prominent symbol (many "pig-dragons," a pig head on one end of an open ring, a pig statue in the apparent shrine, the prominence of a nearby mountain that resembles a pig's head), along with clouds and birds. Chapter 7 is the published version of that paper.

Chapter 7

Ideology and the Formation of an Early State in Northeast China

In China, ideas about the formation of the state, as well as the ideology of early states, differ somewhat from western thinking. In this chapter I would like to highlight some of these differences, and suggest that while both perspectives are valuable, neither is responsive to the ideology of the Hongshan culture, which is crucial for understanding its contribution to the formation of the state. Using feminist theory, and "middle range theory of the mind" (Cowgill 1993), it is possible to approach state formation with fresh eyes. This changed perspective allows analysis of some early characteristics, especially ideology, without other (and in this case later) complicating factors such as irrigation and warfare, often seen as strongly implicated in state formation.

The Hongshan culture was a polity which achieved a three-tier managerial elite, but declined after half a millennium rather than developing further. In spite of the decline, however, continuities in the region suggest that the Hongshan experiment was not completely forgotten, but blossomed again in the Lower Xiajiadian and after another interval yet again in Upper Xiajiadian. The full meaning of these successively more complex societies is not yet known, but the pattern of rise and fall is clear, and appears to be without external cause. Variables within the society may have been insufficient to maintain a three-tier management system indefinitely, and lacking external stimulus to further development, the system gradually dissolved after flourishing some 500 years.

Sarah M. Nelson (1996). In *Ideology and the Formation of Early States*, edited by Henri J. M. Claessen and Jarich G. Oosten, pp. 153–169. E. J. Brill, Leiden. Republished in *Shamans, Queens, and Figurines: The Development of Gender Archaeology*, by Sarah Nelson, pp. 147–160 (Taylor & Francis., 2015).

THE HONGSHAN CULTURE

The Hongshan culture is found in a region that at present includes western Liaoning province and Inner Mongolia, China. It was described in the early part of this century as a group of Neolithic sites distributed along rivers in the vicinity of Chifeng, Inner Mongolia. Because painted pottery is part of the assemblage, Hongshan was believed to be related to the Yangshao culture in the Yellow River valley, and possibly derivative from it. Recent discoveries, however, suggest that Hongshan was a complex society with different roots. Newly discovered Hongshan sites include ceremonial sites with extensive jade carving and elite burials, which are dated by C14 dates to 3500–3000 B.C. The fact that this is sometimes mentioned as "the time of the Yellow Emperor" (e.g. Fang and Wei 1986b) highlights the dominance of writing systems and the privileging of the written word over archaeological discoveries in China in understanding the past. On the other hand the Hongshan culture presents an unexpected array of discoveries which fail to conform to the Chinese past as it has been officially constructed over the last two millennia. These discoveries include the 'Goddess Temple' of Niuheliang, female statues of all sizes, high status burials with iconographic jades, and ceremonial precincts with large altar constructions. In the west, many constructs of state formation which presume that state inequalities are built upon prior inequalities of sex and age need to be reconsidered in the light of the Hongshan discoveries.

In this chapter I will examine the ideology of Hongshan with reference to the historiography of China, the western literature on state origins, and some other avenues to interpreting emblems and statues in their archaeological context. By ideology, I mean the ways in which symbols are manipulated, in this case to maintain a three-tier hierarchy, as well as the related question of the meaning of the ceremonial centres and their contents (cf. Ratnagar 1996). In regard to Chinese history, certain voices from the past have been suppressed, and others augmented, distorting our perceptions in a direction that later Chinese rulers both created and used for their own purposes. With myth and legend to guide interpretations of these unexpected discoveries, Chinese archaeologists are constrained in particular ways. But I will argue that literature on the origin of the state also has a bias, which needs to be reconsidered in the light of Hongshan. An array of various kinds of evidence and inferences must be marshaled to understand the ideology, as well as the political economy of this early complex society.

To briefly describe the problem and anticipate some of the solutions, the iconography indicates an ideology that privileges the female principle, suggesting that women played important roles within the society. This interpretation will be argued more fully later. Here I merely wish to point out that, if correct, it is incongruent with many bodies of theory that touch on the development of complex society, among them not merely Chinese history, as noted above, but also Marxist theory and feminist theory (e.g. Rapp 1977; Rohrlich 1980), as well as much state theory. The Hongshan culture suggests that non-patriarchal models for the formation of the state may be equally valid, and need to be considered.

WESTERN THEORIES OF STATE FORMATION

States are differentiated from chiefdoms using several criteria, many of which are not easily accessible with archaeological data alone. The shift from kinship to territory as the grounds for determining membership, for example, is beyond the reach of archaeology. The criteria for recognizing early states set out by Claessen and Skalnik (1978:640) are more approachable using material culture, but still somewhat elusive. They suggest that legitimate power of a separate group of rulers and an ideology that legitimates their power characterize the early state. The legitimacy of power can only be inferred archaeologically by the lack of overt conflict, and the use of ideology for legitimating power is a second level inference. Claessen and Van de Velde (1985:9 ff.) further introduce the concept of the trajectory of state formation as a slope rather than a staircase, recognizing that "it is impossible to pinpoint the precise moment of the birth of the state". The archaeological data of Hongshan (to be discussed more fully later) show that both intensive agriculture and animal husbandry could produce surplus to support craft specialization and a three-tier political and managerial hierarchy with an ideology that legitimates the rule of the elite.

OTHER THEORETICAL STANDPOINTS

Three characteristics of Chinese archaeology affect the interpretations of Hongshan: the primacy given to written documents, the Marxist formulae concerning the origins of states, and the national sense of the long sweep of Chinese history. These interact in complex ways to produce archaeological interpretations that differ from those in the west.

In China, Marxist thought largely arrived via the Soviet Union, and has tended to be doctrinaire. Thus the scheme of human social evolution laid out by Engels (1972 [1884]) of matriarchy in the early Neolithic followed by patriarchy with the advent of plow agriculture, is included without question or discussion in most Chinese reconstructions of periods that in the west are considered prehistory, or at best protohistory. This construct makes Hongshan a puzzle to Chinese archaeologists, since it appears to be a matriarchal complex society, an oxymoron in the Marxist view, a form which should not occur. Although the problem can be made to disappear by assuming that men ruled while the goddesses were survivals from earlier times, begging the question in this way is unsatisfactory, and has no evidence to support it. A more sophisticated understanding of the role of women in the ideology of the Hongshan culture, as well as their participation in the political and economic spheres, is needed.

If the advent of private property, on the other hand, is to be seen as the "world historical defeat of the female sex", according to Engels' analysis, with the notion that when women became private property they were therefore removed as actors from the public arena, the grounds of the debate are shifted. Some feminist scholars, although willing to concede that the state may be always patriarchal, have seen gender equality as more common in pre-state societies. Leacock (1972, 1978), for example, argues that before the state, gender equality was common and that apparent examples to the contrary were strongly influenced by contemporaneous state level societies through missionization and participation in the cash economy through devices such as the fur trade. This contrasts markedly with a body of literature that sees gender hierarchy in all societies, and suggests that sex and age inequalities are the models for other kinds of unequal access to goods and services (e.g. Service 1975). Although Hongshan seems to have developed its complexity without much reference to other incipient states, and "cluster interaction" (B. Price 1977) or 'peer polity' (Renfrew 1982) concepts are tenuously applicable to this case, if at all, the fact that it was uninfluenced by male dominant societies may be important. The question of private property, and especially women themselves becoming property with the male appropriation of female labor, is an important one which is unfortunately difficult to solve with archaeological data alone. Nevertheless, it needs to be problematized rather than assumed.

Many feminist theorists who were concerned with what appears to some to be universal female subordination (e.g. Rosaldo and Lamphere 1974) relied on these Marxist ideas. Thus it followed that in any state level society, gender stratification would have already occurred (e.g. Earle 1987; Flannery 1972; Lerner 1986; Rapp 1977; Service 1975). Women leaders, however, indeed women rulers of at least incipient states, have been identified in a number of societies. Women rulers of complex societies are now known to be not as rare as was once thought. Queens ruling in their own right occurred in Korea when it had fully developed states (Nelson 1991b, 1993b), in the Celtic world (Muller 1987), and elsewhere (Fraser 1989). Karen Sacks (1979) has argued cogently that belonging to a powerful kinship group is important for women's status, and she uses the concept of sisterhood in contrast to wifehood to illustrate this shift for women in African states.

THE EARLY STATE IN CHINA

Many archaeologists who have some acquaintance with Chinese prehistory would automatically assign the honor of being the first Chinese state to the Shang dynasty of the second millennium BCE (e.g. Wenke 1990), or perhaps would allow the possibility of the Longshan culture preceding the Shang as a state (Patterson 1992). It is in Shang times that a full blown writing system appears on oracle bones and bronze vessels, that warfare is attested in war chariots and weapons as well as divinations on the oracle bones, that social stratification is incontestable with markedly different sizes and depths of tombs as well as palaces and hovels, that long distance trade can be inferred from the cowrie shell money and other exotic items from far afield in literally every direction (Chang, K.-C. 1976, 1980b; Chang, K.-C. ed. 1986).

Some historians of China, on the other hand, might be more inclined to consider the succeeding Zhou dynasty to be the first real state (e.g. Creel 1970), and some would consider the first state to be even later (e.g. Pokara 1978). My proposal to consider a much *earlier* culture as having state-like qualities is thus likely to be controversial among sinologists. Furthermore, the Hongshan culture is not in the basin of the Yellow River, where historic early Chinese civilization was cradled, but far to the north, in what is now Inner Mongolia and the western fringe of Liaoning province, China, in short, in the territory of the 'barbarians', by definition not civilized.

A variety of questions about Hongshan thus need to be addressed. In what sense can it be called a state? If it was a state, why did it rise so early? Even if it was a state, did it have any relationship to the Shang dynasty, later by some thousand years? Perhaps Hongshan is just an irrelevancy, a flash in the pan, a temporary aberration of nomadic northern cultures, with no connection then or later to the Yellow River basin. Furthermore, if China had a goddess-worshipping state in its past, how could all memory of it have been lost? What does the iconography of dragons, clouds, birds, turtles, and pigs have to tell us about the ideology of this early state? And most important, how did the ideology help form the society and keep it together?

THE HONGSHAN CULTURE

Hongshan sites are found in an area of about 75,000 square kilometers, from the Sharamurun River to the Yan Mountains, and from the Mongolian plateau to Bohai Bay. However, the sites are most densely distributed in the center of this region, near the cities of Chifeng and Chaoyang. Two ceremonial sites have been excavated, as well as several dwelling sites and burial mounds. Many other sites of each type are known. Although much attention has been directed to the more spectacular sites in recent years, the first discoveries, made as early as 1908, were simple village sites (Hamada 1938). The villages indicate the nature of the subsistence base of the society, and barely hint at the complexity found in the ceremonial sites. The village sites contain a great many patterned types of stone tools, suggesting a variety of uses for specific tools, especially tools to manufacture other tools of wood and bone, and for farming. Large leaf-shaped stone plows are particularly striking. Both painted pottery and the regionally widespread rocker-stamped beakers are found.

The two partially excavated sites with ceremonial precincts are quite different from each other in their overall structure, but they have elements in common. These common elements include square and round constructions attached to each other in patterned ways, representations of women, and jade pendants carved into specific shapes. The site of Dongshanzui (Guo and Zhang 1984) consists of a large square platform-like construction, with lines of stones on each side, a circular platform in front, and oval stone formations. The site is thought to have been wholly dedicated to ritual, for daily activities are little in evidence. The most common pottery at the site was the large black-on-red painted cylinders usually associated with tombs and ceremonial areas. Small nude female figurines were found in the lowest layer of the stone circle platform. Pig and deer bones might have been sacrificial, and one burial, described as a human sacrifice, contained a single basin placed on its midsection.

Niuheliang, on the other hand, is a more complex site with several distinct ceremonial locations and groups of tombs (Liaoning Province 1986; Nelson 1991a; Sun and Guo 1984, 1986). Completely unprecedented is the 'Goddess Temple', which was built along the slope of a ridge, 25 m. long and 2 to 9 m. wide, in an asymmetrical complexly lobed shape. Traces of painted bas relief in geometric designs suggest a highly decorated building. At the foot of the lobed building the floor of a detached circular building was found.

Inside the lobed building, fragments of life-sized and over-life-sized statues were strewn, mostly depicting human females (some breasts were found, for example). An enormous ear, suggesting a statue three times normal human stature, was also recovered. Other fragments included the feet of a large bird and pig's trotters, both as large as life. Jade pendants were found eroding from this building. A pottery incense burner and shards of large painted cylinders also indicate that ritual events were conducted within the building. A nearby platform, with traces of burning, suggests outdoor ceremonies as well, although the platform might have had other uses, such as constructing and/or firing the over-sized pottery cylinders or making the large unfired statues.

Six areas of tomb mounds were located. Locality 2, which has largely been excavated, revealed complex square tombs and a circular structure interpreted as an altar. One square mound, for example, contained an interior stone square which surrounded the principal grave, and 16 subsidiary burials ranging around it within the larger square. The subsidiary burials, outlined with stone cists, included both primary and secondary inhumations. Between the major grave and the others were double rows of large painted pottery cylinders, probably originally arranged around all four sides of the square. Guo has estimated that 10,000 of these would have been used in the 30 tombs on this site alone (Guo 1995a). The central burial had been destroyed by looters, but most of the additional graves contained several jades. Bones of pig and cattle had been placed as grave offerings, a custom that continued in the north of China for another two millennia.

The jades are patterned, and suggest iconographic meanings. The forms include thick open rings with a pig head on one end and a curved body, which the excavators call the 'pig-dragon' (Sun and Guo 1984), and flat representations of birds with spread wings, turtles, and clouds. Other objects made of jade are roughly tubular, but narrower on one end than the other. They are often found beneath the skull. These artifacts are thought to be some form of headgear, possibly ponytail holders, to create a distinctive headdress for certain classes, or perhaps to identify a subset of the elite.

ICONOGRAPHY AND IDEOLOGY

In recent years art historians have been more concerned with ideology than archaeologists have. A lively debate has arisen regarding the ability to interpret meanings of patterns on Shang bronzes without reference to written documents (Allan 1993; Bagley 1993) which clarifies some of the issues. Allan (p. 162) makes a distinction between images as illustrations of articulated ideas and images (or motifs) which reflect other parts of culture, "alluding to themes" rather than depicting them. Recent archaeological views of objects as not merely *reflecting* culture but *mediating* it, and negotiating by means of symbols the complex interrelationships between groups of persons (e.g. Hodder 1982), are also relevant here. Thus, the question is not merely what artifacts or styles mean, but what they represent to both the owner and the rest of the society, and how they in turn create new meanings (see Ratnagar 1996). In the Hongshan culture, the jades must have been an important reminder of the wearer's place within the society, because they were found on the chest, a highly visible location if worn there in life as well as in death. A society in which visible markers of status are required tends to be large and complex. The jades are not individualized, showing that they are not expressions of individual personalities, but follow patterned forms. Furthermore, the emblems are made of durable material and their creation was labor intensive, implying a managerial elite to direct their manufacture.

The analysis cannot stop here, however. Cowgill (1993:562) has introduced the term "middle range theory of the mind", as an approach to some of these problems. He suggests that we can discover 'local rules' based on the objects that were and were not made. In considering the iconography of Hongshan, and attempting to recreate through it the ideological system, the evidence can be divided into several categories. The female statues are one such group, the jade pendants are another, the architectural shapes can be construed as a third, and the cylindrical pottery is a fourth. These will be discussed in turn.

It is interesting to note that all the pottery human statues discovered so far in Hongshan sites are of women, in so far as they are sex specific. Some are small, representing nude standing figures with arms in various attitudes; these all have breasts, and some may be pregnant. Others are large, sitting with crossed legs. None of the figures is complete, and none of the small figurines, found at Dongshanzui or elsewhere, has a head remaining. They may be votive offerings, perhaps requests for return to health or help in childbirth or for aid in conception.

The large figures, found so far only at Niuheliang, are made of unbaked clay, with a core of coarse clay covered by fine clay smoothed on the surface and then painted. Due to this method of construction, the statues have mostly disintegrated over the millennia, but crossed legs, a breast and a shoulder, a part of an arm, and so forth were found on the floor. These were in various sizes, and belonged to a variety of different statues. None of the statues have any masculine features, although some fragments are in themselves ambiguous as to sex. The most striking fragment is that of a face with blue-green jade eyes and high cheek bones, its wide lips set in a smile. A jade without provenance from the Sackler Gallery of the Smithsonian bears a line drawing of a face which appears to be the same woman (So 1993).

These representations of women do not of course prove that women ruled the society, but they do suggest that women were held in high esteem. Sanday (1981:3) has argued that "each culture has a sex role plan" and that the plan is congruent with the gender of the culture's deities. She develops this theme with cross-cultural ethnographic examples, as well as a few historic ones. Where goddesses fail to represent female power, abundant male gods are found. If it is the case that female gods reflect the society's sex role plan, then these female figures reflect the power of women within the Hongshan society.

The iconographic jades include pig-dragons, turtles, birds, and clouds. All of these either relate to women in some way or are sex neutral. Turtles, clouds, and dragons have traditionally been associated with water in China, and water belongs to the *yin*, or female, principle. Pigs were raised by women in Manchuria, and associated with women, into historic times (Lattimore 1951). Birds have traditionally been considered messengers from the gods or spirits, but do not necessarily carry a gender connotation. However, numbers of jade birds were found in a Shang dynasty woman's tomb, to be discussed below, and the phoenix, a mythical bird, became the symbol of the empress, as the dragon (perhaps changing sexes when it lost its porcine features) belonged to the emperors. Thus, by analogy with later Chinese constructs of gender attributes, the jade pendants can be construed as containing a message consistent with that of the female figures, suggesting the importance of female characteristics, and by extension of women themselves.

It is important to note that the jade pendants are most reasonably interpreted as markers of rank rather than mere decoration, because there are a limited number of shapes, each following a definite form. For example, only the pig-dragons are carved in the round, while the flat birds have outspread wings and the flat turtles are seen from above. If the jades are indeed associated with women, this could indicate either a matrilineally organized society, with the pendants as evidence of ranked lineages, or as tokens of personal rank. In either case, it seems likely that a substantial number of the people holding those ranks were women.

The combination of square and round shapes in altars and tombs is related by Guo (1995a) to the traditional Chinese concept that the earth is square and the sky is round. Round heaven and square earth are represented in Shang dynasty jades, as well as in altar shapes, right down to the final dynasty of China, the Qing, and can still be seen at the Temple of Heaven in Beijing, among other places. The complementarity of heaven and earth is mirrored in the complementarity of the sexes, and may also be an early reflection of the notion of *yin* and *yang*, when male was not better than female, just different. It would be of importance for the argument to know the sexes of the skeletons in the tombs. However, although some are quite well preserved, no sexing has been reported. This leads us to speculate that the square tombs, if they are indeed related to the *yin/yang* ideology, could be expected to contain a woman in the central grave.

The painted cylinders are more elusive to interpret (see also Ratnagar 1996 on the problem of interpretation). Containers are often seen as equatable with women, but these pots have no bottoms, and therefore are not containers. The lack of bottoms could be for practical rather than ideological reasons—e.g. to save clay, to make them easier to fire, or to make them easier to stand in rows—but probably acquired a symbolic meaning which is at least for now beyond our reach. The black-on-red designs of hooks in horizontal lines may represent some kind of vegetation, but it is not entirely clear that this is so, or that it would necessarily be a symbol of women even if it could be determined that plants were intended. It may be the case, since the cylinders are associated with ritual activities in the Goddess Temple, that they were placed in the graves in reference to those activities, rather than directly related to their iconographic meaning.

Thus, given these separate iconographic representations, two expressing female images, one depicting complementarity, and one ambiguous, it seems that gender played an important role in the social arrangements of the Hongshan people. Beyond that it can only be said that it is unlikely, given these sets of symbols with emphasis on the female, that a strongly patriarchal system was in place.

COMPLEX CHIEFDOM OR STATE?

The exercise of pigeon-holing archaeological 'cultures' as either complex chiefdoms or early states is not of primary concern here, but it is useful to consider briefly some archaeologically accessible characteristics of early states in order to have a common ground for discussion. Using some of the criteria put forth by Claessen and Skalnik (1978:625 ff.), I will consider stratification and elites, a subsistence base to support a relatively dense population, craft specialization, and expanding contacts with other polities beyond its borders.

In general, Hongshan can be seen to have been a stratified society, with at least three levels. As I have discussed in more detail elsewhere (Nelson 1993c), both the burial system and the symbols expressed in jade insignia suggest a central elite with at least two levels, in addition to lesser elites in the countryside, and non-elite farmers and artisans. Thus a three-tier managerial system is implied. Although no commoner burials have been discovered, it is clear that the large square stone mounds are extraordinary tombs, in which at least two classes are buried. Village burials with jades indicate local gentry, contrasted with those in the tombs at Niuheliang.

The subsistence base consisted of intensive agriculture and animal husbandry. Stone plows were used for intensive tillage, and cattle bones suggest the possibility of draft animals. Pigs are found in both iconography and in graves as meat offerings, suggesting their importance in the economic system. The excavators of Niuheliang also have noted that a mountain resembling a pig's head can be seen from the Goddess Temple, and may be the reason for locating the temple in that specific place. Sheep bones occur, ritually treated, emphasizing the fact that the Hongshan culture grew up on an ecotone between the pastoral grasslands and the farmed open forests. Sufficient surplus must have been produced to support the jade carvers and potters, whose work is found preponderantly in graves and ceremonial precincts, in the service of the elite.

Craft specialization in both jade and pottery is an indication that skilled artisans existed, although there is no inkling of their social status *vis a vis* either the elite or the farmers, because our knowledge is of the product rather than the producers. Hongshan jades became collectors' items of unknown time and provenance (e.g. Loehr 1975) long before they were discovered *in situ* at Niuheliang. In the unauthorized 20th century trade in these objects, hundreds, if not thousands, have appeared in the world's museums and private collections. They were made in standard forms, indicating specific meanings attached to each type of jade object.

The extent of the pottery industry is indicated by the oversized black-on-red cylinders, placed in tombs and important for ritual. These vessels are 30–50 cm. in diameter. If 10,000 of them were made for Niuheliang alone (Guo 1995a), an organization of considerable size must have been necessary for their production. Procurement of the clay, shaping the pots, making the paint, painting, and firing would have constituted different stages of production. It would be possible to study the vessels for evidence of mass production, with different artisans at work on different aspects of production, but this has not yet been attempted.

The possibility of copper or bronze in Hongshan has been raised before (Nelson 1991a; Guo 1995a), but an earring of copper wire and jade was recently unearthed in a Hongshan site (Han 1993), making the presence of metal conclusive, although in quite a simple form. It remains to be seen whether metallurgy flourished at Niuheliang, but the copper wire suggests external relationships whether the technology or the object was imported. Two other indications of distant contacts can be found in the Hongshan sites. The first is the raw material for the jade insignia. Much early Chinese jade is nephrite, with known deposits in Siberia and Xinjiang (Loehr 1975), hundreds of miles from Hongshan. However, Chinese 'jade' is not necessarily nephrite; it can be any colorful stone which is possible to carve. Quarries for the jade, which is found in a variety of colors, have not been located, but several different materials must have been procured in quite distant and far-flung localities. In addition a small amount of turquoise was imported. Another indication of long distance contact is the painted pottery, which has no antecedents in the local pottery tradition. The nearest painted black-on-red pottery is in the Yellow River basin, in the Yangshao tradition. It has alternatively been suggested that the Hongshan black-on-red pottery was inspired by non-Chinese Neolithic traditions on the western end of the great grasslands, implying a nomadic connection for the Hongshan culture.

It is not necessary for the purposes of this paper to insist that Hongshan was a full-blown state. However, there are lessons for the trajectory of state origins. Not every early experiment in stratified societies blossomed into an empire, and it is useful and important to consider the details of one that failed to do so. A rhythm of cultures, each achieving more complexity than the last one with some devolution between them, appears to pulsate for two thousand years in northeast China. In Hongshan, there is no evidence of coercion, of warfare, of writing. It is, however, important to note that a high degree of complexity had been achieved—a complexity coincident with iconography emphasizing female statues and statuettes, along with other symbols associated with women in later times in China.

Elsewhere in China at roughly the same time, other societies were also becoming more complex. Jade working is present in many of these regions, but none seems to have exhibited the complexity of Hongshan at a similarly early date. Why is there no hint of the Hongshan culture in the Chinese histories?

CHINESE HISTORY

The knowledge of ancient history in China is hampered by the great burning of the books in the Qin dynasty (Wu, K.C. 1982), when Qin Shihuangdi, First Emperor of China, acknowledging the power of the past and its ability to be used in manipulating the present, attempted to erase all but his own officially approved version of history. Historic documents had been and continued to be kept in the palace, inked on bamboo strips and carved in stone, but only the official historians were allowed access to these records. Thus, in the 4th century BCE, the written record of the Chinese past was greatly impoverished (Wu, K.C. 1982).

Official Chinese histories since that time have tended to praise women who knew their place, and to denigrate women rulers (the epitome of women not in their place!); therefore a goddess-worshipping culture from the far distant past cannot be expected to have survived the Qin purge, even if it had been preserved in the historic record up to that time. It is surprising to find even any faint indications of women rulers in the past, but there are a few in myth and folklore.

First, there is Nuwa, the Changing Woman, one of the legendary sages. References to her in Chinese documents include only her name, and the assertion that she was able to change her shape, and that she discovered stones of five colors to hold up the sky. Even Wu (1982:50), working to dredge up every scrap of early history, doubts the existence of any real woman ruler, following the traditional Chinese disregard of women. It is interesting, however, that references to her have persisted, and the fact that they did, in spite of everything, suggests a strong tradition that could not be totally erased. The time period of Nuwa, extrapolating backward from established dates, more or less coincides with the Hongshan era.

On the other hand, Xiwangmu, the Queen Mother of the West, became a very visible deity in the Han period which followed the Qin, appearing as a central figure in paintings and carvings in numerous tombs of lesser scholars and officials. Was Xiwangmu a reflection of Nuwa, a memory simply impossible to erase by burning the books? Was a female culture hero too firmly rooted in Chinese culture to be eradicated?

Some 2000 years after Hongshan, in the Shang dynasty, which had pandemic warfare and known male rulers, a burial of an important woman has been found, identifiable as Fu Hao by inscriptions on the bronzes entombed with her (Qian 1981). Although she was not a ruler, oracle bones suggest that she was both a general who led armies and a lord over extensive land holdings in her own right (P. Chang 1986). This find has of course engendered considerable controversy in Chinese studies, for women were not supposed to have independent status (see papers in K.C. Chang, ed. 1986). It is important to note that Fu Hao's grave is rich with grave goods, including jade carvings that echo those of Hongshan, especially clouds, birds, and turtles. In her grave were also found the only known mirrors of the Shang dynasty, which link her with the 'northern bronzes' (Lin 1986) beyond the mountains—in other words, with former Hongshan territory.

Thus, echoes of the Hongshan culture can be found in Chinese history, but they are both muted and distorted. A past complex society in which the ideology was centered on femaleness became increasingly embarrassing to the official Chinese line, and was increasingly suppressed. Archaeological discoveries, however, provide the missing evidence of one of China's early complex and woman-centered societies. These discoveries can be a corrective to our generalizations about the processes of state formation.

CONCLUSION

The Hongshan discoveries, with their ideological emphasis on women, provide a challenge to both Chinese and western versions of the origins of early states. Inequality in social status was not necessarily preceded by gender inequality, and the roots of social stratification need to be sought elsewhere.

PART VII
Shamans and Ideology

The processual archaeology of my graduate school days not only lacked space for gender, it also eschewed ideology. The spirit world only was readmitted to archaeology after post-processualism made room for it. But that hadn't kept me from being interested in spirit belief in Korea; it only prevented me from trying to publish anything relating the *mudangs* of Korea to the past (Nelson 1993a:7). I was particularly intrigued with shamanism, because it was such an important and active part of the living Korean culture, and because, I had been told, the shamans' chants were so old no one knew what the words actually meant anymore. Could there be some hints for interpretations of ancient sites? It was a question that would have to wait.

In the year I lived in Seoul, besides doing an archaeological survey, I made a study of Korea's cultural patterns, especially the fast-disappearing customs, house types, and even clothing, hoping that all these might have tangible connections with the past. When I returned to Korea a mere seven years later, I was amazed at how much of the material culture I had described and collected was vanishing. Modernization had replaced all the beautiful "grass roofs" of the Korean countryside with red, green, or blue plastic. But shamanism was thriving.

As I learned more about Korean culture, I tried to infuse my University of Maryland classes with my new knowledge and to give my students some firsthand experiences with old Korea. The students in my classes were mixed in age. Some were young American men in the services, some were dependent sons and daughters who had chosen to stay in Korea with their parents, and some were civilians.

The American culture on Yongsan Post was inward-looking. Few of the wives who lived on post drove their cars off the post. They considered me to be incredibly daring to drive in downtown Seoul. I certainly wasn't going to tell

Shamans, Queens, and Figurines: The Development of Gender Archaeology, by Sarah Nelson, 161–168.

them about my adventures in the countryside. But I wasn't entirely fearless. On a sightseeing trip to Japan, I bought a small Buddhist amulet at a shrine to hang on my rear-view mirror to protect my car in traffic. It worked. I never even had a fender scrape, with all the driving I did in Seoul and in the countryside. But twice my car was run into on Yongsan Post, both times when it was parked! I suppose the Buddha didn't have jurisdiction on the US Army post.

I was interested in folklore and ancient history for any light they might shed on the past, but shamanism had the additional importance of being practiced almost exclusively by women. I learned that shamans' ceremonies had been forbidden in cities during the Japanese occupation (1910–1945), and that shamans had been removed from Namsan Hill in the middle of Seoul, to somewhere just outside the walls. Rumor had it that there was a *manshin*, a head *mudang*, who held *kuts* in a house on a hillside just outside the still-standing walls of Seoul. I had heard of other *mudangs* who lived in nearby villages, but this house was accessible to the class.

Korea's hills are not high, but some of them are rocky and steep enough for intrepid mountaineers to train on. The hill along which the ancient Seoul city wall was built is topped by solid granite, in a formation that resembles a pair of monks in cowls. Clearly this had been a sacred place long before Seoul was a city. Below the rock formation, a small rock had been carved with a face, and a flat rock beside it held offerings of fruit and flowers. This path led to the *mudangs'* house.

I took my class to sit on the rocks from which we could look down into the shamans' house. We soon collected a crowd of children, becoming quite noticeable in the neighborhood. When the *manshin* saw us watching, she invited us down to her house to experience the *kut* in altar-side seats.

The healing *kut* was just beginning as we stepped out of our shoes and up to the wooden floor. The class found places on the floor near the percussion trio consisting of two drums and a pair of cymbals. From this vantage point, we could see the altar holding bowls of fruit and bright flowers. Behind the altar, painted saints in poster colors watched over the proceedings. After the *mudang* dances, local women, friends and relatives of the woman being cured, were invited to put on robes and dance (Figure 6). Then the students were invited to dance. One of the young men put on a blue and red robe and whirled himself around the room to the beat of the drums and cymbals. Did he feel that the robe he wore represented the general? He didn't say. The attendees enthusiastically applauded his dance.

FIGURE 6. Mudang dancer

I was not studying the *mudangs*, but I enjoyed the insights of Laurel Kendall, whose early work in Korea involved *mudangs*. I read all her books and papers as they were published, and attended her lectures at meetings. Laurel's talks were always a pleasure. She usually began with a description of an event, and her vivid words invited you there. I wondered if I dared try to make my archaeology papers less dull in a similar way. Mostly I was reluctant to test the small amount of credibility I might have. I felt I was already suspect in some quarters for writing about gender.

Some people argued that *mudangs* were being commercialized and were no longer "authentic," but when I attended *kuts* I saw a living and lively tradition. Once, walking in Seoul with art historian Kay Black, we were enchanted to come across a shaman ritual being performed right in the middle of a street near Seoul National University. A shamanic space had been created with ribbons stretched from a pole in the middle out to four corners of a large platform. The usual percussion players—a small combo of drums and cymbals—sat shoeless on a mat, while one after another the *mudangs* danced in colorful robes.

Fortune-tellers are a wholly different group in Korea. Predictions for one's entire life are made from birthdates and astronomy. Fortune-tellers are rife, and they are especially popular at the time of the national college entrance examinations. One evening, Kay and I got our fortunes told by a computer on the streets of Seoul. For me, the computer predicted that I would become famous in my old age. I am still waiting to be old enough.

On another occasion, I joined a bus expedition of the Royal Asiatic Society, Korea Branch, to Songnisan, a scenic and sacred mountain where Zozoyang, a Harvard-educated PhD architect, had created a folklorist haven. He had gathered lively folk paintings of tigers into a small museum, and sponsored *mudang* rituals in the meadow surrounded by mountains.

The performance at Songnisan was informal, with the audience sitting on mats on the ground, their shoes neatly arranged along the edges. Each dance was announced by a sort of tin trumpet that looked homemade. Different *mudangs* called on the spirits by whirling, leaping, and trancing. But the most amazing performance, the one everyone had come to see, was dancing on sharp knives. Before the final performance of the day, the blades of two sharp butcher knives were bound together, parallel to each other and a few inches apart. These were placed, blades up, across the open top of a large *kimchi* jar, tall enough so the *mudang* had to be helped up to stand on it. I watched agape as she danced on the sharp knife blades. Afterward she showed her feet, which were not cut.

To test further whether the spirits had been pleased by the performance, a whole cooked pig had to be balanced on a *mudang*'s large forked implement. The big fork had a flat base perhaps only two inches across, and was about two feet high. It was amazing to see the *manshin* balancing a pig that must have weighed fifty pounds or more on that unlikely object.

I hoped that both the *mudang* rituals and the early Korean writings/folklore would be avenues into the past, but the beginning of the path was elusive. I thought that perhaps following the strain of animism that still existed in Korea, alongside and even as part of shamanism, Buddhism, and, yes, Christianity, would be fruitful. So when I was invited to a symposium on Religion in Korea at North Park College and Theological Seminary in Chicago, I amassed every reference I could find about animism in early Korea. I read that Koreans believed that stones, trees, mountains, and rivers had spirits, and that each house had a place in the rafters for a spirit, a spirit that needed to be fed. The result of my reading was "The Roots of Animism in Korea" (Nelson 1995b).

I was eager to explore animism and shamanism with archaeological data if I could find the way to begin. In the meantime, a few books about religion in archaeology were published in England. I began to find kindred souls in terms of spirituality in the past, as well as gender. There must have been beliefs, but how can they be identified through material culture without added information from documents? In the meantime, an archaeology of ritual was developing.

When I began to write my first novel, I put some of the current folk practices into the past, to see if they would jar or gel. At the very beginning of my heroine's journey into the past (Part VIII), Clara as the Spirit Bird encounters an image that represents the house spirit, thus using a real piece of material culture to infer a belief, based on current folk beliefs.

With some data on ancient China as well as Korea, I began to think again about gender and religion in East Asia, especially the *mudangs*. But I didn't begin with *mudang* rituals. Instead, I mused on the association of women and pigs in Asia. Perhaps it seems odd that I would think the ideology of pigs would provide another way from the present into the gendered past, but I had scattered additional data to draw on from other sites. Pigs were important in China from the beginning of the Neolithic, and Korean folklore included pigs. Pig figurines in Neolithic northeastern China were very common at some sites. A burial at Xinglongwa of two whole articulated pigs laid out neatly beside a man suggests that pigs were meaningful beyond the provision of food. In recent China, pigs were a symbol of riches (think of a piggy bank), and pigs provided the main ritual sacrifices of the Manchu people of northeastern China, possibly distant cousins of Koreans. Recall that pig balanced on a pole in Songnisan to test whether the spirits approved of the ceremony. Remember the pig heads of the Hongshan culture.

I began to explore this thread by thinking about the meanings of pigs. The first time I ventured into print regarding pigs was a response to an archaeological paper by Kim Seong-Ok (1994) on pigs in a Chinese site, published in *Current Anthropology*, on which I was invited to comment. I found the paper too dependent on the ethnology of New Guinea pigs and without enough attention on pigs in East Asia, especially when there were both ethnographic and archaeological pigs in China to use as models. I pointed out the relationship of pigs and privies in Korea, and wondered if the reported Chinese pits with pigs might represent a similar custom in China. This point was emphasized by David Nemeth, who had studied pigs and privies on the Korean island of Jeju, in his own comments on the paper. In Kim's paper, I worried about the concept that grown pigs would be allowed to walk to market, losing some of their valuable poundage. In making the point, I used as collateral evidence a photo of a pig in Korea going to market on a bicycle. Its snout was tied, but I was told that the pig was usually given a pan of *makkolli,* homemade Korean beer, before being tied onto the back of a bicycle.

Following up on the pig question, and seeking allies, I organized a symposium on the topic for the Society for American Archaeology. The topics varied from current pigs and their treatment to archaeological discoveries of very early pig domestication. I looked for speakers from everywhere that pigs are or once were eaten. Responses to the symposium varied from curiosity to disinterest, but Kathleen Ryan asked if she could publish it in a series on animals in archaeology. We called the volume *Ancestors for the Pigs* (Nelson, ed. 1998).

When I was invited to a Southern Illinois University symposium titled "The Dynamics of Power," I decided to consider gendered power. This inspired my next paper (see Chapter 4) by sending me to the archaeological literature about power—an abundant reading assignment. I thought about the power that shamans have to shape their clients' lives. I thought about monarchs, and whether the gender of the ruler made any difference to their subjects or to the way they might rule. I pondered women leaders of smaller polities (Big Men or Women? chiefs?) and searched the archaeological literature.

My reading led me to the conclusion that different kinds of power can result in different kinds of polities. I looked at shamanic powers and female powers as underappreciated sources of power in the literature on the rise of the state. While I briefly referenced the Hongshan culture in which I had invested more than a decade, most of the power I discussed in this paper was the Shang dynasty in China, a new interest I was beginning to pursue. What kind of power did the Shang queens have, combining divinatory power with female power?

During the discussion, there were no challenges to my paper. Was it too far out for anyone to have a comment? But when I asked the author of a paper on fishers and farmers if he meant to be implying males only, or if all the adults were involved in these activities, I received a hostile reply. I got the impression that, although about half the speakers were women, for some of the audience, power was a male preserve.

Feasting was the center of many discussions on leadership and power. When Tamara Bray asked if I could contribute a paper on Asia (reprinted here, Chapter 8) to a volume she was editing on feasting in archaeological sites, it was a new challenge. I perceived most discussions about feasting as androcentric, since they largely assumed that the feast was thrown by an aggressive individual hoping to aggrandize his position. To provide an alternative view, I considered the literature on feasting in China where there is evidence of feasting at gravesides. I discovered that the ancestors who were feasted at funerals included females as well as males. Although in this group of papers there was no other critique of the feasting theory on feminist grounds, I had once discussed the feasting hypothesis with Rosalind Hunter-Anderson at an IPPA (Indo-Pacific Prehistory Association) meeting, so I was not alone in considering the notion of feasting for the purpose of aggrandizing as more than a little androcentric.

Further research into ancient shamanism in Asia inspired a whole book, a selection of which is included here (Chapter 9). The importance of examining parts of cultures that are less tangible than subsistence and settlement became clearer and clearer as I tried to understand gender in the past. These forays into ideology and religion demonstrate the value of that perspective, whether examining gender is the goal or not. It is particularly important to consider current shamanism, especially as an antidote to the writings on shamanism in Siberia that so influenced Mircea Eliade in his (far too influential) book on shamanism.

Chapter 8
Feasting the Ancestors in Early China

> O soul, come back! Why should you go far away? All your household have come to do you honor: all kinds of food are ready. (from Chuzi, quoted in K.-C. Chang 1977:32)

The importance of feasting in graveside ritual during both the Late Shang dynasty and the slightly earlier Xiajiadian culture is strongly suggested by the numerous vessels found in burial contexts dating to these periods. But it seems to be feasting of a different nature than that described in the classical anthropological literature on pig feasts in New Guinea, which forms the basis of many of our models of the role of feasting activities in traditional societies (Rappaport 1967). Rather than constituting a means of cementing alliances, producing Big Men, and organizing for war, early Chinese feasting activities appear to have had other goals. The evidence for graveside feasting in early Chinese society suggests that enlisting the aid of the dead was of greater importance than forming alliances with the living. In other words, it seems that the deceased, both the recently departed as well as more ancient ancestors, were more powerful and desirable allies than their earthly counterparts.

The graveside feasting activities noted in the early Chinese period are not the only evidence that the ancestors' aid was considered more important than that of the living. As the inscriptions on Shang oracle bones show, propitiating the ancestors, who especially appreciated offerings of wine and food, took place on a regular basis throughout the year, with a particular ancestor always

Sarah M. Nelson (2003a). In *The Archaeology and Politics of Food and Feasting in Early States and Empires*, edited by Tamara L. Bray, pp. 65–89. Kluwer/Plenum, New York. Republished in *Shamans, Queens, and Figurines: The Development of Gender Archaeology*, by Sarah Nelson, pp. 169–184 (Taylor & Francis, 2015).

being feasted on the same day of the Shang ten-day week. Inscriptions on bronze vessels from both Late Shang (ca. 1200–1045 B.C.) and Western Zhou (1045–771 B.C.) periods as well as texts from as early as the succeeding Zhou dynasty echo the mute testimony of the neatly arrayed grave goods, which typically featured vessels for both meat and wine.

Occasionally, the offering of feasts to living individuals is mentioned in the oracle bones, though these feasts appear to have been much less important than feasting the ancestors and the Powers. The more distant and amorphous "Powers," or animistic forces, were called upon only on an as-needed basis to control or predict acts of nature such as floods, or to confer generic blessings for good harvests (Keightley 2000:113–116). In general, however, they seem to have been less important than the ancestors.

The purpose of funeral feasts is known from documents that date to only a slightly later time period than the oracle bones. According to these documents, such feasts were intended to create a new ancestral spirit who would be helpful to his or her descendants by aiding in warfare and weather control, and providing health, long life, and wealth. These blessings could only be obtained through ancestral spirits, by treating them well with sacrifices and ceremonies on appropriate days. It was particularly important that the ancestors were well fed. Chen Lie (1996:272) tells us that, "... the highest priority was nourishment, and we know from texts that food and wine constituted the greater part of sacrificial offerings." Another divergence from the model of feasting to create allies is that the feasts appear to have been family or lineage affairs, partaken of or witnessed only by those who would benefit from feasting these ancestors—that is, descendants and other close kin of the deceased. This is far removed from the notion of public feasting, and deserves closer scrutiny.

The following discussion on the significance of feasting in early Chinese culture is based on archaeological information from both the Late Shang period at Anyang and the Lower Xiajiadian in Inner Mongolia. At Anyang, it is unfortunate that most of the royal burials from the Late Shang period were looted before the era of professional archaeology (Li Chi 1977). Among the rare burials found intact at this site, the best reported and most spectacular are those of queens, especially the grave of Fu Hao, or Lady Hao. This burial, with its large numbers of bronze vessels arrayed around both the inner and outer coffins, allows us to make some inferences about the nature of graveside feasting. Additional evidence can be adduced from the oracle bones and inscriptions on some of the bronzes. Unfortunately, Fu Hao's grave cannot be compared to non-royal graves. The only other well-reported burials from Anyang are those of sacrificed victims, mostly males, without grave goods. Although evidence of ordinary people, and even lower nobility, is still minimal for the Shang, one male burial, about the size of Fu Hao's grave, is crammed with sacrificed humans (Tang 1999:176–177).

The burial ground and city at Dadianzi, an important site of the Lower Xiajiadian culture, can help to fill the gap at Anyang. More than one thousand burials were excavated from this cemetery. Excavators divided these into the categories of 'small,' 'medium,' and 'large' tombs. The quantity and quality of grave goods, as well as features of the graves, make it clear that social ranking and identity were being expressed. The data from these two sites complement each other in the search for the meaning of graveside feasting in the context of early Chinese culture.

The era of the Lower Xiajiadian and Shang is often referred to as the Bronze Age in China. Bronze was used from as far north as Inner Mongolia to as far south as Panlongcheng in Hubei province, and from the China Sea to Sanxingdui in Sichuan province in the west. The extensive use of bronze in China during this period has various implications with regard to the acquisition of raw materials, the organization of production, and trade. Ornaments and weapons were the earliest items produced in bronze, and such items are found, although sparsely, in Lower Xiajiadian burials. By the time of the Late Shang, the primary objects made of bronze were extremely elaborate containers for wine and food, apparently for the exclusive use of the elite, both living and deceased.

NEOLITHIC FEASTING AT GRAVESIDE

The Bronze Age was not the beginning of ancestor worship nor of graveside feasts in China. Several scholars have found evidence for feasting in the Neolithic, especially in those cultures thought to be ancestral to the Shang. Underhill (2000) sees the site of Dawenko as containing evidence of marked status differences but believes that "food and drink were important parts of mortuary ritual for all kin groups, either as gifts to the deceased or for feasting among the mourners" (Underhill 2000:111). That is, whether the status of the kin group was high or low, food and drink were evident in the mortuary ritual. But while all graves contained tools of bone and stone, there were more ceramic vessels in the elite burials. Tall stemmed cups, which are believed to have been used for drinking wine, were the most elaborated form. This suggests that great importance was attached to the activity of drinking at the grave. The consumption of alcoholic beverages as part of these interment ceremonies demonstrates continuity between the Late Neolithic and Bronze Ages.

Underhill (2000:116) suggests that alcohol is important for its ability to transform, "making mourners feel that they could communicate with deceased loved ones." Note that this is not the same as transforming the deceased into an ancestral spirit, which occurs in Shang times. The transformation Underhill is suggesting took place within the consumers of the alcohol, while later uses of alcohol were intended to create cooperative ancestral spirits who would be pleased by the aroma of the wine. There is a difference between creating solidarity among the living by feasting the ancestors and feasting them to turn them into active spirits, although either transformation could be effected by the kin of the deceased. In post-Shang times this immediacy was lost, for the spirits had to be called to the world of the living by special spirit mediums, known as *wu*, who had special training for the task (Ching 1997:8–9; Falkenhausen 1995).

Although Underhill does not address the subject of ancestor worship at Dawenko, Liu (2000) makes a case for ancestor worship in Neolithic China. She finds evidence of three basic changes in mortuary ritual during the Neolithic. One change involves a shift from the veneration of ancestors as a collective group, to the veneration of individual ancestors with high status. Another involves a change in the worshipers from larger village groups to family or lineage groups. Finally, Liu sees a shift in the beneficiaries of the ancestors' attention from the village to the lineage. She presents specific archaeological evidence based on her work on the northern Chinese Neolithic to substantiate these interpretations.

Fung (2000) addresses the question of graveside feasting in the Neolithic using data from the Dawenko culture, rather than specifically from the Dawenko site as Underhill does in her article. Fung notes the ubiquity of ceramic vessels for storage, preparation, and consumption of food and drink in Chinese Neolithic burials. In some of these containers, animal bones and shells were found indicating that food was placed in the grave. His study of Neolithic burials shows that ceramic vessels tend to be placed farther from the body than other kinds of artifacts, with the exception of a particular type of drinking vessel. These are the stemmed drinking cups, which were placed near the chest or head of the deceased. The vessel is typically placed on its side with the top facing towards the head of the grave. Through time, tombs contain increasing numbers of vessels for the storing and pouring of wine. Ding tripods, which have been identified as cooking vessels, tend to be found near the waist or knee of the deceased. Stemmed platters for serving meat are also increasingly prevalent through time, though there are no individual bowls or plates. Fung interprets the lack of plates as a problem for positing individual consumption of meat, although it is possible that meat was eaten directly from a common container. Fung believes his data indicate that communal drinking at the graveside became increasingly common in the course of the Neolithic.

THE BRONZE AGE

Although the historical model of the Bronze Age is that of the Sandai (the three sequential dynasties of Xia, Shang and Zhou), K.-C. Chang (1980b; ed. 1986) has argued that these dynasties actually overlapped in both time and space. Records that purport to be a contemporaneous record of the Sandai are still extant (for a translation of the *Shu Ching*, also called the *Shang Shu*, see Waltham 1971). Although this document cannot be accepted entirely at face value, it is clear that the Shang dynasty was a different polity from the Xia dynasty that it displaced, and the Zhou people who conquered Shang were likewise a separate cultural group. Thus Shang and Zhou must have been present and developing their might during the time recorded as the Xia dynasty. Indeed, for both groups there are lists of named pre-dynastic ancestors. The archaeological evidence likewise suggests multiple polities, with some shared and other completely dissimilar features, jockeying for power during the Bronze Age and variously succeeding. While we cannot know the exact relationships between these polities, the archaeological record does provide some clues.

As noted above, evidence from the Late Shang period at Anyang consists of a rich body of written material, a few spectacular graves, and enormous numbers of unprovenienced bronze vessels. But the site lacks the range of burials found at Dadianzi, a Lower Xiajiadian site in Inner Mongolia. The cultural connection between the Dadianzi and Anyang burials is evident in various characteristics of the graves themselves, although it is not possible to specify in exactly what way they are related (Fitzgerald-Huber 1999).

Lower Xiajiadian (2000–1500 BC) is earlier than the Late Shang, and seems to anticipate Shang styles in burials as well as vessel shapes and decorative patterns. Using Dadianzi to flesh out some details of the Shang may seem surprising to some Sinologists, but I believe that the archaeological evidence of a relationship is clear. To make this relationship more explicit, it is useful to point out that two basic types of tombs can be found in China (Nelson 1997b) before the Qin dynasty, which unified China in 221 BC and enforced standardization in many ways. In one type, the burial is near the surface and is often surrounded by stone slabs and is mounded over with stones or earth or both. The size of the mound and the number of individuals buried within the mound appear to express degrees of eliteness. The other type of tomb also indicates degrees of wealth by the size of the grave, but in this case it is the depth of the grave as well as its overall size that is salient. These larger and deeper graves also contain more elaborate grave goods in greater quantities. Wooden coffins were typically used in these tombs instead of stone slabs, and earthen niches above the coffin often contained additional contributions to the deceased. These two types of mortuary practices coexist both spatially and temporally, and they persist through several millennia.

The earliest known mounded tombs are from the Late Neolithic Hongshan culture, in Inner Mongolia and Liaoning province (Guo 1995a), and they were the burial form of choice for Zhou rulers. But roughly contemporary with Hongshan in Shandong province, the high status tombs (those with the most stemmed cups) are log tombs with a second level ledge, perhaps distantly related to the tombs of Lower Xiajiadian, described below. Thus mounds and deep burials are culturally distinct but contemporaneous beginning in the Neolithic period.

While tomb mounds became more common in China in the course of the Zhou dynasty (1045–221 BC), deep graves can be found even as late as the Warring States period in the Zhongshan culture of Hubei province (530–314 BC), where the tomb of King Cuo was more than 17 meters deep. Thus these tomb types seem to express real differences in cultural patterns, and may well reflect religious beliefs as well as political, social and economic differences among the practitioners of these two burial styles. I refer to the two mortuary patterns as mound burials and deep burials.

It is on the basis of the above observations that I suggest that the assemblages from the Lower Xiajiadian graves at Dadianzi can shed additional light on feasting at graveside, especially when compared with those of the Late Shang at Anyang, in Shaanxi. In burials associated with the Lower Xiajiadian culture, wealth and status are expressed by the amount and richness of the grave goods, as well as the depth of the grave and the number of side niches. In these burials, the coffin tends to be located at the bottom of the grave pit, and food offerings are placed on niches or ledges hollowed out from the sides of the shaft above the coffin. The same variety of deep burials characterize the Shang dynasty at the city of Anyang, though on a much larger scale. Instead of niches, long ramps on which human sacrifices were placed lead into the burial vault. The steps that lead into the burial chamber also contained funerary items. The largest excavated Lower Xiajiadian grave is eight meters deep, while a king's grave attributed to Wu Ding (a Late Shang king) reaches a depth of 13 meters.

But the grave type is not the only reason to connect Lower Xiajiadian with Late Shang. Decorative motifs on the pottery deposited in the deepest graves bear a strong resemblance to those found on Shang bronzes (Fitzgerald-Huber 1999). Furthermore, and most relevant for this chapter, the burial vessels in both cases comprise a suite of shapes that were apparently required for the graveside ritual. The common denominator in both funerary assemblages is a tripod vessel with pouring spout, known in China since ancient times as a container for warming wine.

Given that Lower Xiajiadian precedes Late Shang, it will be useful to consider this culture first. Although there is evidence that the dead were provisioned with food and drink in both cultures, notable differences appear to exist in the details of the feasting practices of the two cultures. These differences highlight specific dimensions of variability in the patterns of feasting that characterized early Chinese states. Anticipating the data presented below, it appears that the most striking difference between Shang and Lower Xiajiadian relates to the fact that drink appears to take precedence over meat as the feasting item of choice in Lower Xiajiadian. This is seen in the variety and elaboration of drinking vessels found in Lower Xiajiadian burials, while the consumption of meat is suggested by the presence of pig and dog bones. But no culinary equipment related to the consumption or serving of meat appears to exist. By Late Shang times, however, containers for meat, and perhaps mixed meat and vegetable dishes, had become nearly as elaborated as those for wine. Both of these container types proliferate through the Shang period in terms of quantity, variety, decoration, and costliness of production.

LOWER XIAJIADIAN BURIAL ASSEMBLAGES

The Lower Xiajiadian culture is centered in eastern Inner Mongolia. Lower Xiajiadian sites are typically hill-top fortresses with extensive stone walls that are readily visible on the landscape. With the recent discovery of Dadianzi, our knowledge of Lower Xiajiadian culture has been greatly enhanced. This site contains an extensive cemetery that has been carefully excavated over the past several years. In addition to being one of the best examples and most thoroughly excavated Lower Xiajiadian sites, work at Dadianzi has also provided us with what we know about Lower Xiajiadian mortuary practices. A small amount of the associated town has also been excavated, with a few trenches cross-cutting the surrounding exterior wall (IACASS 1996).

Over one thousand burials were excavated in the Lower Xiajiadian cemetery at Dadianzi. The graves are laid out in rows. The burials differ in size ranging from graves just large enough for the body of the deceased, to a few that are up to five meters long and eight meters deep (Guo 1995b). Most of the burials are individual and have been classified as either small, medium, or large. Those designated as small have a length of about 1.7 meters, although there are two (M751 and M1213) that reach two meters long. These burials appear to be the minimum size necessary to inter the body. The individuals found in the small graves include all age categories. These graves contain no funerary offerings. Medium-sized graves are larger and deeper than the small burials, and sometimes have traces of wooden coffins. A few have second level niches in which grave goods were placed. The large graves are all longer than 2.2 meters, but their particular distinguishing feature is their depth. They range in depth from three to nearly eight meters. Only large graves were found to contain painted vessels, which are typically located in second level niches near the head or feet, often on both sides of the body. These graves may also contain personal items such as jewelry.

The assemblages from these tombs are described in detail in the report produced by the Institute of Archaeology (IACASS 1996). Pottery vessels that likely represent feasting equipment are found on the single or multiple ledges that are dug into the walls of the burial shaft approximately one to two meters above the body at the foot and sides of the grave. Clusters of vessels are found together in these niches, suggesting use in a particular feasting episode or ceremony. Dog and/or pig bones are also sometimes found in these wall niches.

In the larger tombs, vessels for liquids, often several different varieties, are always present. The most ubiquitous type is the *li*, a tripod vessel with short, fat, hollow legs that taper to a point that often serves as a cover for other vessels, particularly jar forms with flat bases. The tripod vessels are often polychrome painted with patterns that foreshadow the designs found on later Shang bronzes. The assemblages from the medium-sized burials indicate that the basic funerary set was the combination of a jar covered by the tripod *li*. A few additional vessel forms are also present in the larger tombs including footed vessels with pointed lids, jars with handles, and tripod bowls. Tall, thin vase-like containers (*gu*) may also be present. It is clear that the minimum equipment needed for graveside feasts was a set that included a jar with tripod cover, a tripod pitcher, and a small drinking cup.

One example of a large grave (M726) contains three niches. Three vessels were found in the niche on the right side of the body—a tall fluted vase (*gu*), a small jar with a cover, and a jar with a tripod *li* used as a lid. A cup and a lidded jar were found in the niche on the left side of the body, while at the foot of the burial niche was another vase, a *jue* wine vessel, and several smaller objects. The three niches may represent three separate feasting groups at the graveside, since each has its own set of containers. Another individual (M612) was provided with an L-shaped wall niche that runs along the foot and left side of the burial shaft just above the level of the coffin. In this niche were a total of nine pottery vessels, including a large and a small wine pitcher, a jar with a *li* tripod cover, and a small jar at the foot of the burial, and two *li*, and a large and small jar with pointed lids to the left. A few animal bones were also indicated. Burial M905 contained a continuous wall niche around the lower half of the tomb. This grave also had three sets of drinking paraphernalia, as well as two clusters of animal bones and a small pile of cowrie shells. At Dadianzi, all of the larger graves contain at least one *li*-covered jar and one wine pitcher. These pitchers were decorated with thin hatched triangles and bands of alternating hatched lines. Each pitcher has a handle, a spout, and tripod legs.

One reason for interpreting these sets of vessels as remnants of feasting activity at the grave, as opposed to containers for food and drink for the deceased in the afterlife, is that the *li*-covered jars are always standing upright, while the wine pitchers are always lain on their sides. These burials are undisturbed (many of the vessels are unbroken), so the orientation of these vessels must represent deliberate placement. The pitchers had therefore been emptied of their contents before being placed in the grave. Furthermore, the *li*, upside down and used as a cover for a jar, clearly contained nothing. This arrangement is obviously different in intent from what is found in the much later tombs of the Han era in which the food was arrayed on tables for the convenience of the dead and food and wine residue adheres to the containers (e.g., the Mawangdui burials [Qian 1981]).

In the four trenches excavated in the residential section of Dadianzi, four houses and one feature were identified (IACASS 1996). Inside the houses, several different vessel types were found, including *li* tripods, narrow-necked jars, and jars with wide mouths. None of these vessels is painted. A few stone tools were also recovered, as well as several kinds of bone tools, including needles, awls, and projectile points. One particularly interesting discovery was a bone in which circular grooves had been cut into one surface in the same manner seen on oracle bones. It is far from the earliest uninscribed oracle bone, as one has been unearthed at Fuhe, to the north of Dadianzi, that dates to possibly as early as 4000 B.C. (Guo 1995b). But these altered bones nevertheless suggest another interesting possible connection with the Shang. The material recovered in the trench excavations is obviously residential debris, and it is interesting that similar tools and weapons are not found in the graves. This further suggests that the function of the grave goods was to create ancestors by means of a ceremony involving drink and meat, rather than to provide the deceased with equipment for the afterlife.

While some form of libations, as represented by the numerous jars and pitchers, were obviously included in medium and large-sized graves at Dadianzi, the only evidence for the inclusion of foodstuffs consists of animal bones. Pig and dog bones are found both in the wall niches and higher up in the tomb fill. In the largest and most elaborate graves, articulated bones are found, showing that whole legs and in some cases whole animals were deposited in the graves. Poorer graves may contain only inedible parts of the animal, such as the jaw or feet. There is thus a continuum from the richest to the poorest burials, ranging from the presence of whole animals to the complete absence of animal bones. The evident lack of meat containers may indicate that the meat was prepared by roasting, rather than cooked in pots. Unlike the wine, the meat does appear to have been a gift to the deceased rather than the remains of graveside feasting.

The Lower Xiajiadian evidence suggests that wine was imbibed or poured at the graveside, and that the elite, at least, utilized multiple sets of vessels for this purpose. While meat was part of the mortuary ritual, it does not appear to have been consumed at the site. Thus it seems that while food is an important element of the Lower Xiajiadian burial rites, the level of consumption does not constitute a feast. There is no direct evidence that wine consumption at the grave filled the function of transforming the deceased into an ancestral spirit, but the similarities with Late Shang, where the testimony of the oracle bones is available, as well as earlier Neolithic evidence, suggests that this may have been the case.

LATE SHANG DYNASTY FEASTING

The Late Shang dynasty also conducted feasting at graveside, but the food and wine containers were fashioned from costly bronze instead of ceramic. In terms of the burial assemblage, elaboration of both individual containers and the variety of shapes is quite astounding. Another change is that bronze containers for meat were present as well. No longer was it sufficient to lay a roasted pig or dog on a ledge in the grave. Lady Hao's grave even includes a bronze cooking stove, with three bronze cooking pots, perhaps for the preparation of "dishes" (mixed meats and vegetables) or the cooking of grain.

If the painted vessels with complex shapes of Lower Xiajiadian delighted the deceased, how much more honored must the Shang ancestors have been to receive their wine and meat in these elaborate bronze containers. The presentation was made important by the costliness of the serving vessels as well as the food and wine itself.

The importance of bronze vessels cannot be overstated. Nine bronze vessels inherited from the preceding Xia dynasty symbolized the legitimacy of the Shang dynasty, and later the Zhou. These nine bronzes were the tangible evidence of centralized power. Perhaps several kinds of transformations were symbolized. The transformation from ore to molten metal to objects of beauty parallels that of the transformation of grain into wine into a state of intoxication, and from living animals to cooked meat to satiety.

The sheer number of bronze vessels found in Late Shang burials is overwhelming. Only a few royal burials have been found intact, and none of these belonged to kings. But the richness of the queenly burials is impressive enough, even though the sizes of the queens' burials are presumed to be significantly smaller than those of the kings. For example, the tomb of Fu (Lady) Hao, a king's consort who became an ancestral spirit, was 4 × 5.6 meters in plan, and 7.5 meters deep. The personage buried in the tomb is known from inscriptions on many of the bronzes, designating her as Lady Hao. She is also mentioned in many oracle bone inscriptions, allowing many details about her life to be known (Linduff 2002; Zheng 1996).

The 1600 kilograms of bronze found in Lady Hao's tomb included 195 vessels. This was the first undisturbed Shang burial to be excavated; all the known kings' graves had been previously looted (Bagley 1999; Qian 1981; Thorp 1980). Not only the quantity and quality, but also the variety of vessels dedicated to the consumption of wine is highly impressive. Lady Hao's bronze vessels included 40 *jue* and 53 *gu*, both of which are known to have been used for the serving of wine. Food vessels are equally varied, but were fewer in number. Some of these were produced in matched sets, with up to ten bronzes in a set (Bagley 1999). These must have been planned in sets since each mold for bronze casting was unique and could not be reused (Thorp 1980). Some of the sets were from Lady Hao's own store, as indicated by the inscriptions, but others may have been especially ordered by relatives. Most of the large containers were found in pairs. A pair of *fang ding* (square shaped vessels with four cylindrical legs) are particularly celebrated, as they are among the largest ever found in a Shang tomb. Each one is 80 centimeters tall and weighs 118 kilograms.

Bagley (1999:197) estimates that of the 195 bronze vessels, 144 of them were related to wine. This suggests that, like the funeral services at Dadianzi, wine was perceived as far more important to the ancestors than meat. This is further underscored by Bagley's suggestion that of the 56 largest bronzes, only six of them appear to be food vessels (1999:197). The various shapes of wine vessels each had different functions. Some were used for storage, while others were for heating, diluting, pouring, and drinking the wine (Thorp 1980:52). Childs-Johnson (1995) describes the wine offering as "to pour out heated millet wine from the *jue* bronze vessels." A distinction between wine and food is evident in the placement of the bronzes, with wine vessels placed in the inner coffin, and meat containers located between the inner and outer coffins. The "wine" in early China is probably more appropriately referred to as ale (Anderson 1988) or "millet ale" (Keightley 1999c:258)—at least it is clear that it was not made from grapes. An entire Shang industry was devoted to making this beverage. Keightley also suggests that "the offering of wine, whose fragrance and taste, like the smoke from roasting meat, was pleasing to the Powers" (Keightley 1999c:258).

The bronze stove with three *zeng* steamers found in Lady Hao's tomb provides a unique window into food preparation. The soot on it legs demonstrates that it had been used. Although it has not been examined for food residues, presumably grains were steamed, rather than meats or dishes. Rice is still steamed in this way. The stove and steamers together weigh 113 kilograms (Qian 1981).

As for identifying the participants in the graveside ritual, it seems likely that those who would consider the deceased an ancestor would surely have been present. Since the purpose was to create or celebrate a new ancestral spirit, it is highly probable that only family members would have attended. Rawson (1996a:87) suggests that "the large number of different but set shapes suggests a formal meal, with prescribed foods and wines offered in a prescribed sequence."

One avenue to understanding the nature of the funerary feasts is an analysis of the graph *bin*, translated from oracle bone texts as meaning "to invite" or "to host." The graph depicts two persons kneeling on either side of a large vessel, "and appears to have involved the offering of a feast or banquet to a spirit" (Keightley 1999c:260). The word "*bin*" was also used to refer to times "when the king entertained his supporters with banquets" (Keightley

1999c:260). This implies other feasts for which there is no archaeological evidence. It is only possible to say that feasts for the ancestors are mentioned much more often than secular feasts, and that perhaps, given the scene the graph depicts, all feasts were religious in nature. By Period V (1105–1045 B.C.), divining by the king about feasting his supporters through the use of oracle bones had all but ceased.

Another clue to Shang mortuary ritual is derived from objects placed in the fill above the coffin. Two jade bowls, one white and one green, were found on top of the coffin in Lady Hao's grave. The white jade bowl was associated with three eating implements, two of bone and one made of bronze. Tang (1999:174) calls them knives, but the photograph in Rawson (1996b) clearly shows the bowls of narrow spoons. Did the King and perhaps two of Lady Hao's children share one final course with Lady Hao, as she became an ancestor? The fact that the graveside ritual was perceived as including the deceased is further demonstrated by a tomb in which a plate with cattle and sheep legs was placed near the mouth of the body (Tang 1999:176).

During the Late Shang both wine and food were part of funerary feasts, but the emphasis was decidedly on wine, to judge from the number and variety of wine-related vessels. Many of Lady Hao's bronzes bore traces of fine cloth, as if they had been wrapped up. It seems that after the feast, the dishes must have been washed, and the vessels stacked in the grave after washing. The graveside feasting was elaborate, and must have required the labor of many servants to make preparations as well as to tidy up afterwards. The various steps involved in the preparation of the wine, including heating, pouring, and consuming, must have been laid out for the officiant. In so important a ceremony as feasting to create an ancestor, the proper rituals would have had to be strictly observed.

It is interesting that ritual feasts were more common than banquets for allies. It seems that the politics of the Shang were so enmeshed in ritual that the ritual itself showed that the Shang kings were in control. Enormous amounts of energy were invested in divining about the ancestors, and keeping them supportive of the Shang state. Warfare was continuous, and trade, glossed as tribute, is evident in the artifacts of Shang. But ceremony appears to have been the secret weapon, keeping the rites was an end in itself.

CONCLUSION

The gradual change in mortuary treatment in China, from the Neolithic to the Bronze Age, indicates that through various paths, feasts for the ancestors at the gravesite became the process through which the immediate and future beneficence of the deceased was insured. K.C. Chang demonstrates that in the Zhou Li, an ancient book describing many kinds of ceremonies, "food cannot be separated from ritual" (Chang 1977:11). Chang suggests that Chinese people are "preoccupied with eating," and naturally the ancestors would be, too. In fact, David Keightley asserts that "the great wealth of ritual bronzes buried with dead elites was presumably provided so that the recently dead could continue their sacrifices to the more senior ancestors" (Keightley 2000:101).

In addition to graveside feasting, regular ceremonies were necessary to keep the attention of the ancestors and to seal their allegiance. Although secular feasting also occurred, less is known about these events, as they are mentioned infrequently on the oracle bones, and no archaeological evidence has been discovered. This is probably because the oracles bones were concerned with sacrifices that would be pleasing to the dead, not the living, and it was the responsibility of the king to discover what animals and how many would be acceptable to the spirits on particular occasions (Chang 1977:19).

Feasts for the dead were held for everyone at many Neolithic sites, although differential treatment is evident even in this early period. By the time of the Lower Xiajiadian, only some people (those buried in medium and large graves) were feasted, while others were interred without wine vessels or meat bones. It appears that by the Late Shang, ordinary people no longer became spirit ancestors. The differences noted between the mortuary rituals at Dadianzi of graveside feasting and Late Shang practices can be interpreted as emphasizing the royal ancestors (although it must be admitted that no non-royal burials, other than human sacrifices, are known from the latter period).

These changes are expressed in several specific ways. First, it is clear that wine was the most important element in burial rituals throughout the earlier periods, based on the relative number of containers for wine in comparison to food. The addition of food vessels in the Late Shang period indicates a new attention to meat and other foodstuffs. One of the common topics of oracle bones is animal (and human) sacrifices. Perhaps the sharing of the food in the form of cooked offerings among the relatives at the gravesite was meant to remind the ancestor of family ties and obligations. The consumption of meat at the gravesite may have contributed to the creation of a sense of community among the descendants who would share in the hoped-for blessings from the new ancestor.

Second, by the Late Shang period there is no evidence of wine or food being given directly to the deceased. In Dadianzi, the wine was consumed during the burial event but meat on the bone was left for the deceased. In Shang, while the newly created spirit may have partaken of the essence of the wine and food through the insubstantial means of aroma and smoke, no food seems to have been left in the grave, only the cleaned vessels. This suggests a diminished sense of the corporeality of the deceased. More importance appears to have been attached to the bronzes (many of which were inscribed) than to their contents. Food was so important by this point that a bronze cooking vessel was the symbol of the state (Chang 1977:11).

From the Neolithic to the Late Shang, there is a shift in concepts pertaining to the dead and their role as ancestors. By the Late Shang, the power of the ancestors is believed to derive from the world of the spirits and the use of their powers to aid descendants is no longer automatically assumed. The food and wine offered to the dead function to keep the ancestral spirit attached to the living. The quote at the beginning of this chapter emphasizes this attitude. "O soul come back," begins the incantation, not "please go away and don't bother us."

Finally, the contexts of feasting multiply in Late Shang. Graveside feasting likely included only members of the immediate family, those who could expect blessings from the feast, though a huge retinue of servants and officiants must necessarily have been present as well. While the feast was elaborated for the sake of the ancestor rather than spectators, there undoubtedly must have been a highly visible procession to the gravesite with servants carrying the food vessels and other offerings. Worship at the ancestral temple, built on the gravesite, took place according to the appropriate day in the ten day cycle, presumably with prescribed ritual actions performed by specialists.

The changes noted correspond to the different sociopolitical contexts of the Neolithic, the Lower Xiajiadian, and the Shang. Neolithic societies were socially differentiated but all the dead were treated as ancestors for the sake of the entire village or clan. Lower Xiajiadian society appears to have been ranked based on the differential treatment of the dead, with distinctions expressed in the size and depth of the graves, as well as the number and elaboration of the funerary offerings included. During this period, only some of the dead were feasted, presumably those who had more influence and wealth. Late Shang burials follow this same pattern only on a scale several orders of magnitude grander. By this point, social stratification is so marked that only royalty are feasted and only the royal dead can apparently become spirits.

It is likely that the prosperity of the Shang royal lineage was construed as evidence that their ancestors were the most powerful. It became then imperative for the lineage to maintain their wealth and to display it in ritual ways.

The royal ancestors were active contributors to Shang prosperity, and it was this prosperity that at once conferred the right to rule as well as demonstrated the power of the ancestral spirits. Changes in mortuary practices through time indicate that graveside feasting gradually became the prerogative of the elite, and finally, perhaps, only of the royal clans. Chang (1977) believes that the distribution of food resources underlay social stratification in the early state in China. Although that proposition cannot be demonstrated with the data relevant to feasting, it is certainly "food for thought."

Chapter 9
What Is a Shaman?

Earlier (see Chapter 6, this volume) I opened a paper with two contradictory quotes—one by Basilov (1997:3) and one from the *Guo-yū, Chu-yū* (part 2, 18:1a, translated by Ching 1997:14-15), describing two poles of opinions about shamans.The discrepancy causes me to wonder, what images of shamanism do archaeologists hold in their heads? Is a shaman some scruffy reindeer herder wearing a tattered costume, beating a homemade drum and pretending to contact spirits? A woman with wild hair and chains sewed to her coat, clanking as she dances? Or is the shaman a leader of the community, a respected person whose ability to contact spirits offers proof of the ability to lead while conferring the right to do so? These are not trivial questions. The mental image that the word "shaman" elicits is surely a factor in admiration or distaste for shamans in the past, which influences the willingness (or lack thereof) to consider shamans as leaders instrumental in state formation. Unfortunately, archaeologists and historians of China as a rule do not describe their perceptions of shamans, nor do they usually attempt to imagine (at least not in writing) the details of the rituals or other activities of the shamans whose existence they posit or deny. In the absence of such statements it is impossible to know, but it seems likely that competing versions of shamanism underlie the ongoing debate about shamans as early rulers in East Asia.

Sarah M. Nelson (2008a). In *Shamanism and the Origin of the State: Spirit, Power, and Gender in East Asia*, pp. 51–75. Taylor & Francis, Walnut Creek, CA. Republished in *Shamans, Queens, and Figurines: The Development of Gender Archaeology*, by Sarah Nelson, pp. 185–206 (Taylor & Francis, 2015).

Although ethnographic writings on shamanism usually treat shamans with respect (occasionally mixed with skepticism about what "really" happens in shamanic events known as séances), the disheveled Siberian shaman is probably the image most archaeologists tend to visualize. It is the popular image, the one that is evoked by Eliade's (1964) influential *Shamanism: Archaic Techniques of Ecstasy*. The prevailing image is the shaman as psychopomp, not the shaman as knowledgeable community leader. Although many current scholars of shamanism find Eliade's work flawed (e.g., Howard 1998; Kehoe 2000; Thomas and Humphrey 1994), his version of shamanism has held strong in popular culture. Furthermore, much that has been written about shamanism in the former Soviet Union was filtered through Soviet eyes, which, officially at least, considered shamanism to be a superstition needing to be stamped out, along with all other superstition and religion (Balzer 1997:xiii–xiv). Siberian shamanism, often taken to be the most ancient and definitive form, was distorted by the persecutions of the Stalin era. The resulting poverty and dislocation of many groups with shaman leaders often made the leaders less effective than they had been before Russian contact—and, what was more disruptive, séances either ceased altogether or were held in secret. For the most part, Siberian peoples with shamanistic beliefs and rituals were shamelessly abused (Reid 2002:157–166), and the remnant Siberian and Central Asia shamanism recorded today must be a shadow of its former self.

We cannot reclaim the earliest histories of Siberian shamanism beyond some stories and myths (Nowak and Durrant 1977; Van Deusen 2001, 2004), and some pre-Soviet records describing the earliest encounters with shamanistic séances (Balzer 1990; Glavetskaya 2001; Znamenski 2003). These snippets focus on séance events, rarely allowing a glimpse of the shaman's standing in the community. In considering the archaeological past, a broader understanding about what shamans did within the community is needed.

The archaeology of East Asia has produced many artifacts and sites that cannot be entirely explained in terms of economy and ecology. Some artifacts seem to have nothing to do with acquiring food, staying out of bad weather, or other practical concerns. These unusual objects or unexplained features in archaeological sites tend to be labeled as shamanistic, a trend that runs throughout East Asia. The largest numbers of sites believed to reflect shamanism in the Neolithic and Bronze Age are found in China, but China does not have a monopoly on apparent ritual. Many sites and artifacts in the rest of East Asia and contiguous regions are also designated as shamanistic. These sites present a variety of features. Rock art in the Russian Far East is said to portray shamanistic elements, including humans and animals with visible skeletons depicted inside the skin and sun-like faces surrounded by rays (Okladnikov 1981). Scenes with humans wearing flamboyant costumes in Siberia and Central Asia are believed to portray shamans (Devlet 2001).

Just north of China, the ancient "deer stones" of Mongolia may be interpreted as shamanistic (Fitzhugh et al. 2005). Several protohistoric sites in Korea and Japan are believed to represent shamanic activities, ranging from shell masks in coastal Korean sites (Im and Kwon 1984) and *haniwa* tomb figures believed to represent shamans in Kofun period Japan (Kidder 1965), to bronze artifacts—especially mirrors and bells, which are often attributed to shamanistic rites in the early Bronze Age of both Korea and Japan (Kim W.-Y. 1986; Seyock 2004).

It is easy to understand why the attribution of ritual behavior to shamanism would be attractive in East Asia. The supposed homeland of shamanism is Siberia, a region which shares some archaeological attributes with East Asia in the Paleolithic and Neolithic and which is not so far away that it is unreasonable to posit connections between the regions either in the form of movements of people or the spread of ideas. But before examining the specifics of archaeological discoveries said to represent shamans, it will be useful to have a brief look at how archaeologists interpret religion in general, and shamanism in particular.

The Archaeology of Religion, Magic, and Ritual

Very little that is analytical has been written about the archaeology of religion—and even less about shamanism in archaeology. Archaeologists are not uniform in their understanding of shamanism, or of religion, or even of ideology. More attention, however, is being paid to ritual in recent years.

Although explanations of archaeological sites and materials as related to ritual has been one of those perennial jokes in archaeology—"if you can't identify it, call it a ritual object"—the topic of religion is beginning to receive more serious consideration in mainstream archaeology. For example, Ralph Merrifield, differentiating religion from magic, defines religion as "the belief in supernatural or spiritual beings," and magic as "the use of practices intended to bring occult forces under control and so to influence events" (Merrifield 1987:6). These definitions separate ideology from activities, perhaps as a result of focusing on rituals more than on religion (Merrifield 1987:xiii).

Rituals, in Merrifield's usage, are not necessarily religious, but are "prescribed or customary behaviors" that could be simply magical or might have social functions. The purpose of rituals is "to gain advantage or avert disaster by the manipulation of supernatural power." Shamanism falls within these broad parameters both as belief and as practice. Unfortunately for East Asianists, Merrifield's archaeological examples are largely drawn from Europe and tend toward intermittent events, such as depositing votive offerings in wells. Little help is available for recognizing shamanism in East Asia.

Although attention to religion as a phenomenon in the archaeological record is relatively new, even when religion is the topic of interest shamanism is not likely to be in the foreground. In a recent book on the archaeology of religion, Timothy Insoll (2004:43) allocates only a few paragraphs to shamanism, preferring to examine the more general question of religion and archaeology rather than any specific religious beliefs or practices. However, in his brief discussion of shamanism, Insoll makes an important point about archaeological attitudes toward shamanism, one which is directly relevant to East Asia. He notes that shamanism was seen as low on the evolutionary ladder by most writers about early religions, with shamanism falling between totemism and anthropomorphism (e.g., Tylor 1865). This evolutionary perspective may help explain why shamanism tends to be almost exclusively discussed in the company of other "primitive" religions, but it needs to be revisited.

Insoll does not attempt to define shamanism. He only suggests that shamanism can be better approached by archaeologists through context rather than definitions. That advice is well taken, because context—whether or not other evidence of shamanism is present—certainly provides the determining factor of whether a given site or object is reasonable to interpret as relating to a performance of a shamanistic ritual. Several items of material culture have been used as possible evidence of shamanism in archaeology. Since performance has received most of the attention in scholarly writing on shamanism, a context that suggests ritual performance can help differentiate among the possible uses of those artifacts.

Although often simply called shamans, there is disagreement about which word best conveys the essence of these early leaders. Tong (2002) feels more comfortable using the Chinese word *wu* to describe these practitioners in China rather than referring to them as shamans. He uses instead the concept of "wuism" (after DeGroot 1910) to emphasize the particulars of Chinese practices. In his discussion of wuism, Tong defines religion, simply, as relating to the supernatural world and the beliefs, duties, and practices that pertain to the interaction between the human world and that of the spirits. Tong cites thirty-six classical Chinese texts that pertain to wuism, and it is reasonable to assume that he found and assembled the majority of ancient Chinese references to the *wu* in the *Shanhaijing*, which is considered a manual for shamans. Such texts demonstrate that ancient people were well acquainted with *wu* and their practices. Tong observes that the meaning of the term *wu* changed through time, suggesting that the word was applied to shamanistic practitioners earlier, and "priestly" ones later.

Tong (2002:31) uses "magicians" as a larger category that includes shamans, but I am not comfortable with this taxonomy. Perhaps the Chinese word led Tong to this conclusion. *Wushu*, or the art of the *wu*, is translated into English as "magic." While some shamans may practice sleight of hand, ventriloquism, and other magic tricks in séances, magic is not the basis of wuism. In any case, Tong does not emphasize magic in his discussion of wuism. He defines shamans as "part-time religious practitioners, either male or female . . . [with] the ability to communicate with spirits through divination, sacrifice, exorcism, or spells." His emphasis is on communicating with spirits rather than the performance of magic. In late antiquity the *wu* were not primarily performers, but instead belonged to the intelligentsia. In this regard, Tong discusses the *wu* as possible originators of important facets of Chinese culture, such as the Chinese script, astronomy, and music. These are salient characteristic in the context of archaeology.

Archaeological attention to shamanism is beginning to affect mainstream archaeology somewhat, in spite of a slow start. A recent introductory archaeology text mentions shamanism several times in more than ten contexts. Shamans are defined as "men and women who serve as intermediaries between the living and supernatural worlds and are thought to have magical powers. . . . They are sometimes called *spirit mediums*" (Fagan 2007:460). Neil Price (2001) edited a volume specifically dedicated to describing shamanism in archaeological contexts. Regrettably, East Asia is not covered in these pages, although neighboring regions of Central Asia and Siberia are represented. Describing the archaeology of shamanism as being one of "altered states," Price discusses shamanism as a way to deal with a world full of spirits that must be placated.

European archaeological data that is believed to reflect shamanism is compiled in a volume that specifically seeks shamanism, not religion in general, through archaeology (Aldhouse-Green and Aldhouse-Green 2005). This book minimally defines shamanism as an ecstatic religion involving soul journeys of persons chosen by the spirits, thus following Eliade's overly specific and dated definition. Based on Eliade they likewise assert that shamans are able to induce the trance state in themselves in order to intercede with the supernatural world, thus promoting the prosperity and success of their group. The Aldhouse-Greens stress a worldview in which "souls may inhabit trees, rivers, mountains, and stones, where everything around them possessed (or was possessed by) a spirit force, whether sky, sun, river, mountain, rock outcrop, cave, house, or hunted creature" ([pp.] 10–11). Archaeological examples from Europe offered by the Aldhouse-Greens are ordered by time period. They include possible evidence of shamanistic beliefs—such as red ocher burials, rock art, megalithic monuments, bog bodies, and representations of humans wearing antlers—but they do not discuss what these might have meant to the overall culture, or to leadership.

Archaeologists thus use varying definitions of shamanism, including both beliefs and activities. Can archaeologists distinguish shamanism from other rituals or religious beliefs? For that matter, how do ethnographers draw the line between shamanism and other ways of dealing with an unseen world?

The generalizing of shamans through time and space can be laid at the door of Eliade (1964), who characterized shamanism as "archaic techniques of ecstasy." Emphasis on ecstasy remains the most central definition of shamanism for many archaeologists. Not only is the trance state perceived as a defining characteristic of shamanism, but so is "archaic," putting shamanism, as noted above, low on any religious evolutionary scale.

Because it is perceived as a primitive religion, many who study shamanism seek its origins (e.g., Tedlock 2005). Like Eliade, they find in the Paleolithic the source for all shamanism. However, for this exploration of shamanism in East Asia it is not necessary to seek either an original time and place of shamanism or a primal form of it in the ethnographic present. Changes are to be expected in cultural forms, and shamanism, even in its narrowest definitions, has changed through time and with different circumstances. To chase a "pure" shamanism of the distant past is to chase events as transient as a séance itself. It is more appropriate to allow for varieties of shamanism than to try to shoe-horn all shamanisms into one reindeer herder's boot. On the other hand, it is important to bear in mind that not all forms of "primitive" religion must be related to shamanism. For example, while animism and ancestor worship can exist without shamanism, the work of shamans can also partake of and enhance animism and ancestor worship. This topic is discussed further below.

SHAMANS IN ETHNOLOGY

Definitions of Shamanism

In seeking a useful definition of shamanism for archaeological interpretations, problems arise if definitions are either too broad or too narrow. Broad uses of the term allow shamans to be identified in cultures worldwide (e.g., Eliade 1964), but narrow ones can hardly be applied outside their supposed homeland of Siberia. A middle ground is needed. While generally it is agreed that the word shaman comes from the language of the reindeer Tungus of Central Siberia (e.g., Price 2001:3), the concept has been applied to many peoples who are far from any reindeer. The prevailing tendency is for the term shamanism to be used broadly in many ethnographic accounts. Kehoe (2000: 2) says that shamanism "is used so loosely and naively by anthropologists no less than the general public, that they convey confusion more than knowledge."

Defining shamanism is not only an archaeological problem. In a summary article about shamanism from an anthropological viewpoint, Atkinson (1992: 308) voices skepticism. "Among cultural anthropologists there is widespread distrust of general theories of shamanism, which run aground in their efforts to generalize." If ethnographies fail archaeology as a source of usable definitions of shamanism, romanticizing of shamanism fails even more. "The magnetism of shamanism is not just a strand in pop religion or an aesthetic. . . . Shamanism is more of an exotic essence . . . than a scholarly category that can stand up to any sustained interrogation" (Thomas and Humphrey 1994:2).

Shamans are said to have many purposes. "Traditional shamans provided psychotherapy, cures, and leadership for their communities, along with poetry and entertainment" (Balzer 1997:xiv). Shamanisms have been identified on most continents (e.g., Tedlock 2005), but sometimes it is difficult to say exactly what it is they have in common. Laurel Kendall (1985:27–28) suggests that the term shamanism is often "sloppily applied," and others who discuss Korean shamanism agree (Howard 1998).

Shamans vs. Priests

Shamans have been contrasted with priests in order to define both categories. Often shamans are said to be individual leaders with access to spirits, while priests are those with a written tradition and set rituals. For example, Takiguchi (2003:122) proposes that shamans are "inspirational individuals, and [priests] are institutional functionaries in some kind of religious hierarchy." However, not everyone uses these concepts in the same way. Sarah Allan (1991:85) considers the *wu* of the Shang dynasty to have been "specialized priests who could call the souls of the dead." She does not use the term shaman; instead she considers the thinking of Shang to be "mythic."

Shamans as Spirit Contacts

Some scholars make a distinction between those who are believed to journey to the spirits and those in whom the spirits descend. The former are called shamans; the latter are spirit mediums. However, this is not always a useful distinction. For example, some Korean shamans call down the spirits and some Siberian shamans' souls journey to them, but otherwise they perform similar actions. In either case the shaman is personally in contact with spirits, and that is the characteristic that is important for Korean shamanism. Perhaps the simplest way to distinguish shamans from other religious practitioners is that the shaman's soul must contact spirits.

Shamans and Knowledge

Shamans are often described as knowledgeable people. Kehoe (2000) explains that the root "sa" as found in the original Tungusic word *saman* means "to know." "Knowledgeable" is a useful way to think about *wu* and *mu*, especially as they became leaders in increasingly complex societies. Hsu (1986) makes the same point about those who read the oracle bones in Shang China, noting that they were knowledgeable specialists. Of course being knowledgeable is not sufficient to define a shaman, for many people had various kinds of knowledge. Shamans, though, had specialist knowledge about spirits, presumably based on keen intelligence and observations of other people in the context of their lives.

Emphasis on the shaman as a political actor as well as a religious practitioner is critical to the question of the shaman's sociopolitical position. The shaman as leader is particularly a propos for East Asia, for it has been argued based on both texts and archaeology that in the process of state formation "charismatic power may be appropriated and incorporated in the center" (Thomas and Humphrey 1994:4). Several archaeologists believe this appropriation describes the sequence in China.

Shamans as Healers

Treating illnesses is an important shamanistic activity often performed in the context of séance. For example, Balzer (1997) calls shamanism an "ancient medical system." She highlights the intention to cure as follows:

> Many writers would agree that shamans are medical and spiritual practitioners. The term "Medicine Men" applied to Native Americans, suggests the same combination of abilities and activities (and the usual gender mistake). Blessing, foretelling the future, and dancing for rain are among other specific activities that are connected with shamans, but they may also be seen as sorcerers, with the potential to do evil. But mostly they are intermediaries between two worlds: the spirits and humans. (Balzer 1997:xiii)

Balzer thus defines shamans as both healers and leaders. She discusses several debates about the nature of shamanism, including whether the healing is "real" (Balzer 1997:xvii). These debates center around the "political, mystical, and religious roles" played by shamans.

Ching (1997:13) also considers healing an important aspect of shamanism, defining the shaman thus: "He or she serves the community by divination and healing, although in China, praying for rain has been a principal responsibility." Indeed, as will be seen in the context of Shang and Chu shamanism, praying for rain looms large in texts as a shamanic activity.

The Shaman's Drum

Kehoe describes shamans as "religious leaders, men and women, who serve their communities by using hand-held drums to call spirit allies" (Kehoe 2000: 15). The limited version of Siberian shamanism is too simple for exploring the varieties that became the Chinese *wu* and Korean *mu*, as well as many other East Asian traditions. While the statement about serving their communities is one that is important for East Asia, focusing on the hand-held drum is too specific. It omits much that is salient for shamanism as it is practiced in East Asia in the present. For example, drums are used in shamanistic séance almost everywhere in Asia, but they are not all hand-held drums, and even when drums are held, the shaman is not necessarily the one holding the drum. There are even shamanic traditions in which the primary instrument is not a drum at all. In Korea a member of the percussion band beats the two-sided large red drum, and others play smaller drums and cymbals as well, often in a trio sitting on a mat on the shaman's heated floor.

Drums found in archaeological contexts in East Asia are likewise of several kinds. Wooden drums stretched with crocodile hide were prominent in the Longshan Neolithic, and there are possible ceramic drums in Hongshan and Longshan. Red hourglass-shaped wooden drums with hide ends feature prominently in Korean rituals. The same red drums are used in recreation involving circle dancing. These drums are available to rent for a picnic with drinking and dancing on temple grounds in Korea. The huge decorated bronze drums in southern China and southeast Asia in the Bronze Age must have been used in ceremonies and rituals. Even allowing for the importance of percussive instruments, a problem for archaeologists may arise when hand-held skin drums stretched on a wooden frame left no traces, being made entirely of perishable materials. But even in cases where hand-held drums were not used, the *wu* and *mu* certainly had rhythmic ways to call up their spirit allies. Even hand claps can be used, as they are in some Buddhist temples. One must conclude that drums per se cannot be seen as the defining characteristic of East Asian shamanism, although at least some sort of rhythmic percussion does seem to be imperative for ritual dancing.

SHAMANS IN HISTORY

Inner Asia

Excellent reviews and translations of writings about Siberia and Central Asian shamanism have been published in English (Balzer 1997; Knecht 2003; Znamenski 2003). This is not the place to detail the history of encounters with shamans, although the variability of shamanism is instructive. Reid (2002) effectively describes the terrible experiences of native groups in Siberia during the Stalinist era, and how shamanism was affected—as well as the dismal results for the careers and even lives of the ethnographers themselves. The point to be made here is that shamanism changes according to circumstances, as do the outsiders' responses to shamanism.

Chinese Wuism

If the word shaman can be used only to describe religious practitioners among the reindeer Tungus, then another concept is needed to apply within East Asia. This is probably the reason that the Chinese word *wu* is used for Chinese ecstatic religious practices and the neologism wuism, rather than shamanism, is preferred by some. However, not all scholars who use the word shaman to translate the character *wu* would agree that the *wu* mainly represent "archaic techniques of ecstasy."

Shuowen, an ancient Chinese dictionary, defines the character *wu* as follows: "*Wu* are Chu, female, capable of serving the formless [spirits] and dancing to bring down the spirits. [The character] is composed of a person extending the two sleeves in the act of dancing" (Ching 1997:20). Chang has suggested that the oracle bone version of the character depicts an instrument used to draw circles and squares, which represent heaven and earth, respectively. He thus proposes that *wu* had access to earth and heaven by virtue of geometry, being able to draw circles and squares, which had magical meaning (Chang, K.-C. 2005). Fuxi and Nuwa, mythical founders of China, are sometimes depicted holding the compass and square rule. "Thus, the shamans of the Shang and Zhou periods were mathematicians who understood the heaven and earth and were sages and wise men" (Tong 2002). Yet another suggestion regarding the character *wu* is that it represents yarrow (milfoil) sticks, which were thrown in ancient China for divinatory purposes. Keightley (1982:299) reports with skepticism that Akatsuka sees the graph for *wu* as "a picture of the altar stand possessed by the spirits summoned from the four quarters." The graph thus functions as a Rorschach test for sinologists. So much has been seen in this simple character of six or seven strokes (the oracle bone version of the character differs slightly from the current character) that it seems wise to avoid interpreting the graph as an image, but consider it a concept.

Wu and *xi* also can be represented as "brilliant descendants of past sages" who have much occult knowledge. These descendants managed ancestral temples and knew the names of rivers and mountains. They could recite lineages leading back to distant ancestors, and their knowledge allowed proper ranking of generations. *Wu* were therefore historians, guardians of knowledge of the past (Wu, K.C. 1982:12), even when it was remembered through oral history.

Other Beliefs and Rituals in East Asia

The problem of slippery definitions of shamanism in archaeology is even wider than the attribution of shamanisms to all manner of interesting discoveries. Other anthropological concepts—such as totemism, animism, and ancestor worship—are often evoked indiscriminately and likewise without definition. It is worth a brief look at these other religious concepts that become intertwined with shamanism to see to what extent they are useful or whether they contribute "noise."

Totemism

While totemism is not usually defined when evoked in East Asian archaeological contexts, the mere presence of animal depictions seems to be sufficient to call forth this response. Totemism is the belief that a particular group of people are related to a specific kind of animal and may include taboos related to that animal, whether it is a wolf, a kangaroo, or a worm. This is a group belief, not at all resembling the animal spirit helpers of some individual shamans. Often art historians and archaeologists use the word totemism without any explicit discussion about its relationship with shamanism. Since totemism as a useful concept has been discredited in anthropology (Atkinson 1992:308), its lack of definition when called upon in Asia need not give us further pause. It is not relevant to the question of shamanism in ancient East Asia and can be safely ignored.

Animism

Animism does relate to shamanism, although the presence of animism does not presuppose shamanism. Essentially, animism is a worldview that sees everything as alive in some sense, with an independent spirit. Rocks, trees, springs, rivers, mountains, and even diseases may thus have spirits, as well as buildings, birds, and hearths. Animism may underlie some shamanistic beliefs, such as the belief in spirits of mountains and rivers, wind, and rain, but without written documents it is impossible to recognize animism directly from archaeological discoveries.

Where archaeology fails, however, texts can be used with caution. Korean myths and legends, for example, strongly suggest early animism in the Korean peninsula (Nelson 1990b). On the other hand, spirits can inhabit a stone or a tree without the stone or tree itself being a spirit. It is unlikely that archaeological materials will ever be able to make this subtle distinction, but it is important for understanding beliefs about spirits.

Myths that assert the prestigious ancestry of queens from goddesses of mountains are intended to establish the relationship of queens to mountain spirits anthropomorphized as females (Nelson 1990b). Spirit shrines were (and are still) often erected on mountains, even if the mountain top also supports a military look-out post (Kendall 1998). A shrine can be as simple as a pile of stones—or a tree or rock with ribbons, paper, or straw attached. The marking of shrines can be too ephemeral to appear in archaeological contexts.

An example of a sacred place inhabited by spirits in ancient Korea is that sacred groves called *sodo* in southern Korea were marked by a tall pole, drums, and bells (Parker 1890). It is reasonable to suppose that these numinous places were inhabited by spirits who lived among the trees, although the text is not specific on this point. As recently as the mid-twentieth century, even after the Korean War and deforestation caused by poverty and limited access to fuel had destroyed most of Korea's forests, many Korean villages surrounded an old sacred tree that escaped the axes of villagers desperate for firewood. Some revered *mudangs* outside the walls of Seoul kept a large tree by their shrine to which strips of colorful cloth were tied. Old Korean villages had a pair of wooden guardian figures called *jangseung* on each road leading into the village. Inscriptions on the posts named them the Earth Grandmother and the Sky Grandfather. Since similar figures in Cheju Island and parts of the southern coast are made of stone, their ability to guard did not derive from the trees from which they were cut, but from rituals related to their manufacture and placement.

As for activities in sacred places, in texts written in the early centuries of the Common Era (Parker 1890), Korean rituals are said to have included singing, dancing, and drinking alcoholic beverages as ways to worship the gods. The place for such activities was specifically noted to be a cave in the case of Puyo—surely a place imbued with spirits. For that matter, many caves in China containing Paleolithic and Neolithic remains are called Xianren Dong, Spirit Cave, suggesting that these places were believed to harbor spirits related to ancient relics. Daoism in China preserves remnants of animism as well (Allan 1997). It seems that mountains, rocks, water, and trees are home to spirits throughout East Asia.

Ancestor Worship

Ancestor worship is yet another Chinese concept that sometimes has been alleged to be interpretable in prehistory and occasionally is conflated with shamanism. A belief in spirits of the dead who need to be fed and who can influence the living (Allan 1991) is connected to shamanism because some shamanistic spirits are ancestors. Ancestor veneration is probably the most accessible of these rituals to archaeologists, as well as being a known indigenous belief in East Asia. Neolithic evidence for ancestor worship is usually adduced from grave goods, which are interpreted as evidence of graveside feasting to appease the spirits of the recently dead (Fung 2000; Liu 2000; Nelson 2003a).

However, while feasting may involve intoxicants and riotous behavior, it is not the same as a séance. Ching (1997:25) notes that the graph *wu* appears in the context of sacrifices to nature powers, especially wind and rain, but not to ancestors. On the other hand, Keightley (1983:555) puts the emphasis on ancestor worship, not nature or the powers, as "the organizing metaphor of Shang life." Ancestor worship can exist without shamans, but the two may be intertwined. Spirits of the dead are among the pantheon of spirits called upon by shamans. Korean shamans to this day perform a separate *kut* for the dead, calling back their souls (Janelli and Janelli 1982).

Ancestor worship may have contributed to political consolidation. Tong (2002:43) specifically connects ancestor worship with the rise of the state: "In the course of state formation, if a clan or family became the ruling group of a polity, then its ancestors would become the gods of the whole polity." This apparently occurred in the case of the Shang kings. Tong points out that in the Zhou dynasty, "towns having an ancestral temple, with the spirit tablets of former rulers, were called capitals. . ." (Tong 2002:43). Having ancestral spirits thus *defines* a capital. Akatsuka further suggests that the town, the clan, and the ruler all had the same name (Keightley 1982). The identification of the elite and their ancestors with the religious ideology was thus complete.

It is clear that each of these belief systems—animism, ancestor veneration, and shamanism—is an independent variable. Each needs to be demonstrated separately; none implies any other. Animism, ancestor worship, and a belief that spirits of the dead exist and can interfere with the living are independent of shamanism, although they may coexist. It is inappropriate to use either animism or ancestor worship alone as evidence of shamanism in the past.

However totemism, animism, and ancestor worship are not the limits of concepts that have been related to shamanism in East Asia. Cosmological concepts are also implicated. Evidence for ancient astronomy is often tied into cosmological concepts of later East Asia (e.g., Nelson et al. 2014). Since the purpose of early Chinese astronomy was to discover the will of heaven (Pankenier 1995; Sun 2000), reading the sky is closely related to other kinds of divination.

Archaeologists have used Chinese cosmological concepts to interpret prehistoric sites. For some archaeological examples, the ancient Chinese belief that heaven is round and the earth is square has been used to explain several kinds of archaeological objects and features. Square and round constructions, especially flat-topped altars and rounded burial mounds, are said to be evidence for the antiquity of this cosmological belief (Sun and Guo 1986). Round jade objects (*bi*) and square ones (*cong*) are likewise implicated as cosmological symbols.

These are all interesting ideas, and I am not suggesting that they are wrongly applied, only that the synergy between other religious concepts and shamanism needs to be queried in each instance, and the connection made explicit. In order to examine the question of shamans as leaders, it is necessary to ask what aspects of shamanism can be teased out of archaeological sites, what activities occurred, and how shamans brought about the desired effect.

Practices of Shamans

If ethnographers—with live people and events to observe and describe, and participants to question—cannot be specific about what is and is not shamanism, what hope is there for archaeological explanations, with our much more impoverished catalog of material objects and their relationships to describe and explore? We are warned that "shamanism should not be thought of as a single centrally organized religion, as there are many variations" (Stutley 2002:2), which is no doubt good advice for ethnographers, but difficult for archaeologists. For archaeological interpretation, it is important to focus on practices and the associated material culture used in shamanistic séance.

The literature of shamanism suggests that the major activity of shamans is staging dramatic events, which ethnographers often call séance. Balzer calls séance "the heart of shamanism." The activities of séance include music, dancing, trancing, and audience involvement, as well magic and special effects. Balzer's (1990:xvii) insistence on public performance is a key to interpreting archaeological sites. If there is no audience to see the séance, is it shamanism? For example, audience involvement is important in Korean shamanism, but not, as far as is known, in the oracle bone divinations of Shang China. Divination was not usually performed before an audience (Keightley 1982), but was there an implicit audience? And even if there was no audience for the act of divination, were there other public events? Were there announcements to the public that the ensuing sacrifice was to Ancestor X in order to cure the king's toothache? Who watched the sacrifices to the powers that were the subject of divination? These questions are not answerable with present data.

Still less is known about performances of Neolithic shamans. In contrast to activities of Siberian shamans and later shamans in East Asia, there is no written description of what alleged Neolithic shamans may have done. A catalog of activities of the *wu* is found in an Early Zhou document (Falkenhausen 1995), which implies differences from Siberian practices, but continuity nevertheless from a time when séances were part of the repertoire of the *wu*. Activities listed include rain-making, star-gazing, medicine and healing, divination, music and dancing. In later times and in various places, these practices are sometimes divided among different kinds of practitioners. For example, in Korea fortune tellers, who use a number of devices including astrology, are not the same as those who dance to heal and to learn the reasons for ill fortune of other kinds. As a general rule, neither group includes rain-making in their repertoire.

Practices performed by shamans may be carried out by other ritualists as well, so that in many cases archaeologists may be able only to recognize ritual, but not specifically shamanism. Nevertheless, it is still helpful to consider shamanistic activities and the items of material culture that might indicate shamanism. While many take trancing (or ecstasy) as the essential element of shamanism, trance and dance leave few archaeological traces. What can an archaeologist hope to find to indicate shamanism?

MATERIAL CULTURE OF SHAMANS

Archaeologists need guidance about the kinds of material culture to expect, dependent as we are upon the material manifestation of ephemeral events that relate to the question of performance. The objects said to represent shamanism in East Asia include a variety of artifacts. The underlying logic to the claims of shamanism in archaeological contexts relates to both practices and beliefs. The problem is that shamanistic artifacts often have no continuous thread. The dazzling gold crowns of the Silla kingdom of Korea seem to have little in common with the depictions of possible animal masks on Shang bronzes. While it is important to consider each within its own context, it would be reassuring to find repeated patterns.

As we have seen, Kehoe (2000) takes the shaman's drum as the central feature of shamanism. She likewise emphasizes the reindeer livelihood of those whose language gave us the word shaman. But—although I will argue for the importance of antlers as a shamanistic symbol—even reindeer symbolism cannot be depended upon as universal in the symbolic language of shamanism. Antlers do occur in possibly shamanistic contexts in East Asia, even away from reindeer territory. Antlers are obvious on Silla crowns in Korea, where reindeer did not roam, and antlers attached to noncervine creatures also appear in Chu statues of southern China, which was not reindeer country either (although the antlers may represent those of local deer, not reindeer). In any event, deer in Korea are symbols of long life, related to the supposed medicinal value of the antlers.

Shamans' clothing is usually intended to attract attention—not only the attention of the participants but of the spirits as well. Costumes may be colorful, fringed, or feathered—and likely to make noise as well. The shaman's hat may be intended to convey the spirit is being called down, or may simply be another focal point for the display of symbols. Shamans' clothing and symbols vary widely, even among Central Asian shamans, and should be expected to have different characteristics in different regions.

Paraphernalia of shamans used in séance can include masks for impersonating spirits, bells and rattles, flags, fans, or bowls of wine. Some events call for whole cooked pigs, or parts of them, and some use dried fish. Shamans may also have altars or shrines, with simple objects such as pebbles, or perishable materials like food, which the archaeologist may not discover at all or may find difficult to interpret.

Another problem for archaeologists is that few objects that are used by shamans are exclusively shamanistic. Drums can be used for communal dancing as well as séances. Fancy clothing may mark the elite. Food for the ancestors may be difficult to distinguish from feasts for the living. It is therefore necessary to argue from the total context, rather than having any single mark of a shaman that will appear in an archaeological site. However, once the archaeological hunt is on, the material accouterments of shamans are seen to be many, and involve most of the senses. For example, *wu* might have left evidence of sound-makers of various kinds. Rhythmic sound can be produced by drums, chimes, and bells, while haunting melodies can be played on flutes, not to mention other more complicated percussion and melodic instruments. Sound can also be produced by jingles and rattles attached to clothing, which are activated by the shaman's dance. The kinetic sense of course also would be represented by dance, which can be inferred not only from musical instruments but, some allege, by the early forms of some Chinese characters. The *wu* dance with long sleeves, arms extended, as shown in later paintings. The sense of smell might be activated by smoke from aromatic plants or incense and taste by wine and food.

Whether narcotics and/or stimulants might have been ingested by the participants and onlookers at rituals as well as the shamans is unknown. Hemp seeds and leaves were certainly available, although there is no evidence that any part of the plant was used to create euphoric visions. Some hemp seeds were found in a burial context in Siberia that suggest a final rite for the deceased that involved burnt hemp seeds (Gryaznov 1969:136). However, the drug of choice among the Shang and at least some of their Neolithic predecessors seems to have been wine. It is usually described as most probably made from fermented grain rather than fruits (Underhill 2002).

Visual effects would have been many, including colorful costumes. Parts of costumes that swirl, dangle, or glitter—and showy or sharp paraphernalia—are often part of the shamanistic show. Shamans have favored headgear that attracts attention: hats that are tall, or colorful, or include antlers or other animal representation suggesting spirit helpers.

Styles can alert the archaeologist to the possibility of shamanism as well. Depictions of birds or wild animals, drawings of the sun with rays, and the indication of bones inside the body of humans or animals are often seen as shamanistic traits (Okladnikov 1981). Transformations from one type of being to another, as well as composite animals, are also interpreted as indicating shamanism (Chang, K.-C. 1983, 1994b; Childs-Johnson 1995).

Archaeological features that can be examined for possible shamanic indications include extraordinary burials, rock art depicting shamanic symbols or activities, mural paintings in tombs, early writing or symbols on pottery, and the landscape (as its usage may reflect rituals). Artifacts and their contexts also are important, because objects with daily functions may take on shamanistic meaning in a ritual context, and in that context may be larger than their functional analogues and/or made of impractical materials.

Neolithic archaeology in China is vast and varied, including the contents and layout of burials—as well as ritual buildings and landscapes, statues and figurines, and carved jades with symbolic meanings from several regions. Altars and the placement and shapes of graves also help to understand Neolithic shamanism in East Asia. Shang shamanism is another possible touchstone, for it has been adduced from several different sources: writing on oracle bones (Keightley 1978b), documents from the Zhou or later (Falkenhausen 1995; Pankenier 1995), symbolism depicted on bronzes (Chang, K.-C. 1983), and from other symbolism, especially on jades (Childs-Johnson 1995).

CURRENT SHAMANISM IN EAST ASIA

There are several reasons for restricting this archaeological exploration of shamanism to East Asia. First, this is where shamans have been said to become leaders and rulers. Second, through time many elements can be found in common among the people of East Asia, although there are significant divergences. Third, I avoid implications of relationships with far-flung alleged shamanisms, for example in Europe (Aldhouse-Green and Aldhouse-Green 2005) or South America (Tedlock 2005). Finally, the East Asian cultures have interacted with each other for millennia, making the differences among them of interest as well as their similarities.

But even limiting the discussion to East Asia, close to the possibly "original" shamanism of Siberia, the question of what is shamanism remains. The scholarly concept of shamanism is based on Siberian data, and Siberian shamans were taken to be "living fossils" who allow a glimpse into deep antiquity. When it comes to other current shamanism, the question of which groups are "really" shamans can become heated. Howard (1998:12) suggests, "in Korea the brush we use to paint our descriptions of shamanism needs to be broad." If ethnographers studying living Korean practitioners who go into trances and call down spirits can't agree on whether or not they are shamans, what chance do archaeologists have of teasing out shamanism from scattered and impoverished bits of material culture? Although the difficulties are many, it is an effort worth making because of the light it may shed on paths to rulership and the rise of states.

While linguistically Chinese is unrelated to Siberian languages, the other East Asian languages spoken where shamanic rituals were practiced in state level societies, especially Korean and Japanese, are usually considered to be anciently related to Tungusic or Siberian/Manchurian languages (R.A. Miller 1971, 1980). There may be a more direct link between peninsular and island forms of shamanism with the northeast than between Siberia and China, but influences from China (as well as Buddhism and Christianity) are also part of the mix. "Religions" in Asia lack the exclusivity of the religions of the Bible lands.

Shamans, even those of Siberia, may be either born into a shamanic family or "called" to it later in life. In China, Wu even became a family name, and shamans with the surname Wu are mentioned in the Shang oracle bones. In Korea, two types of *mudangs* have been described—*kongsin*, who are called by the spirits, and *seseup mu*, who are born into shaman families (Kim S.-N. 1998:33–34). Another group of *mudang* lives on Jeju Island. Called *shiumbang*, they belong to *mudang* families but also use trance. The performances of these groups, however, are similar enough for all of these shamans to be called *mudang* by most Koreans.

In desiring to distinguish Korean *musok* from other forms of shamanism, Tae-gon Kim (1998:19) produced a definition of the general term, which was based on his observations of and participation in shamanic events from many parts of Central and East Asia. This is a useful understanding for archaeologists to work with:

> Shamanism is a traditional, religious phenomenon tied closely to nature and the surrounding world, in which a practitioner endowed with the special ability to enter a state of trance-possession, can communicate with supernat-

ural beings. This transcendental power allows the practitioner, the shaman, to satisfy human cravings for explanation, understanding, and prophecy.

VARIABILITY OF SHAMANISMS IN ANCIENT EAST ASIA

In accepting Kim's definition of shamanism, I should make it clear that I am not positing an ancient religion from which Chinese *wu*, Korean *mudang*, and others descend. Many scholars who investigate living shamanism today disagree with the approach of Eliade (1964), which suggests that shamanism is both primitive and timeless. Kehoe is among the scholars who warn against this approach. Shamanism should not be placed "in a time warp outside of history" (Kehoe 2000:39). It will be useful to keep in mind Kehoe's dictum that "ethnographic particularities are highly significant clues to societies' histories" (Kehoe 2000:15). It is necessary to recognize that the *wu* and *mu* were specific to times and places. Seeking their antecedents or successors is not meant to imply a lack of change throughout this spread of time.

Others have emphasized the situatedness of shamanism. Thomas and Humphrey (1996:2) find Eliade's work inadequate because to him shamanism reflects "a romanticized inversion of Western rationalism." They hope to "recover and analyze the diversity that essentialism has masked." Kehoe (2000:4) makes the point that it is important to "historicize shamanic activities by understanding their particular manifestations as results of historical processes."

A characteristic of shamanism in northern Asia as well as East Asia is that the "concept of heaven or the sky as the all-encompassing principle of cosmic order and human destiny" that is held in ancient China is similar to that of Mongols and Manchus. Deities are sky deities, and the sky itself is a source of power (Humphrey and Onon 1996:197). This emphasis on the sky ties observations of the heavenly bodies closely to East Asian shamanism and the practices that became Daoism.

K. C. Chang suggests a similar definition, but he emphasizes a version of the world particular to China, in which heaven and earth are equal spheres. "In the context of ethnography, a shaman is defined as someone who can communicate with both heaven and earth, in other words, with both gods and humans, and this ability is considered to be inborn" (Chang 2005:129). However, in describing Shang kings as shamans, Chang does not emphasize trance or ecstasy, but foretelling the future, utilizing animal helpers, and communicating with spirits of the dead. It is not known whether these practices were performed in the context of trance, although reaching the spirits was the goal (Chang 1983, 1994a, 1999, 2005).

Ching is less interested in the ecstatic than she is in the mystical. The fact that "the human being is open to the divine and the spiritual . . . this was the primeval experience of the shaman" (Ching 1997:xi). Although she defines shamanism as relating to "the claim of spirit possession and the ensuing ecstatic experience" during which the "shaman controls the spirits" (Ching 1997:13–14), it is ultimately the way that shamans became rulers that is of interest to her. "Charisma associated with shamanic ecstasy created the aura for the office of kingship" (Ching 1997:xii). Shamanic figures—original, spontaneous, and charismatic religious individuals—were often, although not always, also the political leaders, or kings, assisted by other, lesser, shamans (Ching 1997:xiii). It is important that, focusing on the Chinese case, Ching also looks at divination and the knowledge of stars as an important element of shamanism in China. Both have left traces in Neolithic China.

Let me reiterate that in discussing shamanism in East Asia from the Neolithic to the present, I am not implying that shamanism remained unchanged though time and space. The point is only that shamans in this instance were able to claim exclusive ability to reach the spirits, and hence had the power, or even the mandate, to become secular as well as spiritual leaders in the community. The populace would have wanted to follow them to enjoy the benefits from the spirits and the protection from harm that the spirits could grant. It is an "ethnographic" approach, based primarily on archaeological, historical/textual and ethnographic data, and considering variations through time and space. What began with shamans as rulers became bureaucracy, with *wu* sometimes performing as priests. This occurs earlier in China, and later in Korea and Japan, under the influence of Chinese Confucianism. But shamanism stubbornly, and interestingly, survives alongside.

The Korean *mudang* were seen to be powerful because they could call down the spirits and control them (Hogarth 1998:47). But this power goes beyond the personal possession of spiritual power.

> If a *mudang* experiences ecstasy, a non-ordinary personal phenomenon, it is interpreted as evidence that he or she has spiritual power. However, this power stems not only from personal innate competence; it can also be understood as a cultural and social construction. It comes from the authority or prestige that believers and clients acknowledge in the *mudang*, authority or prestige which they assign for personal or collective interests. Both the belief system and the presence of this power in the ritual context—in keeping with the demands of the clients—are necessary ingredients for the comparison and judgment of spiritual efficacy. (Kim, S.-N. 1998:41–42)

CONCLUSION

Ethnographies thus warn interpreters of archaeological sites that the phenomenon called shamanism in various places around the world has multiple beliefs and practices. It is a familiar term with too many meanings—or better, a potpourri of practices. This makes the archaeology of shamanism an even more slippery subject than "sloppily applied" ethnographic attributions may suggest. While for the purpose of this book it is important to delineate what a shaman is (and is not) to have a measuring stick to recognize shamanism in archaeological discoveries, probably more useful for the understanding of the past are the spin-off questions. What do shamans do? How can shamanistic practices be recognized in ancient sites, burials, and artifacts? When shamanism has been identified, what can be inferred about the society? What is the nature of shamanistic leadership, and is it different from other leadership?

The basic aim of this exploration is not to discover whether or not shamans were rife in ancient East Asia. It is ultimately to ask, why would it matter whether or not there were shamans? Shamanism is magical and mystical and mysterious. As such it is attractive to researchers as well as to the general public. Can we move beyond the mysteries of shamanism to inquire about leadership? What is the context in which shamans flourished (when they did), and how did shamanistic ideology affect the organization of society, economics, and politics? Were shamans leaders in East Asia? If so, what kind? Did shamans or shamanistic families become the elite, or did they stand in opposition to persons and families with budding economic and political clout? To begin to address these questions it is necessary to be more specific about what is being sought. In particular, we need to ask, can shamanistic power be instrumental in the formation of states?

PART VIII
ARCHAEOLOGICAL STORIES

LONG AGO, WHEN I READ JAMES MICHENER'S *THE SOURCE*, I was enchanted with the way each story developed from an excavated artifact, and the way each episode traveled further back in time than the one before, being deeper in the dig. I didn't immediately decide to be an archaeologist because of this story—it didn't seem to be a profession available to girls. At the time, I was aiming to be a lawyer and/or a writer. If John Grisham had already been writing, he would have been my idol. Nevertheless, *The Source* was a belated inspiration.

My first push toward writing archaeological stories was Jean Auel's *Clan of the Cave Bear*. The story details made it clear to me that Jean had read a lot and thought a lot about the archaeology of southern Russia. She wove some of the archaeological discoveries directly into her story. I thought she did a splendid job of keeping the reader interested and being reasonably true to the archaeological record.

I once had a long and interesting telephone conversation with Jean Auel about *Clan of the Cave Bear*. I had written to her, asking her to support the Womankind Museum which I was attempting to found. I wrote each appeal individually, and in my letter to Jean, I told her I had read and enjoyed her novel but thought the way she depicted Neanderthal sex was physiologically unlikely. So, on her dime, we discussed Neanderthal sex for an hour at dinnertime, while Hal ate his dinner, bemused.

While I perceived that Neolithic Korea didn't have the inherent appeal of the overlap period between Neanderthals and modern humans, I thought I could write an accurate yet interesting novel using my own material. Since Jean Auel's book was enormously popular, I thought maybe readers were ready to enjoy other tales of the prehistoric past. Of course, I would have been

Shamans, Queens, and Figurines: The Development of Gender Archaeology, by Sarah Nelson, 207–218.

delighted to follow in her footsteps and have *Spirit Bird Journey* on the best-seller lists. Well, we can all dream.

SPIRIT BIRD JOURNEY

I began to sketch out a novel about the Korean Neolithic. My material was thin, so I included all the known Neolithic sites in Korea—house details, village arrangements, artifacts, and so forth. Each location of the novel is an actual archaeological site. My tale combines previous observations about subsistence and settlement with a gendered theme.

At first my story was a test to see if positing a woman chief in the past would at least not violate any of the archaeological evidence. I created a heroine with a name, a description, and a life story. I named her Golden Flyingbird. Her village belonged to the Golden clan, and she was named Flyingbird for the Spirit Bird who came flying in at the moment of her birth. Koreanists will recognize that Kim, the commonest name in Korea, means "gold," and that the royalty of the Korean Silla Kingdom were surnamed Kim, as were heads of some Kaya polities. And, as many people in Western cultures know these days, in East Asia the family name comes first. There are other clans in the story—Red (Hong), for example, and White (Bai).

In my novel, the Golden clan lives along the west coast of Korea, and they fish in the deep waters of the East Sea (Japan Sea on some maps). The villagers have boats to travel along the coast, and people from the small villages can gather in larger groups for festivals. Travel by boat is inferred from the fact that the coast is steep, with mountains coming down to the sea in places, cutting off one village from another by land. Boat travel is further derived from very large fishhooks, implying large fish caught in deep water, for which watercraft would be needed.

In Flyingbird's matrilineal society, as the first daughter of the village leader, she was born to be the next leader of her village. I called her village Bird Mountain Village, after Osanni, the archaeological site on the coast where the early action of the story takes place.

The story became thicker by adding the element of ethnicity. I had written a paper about pottery styles in various regions of Korea (Nelson 1990b) and was interested in the question of whether the styles marked ethnic groups. I posited two Neolithic groups in the Korean peninsula who were physically as well as culturally different. I chose the Ainu of Hokkaido, northern Japan, as a model for the group that lived on the east coast of Korea, inhabiting the sites of Osanni, Tongsamdong, and Sopohang. Details of these sites appear in descriptions of the villages. I supposed that the fishing people along the Korean east coast must have spread along the littoral, forming small clusters of households, each cluster with a leader. But there was no perishable material at Osanni to guide descriptions of their clothing and other perishables. The Ainu I had selected as a model are Europoid in some respects—abundant brown wavy hair and no eyefolds, for example, so they made a good contrast with the people of the west, with straight black hair and Asian eyes.

I read about Ainu clothing, tools, and food habits, as well as rituals and beliefs. I learned that some Ainu groups recalled important past events by means of songs; thus, in my novel the people of Bird Mountain Village sing about their ancestors and create songs from the major events of their lives. They carve figures on song sticks as aids to their memories; each carving refers to a song.

Some Ainu groups were known for their bear cult. Sometimes they captured a bear cub when its mother was still hibernating. They raised the bear as a spirit and sacrificed the full-grown bear at a ceremony with dancing and feasting. When Flyingbird is young, she is charged with feeding the bear and keeping its spirit happy. Her mother nursed the tiny female cub, and Flyingbird calls the cub "Sister Bear." They play together. Flyingbird does not know Sister Bear is destined for sacrifice.

For contrast with the coastal fishing people, I imagined that the people in central Korea, living at Amsadong and Misari, were related to groups of forest dwellers in Manchuria. In the novel they wear leather clothing, speak a language unrelated to that of the Golden clan, and grow millets. Eventually they get domesticated pigs and dogs from kin in Manchuria.

The clash of cultures is intensified by the fact that, although Flyingbird is already married to Big Bear, Tigertail is required to become her second spouse, for cultural reasons described in the story (I made this up). This bit of plot was created to account for a large house floor with two hearths at Osanni.

While my writing may have been too "graceful" for the scholarly world, it wasn't literary enough to interest a literary agent. After trying unsuccessfully to interest an agent, I realized that I had to learn more about writing for the public if I wanted to find a trade publisher. I enrolled in a fiction-writing course, which helped refine my plot and dialogue, but I wasn't altogether pleased with the result. My story didn't flow the way I wanted it to.

The novel project was set aside for several years while I researched in China, taught my classes, and wrote papers, much easier activities than writing fiction. Off and on, I would add chapters to the novel in progress whenever I was on an airplane with no papers to grade or grant proposals to write, but the novel was still on my things-to-do list.

The first readers of the early novella, as it then was, were the volunteers sent by Earthwatch to work with me on a Neolithic project in Korea. I handed it around for my crew to read at the end of their Korean adventure. Dr. Eleanor "Fuzzy" Downs said the novel explained the sites they had worked on in a new and exciting way, which encouraged me to keep developing my story.

After sending the Neolithic tale around to friends and family and getting feedback, I realized that the archaeology part of the story needed explaining. I didn't want to be the omniscient author, so I added a current story to provide a narrator for the prehistoric events. Clara Alden's tasks were both to tell the prehistoric story and to describe the archaeological digs, thus allowing readers to connect the prehistoric past with the present. Clara as the Spirit Bird becomes entangled in Flyingbird's problems and appears at her side to help however she can in any crisis.

Since the novel hinges on ethnic differences in the past, I had Clara represent ethnic differences in the present. Clara is Korean-born, adopted as an infant by an American couple. She is culturally American but looks Korean. She goes to Korea to work on an archaeological site, but she is also fleeing her college beau, because his mother has been unable to accept her Asian face.

As I was writing, Clara became the glue between the present and the past. When I wanted to describe parts of Korean culture that not every visitor sees, I enlarged Clara's duties to include visits to Buddhist temples and scenic areas, museums, and antique stores while she digs at the archaeological site of Osanni. It seemed like a cliché to have Clara searching for her birth mother, so in my story she completely belongs to her American family. (I felt comfortable with this since there are adoptions in my family.) But I do allow Clara to find out something about her birth parents, through a chance meeting with a Buddhist monk.

Clara's adventures in Korea help to remind the reader of the different demands of nature and nurture. Clara has to study the Korean language and negotiate Korean culture at the same time. She is aware that the kind of archaeology she learned as an undergraduate is different from local practices. She doesn't want to be openly critical, but she wants to uphold the highest standards of research. Her part of the excavation has been selected from a random sample at her request, so she can excavate the way she learned at her student digs. Readers of my novels have asked if my heroine, Clara, is my alter ego. My answer is that Clara belongs to a different generation, but I gave her some of my experiences. She is more feminist and self-assured than I was after college, so Clara is definitely not me, but to some extent she inevitably sees Korea through my eyes.

By now I had written a complex story, with three layers. I began to worry that readers would get lost in its complexities. I created three logos as guideposts for the reader. On the back cover, I explain that a tiny trowel indicates archaeology, Flyingbird's story is indicated by a bird, and a lattice window design marks Clara's adventures, since Clara's only memory from infancy is seeing a lattice window while hearing angry voices.

I did find a literary agent for *Spirit Bird Journey*. Lettie Lee sent it around to several publishers. One editor liked it but declined because she had just signed another novelist for a story about Korea. I have assumed that that novel was *One Thousand Chestnut Trees,* by Mira Stout, which I enjoyed reading. It is true that Stout's story took place in many of the same places as mine; otherwise, our two books had little in common. But that's the way it is with impressions of Korea. Nobody would think one novel about China was enough.

When I decided to self-publish *Spirit Bird Journey*, I joined the Colorado Independent Publishers Association, bought books about how to self-publish, and using my new knowledge created RKLOG Press, with a trowel for a logo (what else?). *Spirit Bird Journey* (Nelson 1999) became an indie book.

After I printed *Spirit Bird Journey,* I took copies to my husband's medical meetings as well as to archaeology gatherings, and sold them sitting at a table or grabbing friends in the hall. Sometimes at SAA meetings, Bob Whallon was kind enough to show them on his table. I probably sold a thousand copies in this tedious way. That may sound like success, but I was overly optimistic with the original print quantity, ordering 5,000 copies. Advice: don't print so many copies if you write a novel. However, it's easier to self-publish these days and to advertise the books on the Internet. Besides, now there is print-on-demand, to take care of the print quantity problem.

The opening chapter to *Spirit Bird Journey* is presented in the first part of Chapter 10 of this book, in which the reader is introduced to Clara at a *kut,* a ritual of Korean shamans, and through dancing herself into a trance Clara becomes a bird spirit.

The prehistoric story was the heart of the novel, but I wanted Clara's strange transformation into a bird taking part in the prehistoric past, recognized by the villagers as a Spirit Bird, to be established at the beginning. Readers who were offended by this piece of literary magic would know to read no further. Naturally, I hoped most readers would become entranced themselves.

I used a shaman ritual to send Clara into the past in order to make several points. One was that the shamans themselves were connected to that past. Another is that ancient rituals are a part of living Korean tradition. Clara returns to the shaman rituals several times, but they are not the only device that ties the present to the past. Flyingbird has to collect six amulets, and must know how to use them, before she can become the village leader. These same objects may also send Clara to Flyingbird's aid when she is in trouble.

Story elements are inspired by and built around other artifacts. A large mask-like shell, brought into Bird Mountain Village by a bride, turns out to represent evil. Clara as a bird flies into her house, clasps the shell in her claw, and deposits it where it can do no further harm. In this way, I mix fantasy with daily events, but only three artifacts are invented for the story. One is a golden crystal, which exists in Korea (called smoky topaz). Her father presents it to Flyingbird at her birth. The second is a bone figure of a bird, which Flyingbird wears as a hairpin. Bone objects were found at both Tongsamdong and Sopohang but not at Osanni. Hairpins were used later in Korean culture if not at this time (but they could have been). The third is the only object that penetrates between Clara's two worlds. Clara loses an amber bead at the *mudang's* house, which turns up on a mountain trail above Bird Mountain Village, saving Flyingbird from a snare intended for deer.

I mapped out the plot to cover all the Neolithic Korean sites I knew well, and included a site in Manchuria. Only one site I hadn't visited appears in the novel. The Heavenly Lake is on the border between North Korea and China, and at the time it was impossible for me to visit either the Korean Autonomous Region of China or North Korea. This large crater lake in the Changbai Mountains was too tempting to omit, as it is known as the birthplace of both the Korean culture hero Tangun and Kim Il-Sung, North Korea's first leader. In fact, the locality so drew me that Flyingbird visits it twice and finds out that it is a sacred place for Tigertail's people as well as her own. I was able to visit several years later, and I found I had done a reasonable job of describing it.

JADE DRAGON

When RKLOG Press published Peter Bleed's wonderful novel, *National Treasure,* I was smarter than when I printed *Spirit Bird Journey,* and this time ordered only 2,000 copies. By the time I wrote my second novel, *Jade Dragon,* I had an even better sense of the economics of publishing and printed only 1,000 copies. Besides, lugging books around to conferences was a big chore, and I grew tired of it. Possibly friends were growing tired of me and my books. In 2003, I closed RKLOG Press LLC and was delighted when Left Coast Press offered to advertise and distribute these three novels.

After writing about the early Neolithic in Korea, I began working at Niuheliang, the central site of the Hongshan culture (Part VII). Clara's next adventure occurs in northeastern China. I wrote *Jade Dragon* in only a year, because Randee Mansfield, who was organizing speakers for the medical wives' group, asked me to speak about my next book for the next year's program. So I had to hurry to write a sequel to *SBJ.*

In *Jade Dragon*, the girl Clara watches over as her Spirit Bird, is a distant descendant of Flyingbird through the matrilineal line, and Jade is heir to her mother's shaman lore as well as her position as leader of a group of villages. The dragon in the title comes from the thick jade rings with pig heads, which are locally known as pig-dragons. *Jade Dragon* takes place in northeastern China and Inner Mongolia, as well as at the site of Niuheliang. Clara still dreams about the ancient past, while China is the venue for her adventures in the present.

As the reader will know from Part VII of this book, the Hongshan culture has vastly more story potential than Neolithic Korea. It is complex enough that several researchers have seen the remains as representing a state, and yet its most distinctive feature is a woman's face with inset jade eyes. Many elegantly carved jades have been found, mostly in burials.

As described in Part VII, pigs were important in Hongshan iconography, and therefore a pig had to play a big part in the story. A pig jaw fragment from a statue found in the "Goddess Temple" confirms the high importance of a pig, and a large bird claw and parts of female statues include the face. My story would have to involve a woman, a bird, and a pig. Of course, Clara would fly in as a bird, so all I needed to add was a trained pig and a heroine. Famous stories from ancient China involve a pig as one of the lead characters on a journey to the west, suggesting that travel should be part of the story.

Jade's task is larger and more complex than Flyingbird's, as is her polity. Jade's mother, Wise Owl, is the chief of many smaller communities. She holds ceremonies for her village as well as larger rituals at Niuheliang. In my novel, Jade trains a piglet she calls Piggy.

Jade and Piggy, with Clara as the Spirit Bird, make journeys in four directions to learn about the neighboring people who are not part of their chiefdom. This device allows me to describe other sites in the region. A mysterious stranger on a horse provides the love interest. Jade is a shaman and becomes leader of her polity. After she dies, her people erect statues of her in a shrine, which also commemorates the bird and the pig who were her traveling companions.

Horses were described in the eponymous Hongshan site, although most archaeologists now believe they do not belong to the Hongshan culture. However, some of the "pig-dragons" are larger and thinner, with long heads, no fangs, and wavy manes. What could they be except horses?

The modern story involves a small university crew using ground-penetrating radar at sites near Niuheliang. They see the tourist sites of Beijing and talk with the local archaeologists about the site before driving to Liaoning. Other characters include Evan, interested in archaeoastronomy, and Lars, who hitches a ride with them without offering an explanation. Others in the cast of characters are Korean archaeologists who appeared in *Spirit Bird Journey*, and Chinese archaeologists.

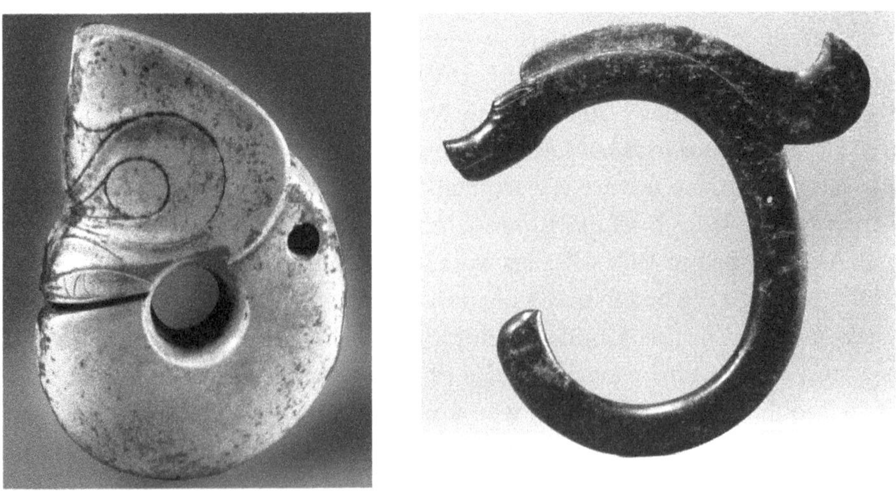

FIGURE 7 Pig-dragon and horse-dragon

Looting is a huge problem in Chinese archaeological sites. Once when I was working at Niuheliang, a large white van drove into the site, and six hefty men got out, bringing shovels and pails. The guard pointed in our direction, and seeing foreigners, they drove away. It wasn't hard to infer their intention. This kind of destruction of archaeological sites is rife. Looting is part of the current story of *Jade Dragon*. Clara and Ashley are captured by looters whom they have come across by chance. Not wanting to draw attention by killing the girls, the looters tie them up, force them into the van, and take them with the loot to Hong Kong. The Korean archaeologists, who have been touring Chinese sites in a bus, stop to visit Niuheliang. When they realize that Clara and Ashley are missing, the bus driver finds the van and follows it, afraid that any direct action will cause the girls to be harmed.

For this novel, I still use the trowel logo to indicate archaeology. A horse-dragon indicates scenes in Hongshan times. The current story is designated by a chopsticks logo. Eating is important in China.

The prologue sets up the looting problem and explains how Clara, who began her archaeological research in Korea, has come to China. In Chapter 11, we eavesdrop on archaeological conversations involving women archaeologists and the gender of the skeletons at Niuheliang over a Chinese banquet after the crew landed in China.

THE JADE PHOENIX

I didn't have to invent Lady Hao, the heroine of my third archaeological novel. One of the wives of King Wu Ding of the Late Shang dynasty, around 1250 BCE, Lady Hao led troops to battle, owned land, and was the mother of at least three children. She must have been an amazing person to know.

Lady Hao's tomb is the only intact royal grave found so far that dates to the Late Shang period. Her final resting place reveals many details about her life. She was buried with a plethora of varied artifacts, including inscribed bronze vessels to honor her as an ancestor after her death, finely carved jades, weapons, jeweled hairpins, and mirrors. One of those artifacts, a phoenix carved from yellow jade, inspired the title. It's the same bird I used for Clara's bird logo in the previous two novels and on the cover of *Spirit Bird Journey*. This yellow jade phoenix, the most beautiful object from Lady Hao's tomb, lies at the center of both present and past tales in this novel.

FIGURE 8 Jade phoenix

Lady Hao's well-furnished tomb is not the only information available about Lady Hao. The Shang had a writing system, which must have been considered sacred, for they sent messages to their ancestors by means of writing on shoulder blades and turtle shells, inscribed with the questions to which they desired answers. The characters used are an early form of written Chinese; thus most of them can still be read. Although King Wu Ding had other wives, he inquired about the health and activities of Lady Hao more often than of anyone else. Two of Lady Hao's babies were recorded on the oracle bones as "not auspicious," presumably meaning they were girls. Her son, Zu Jia, became a king. Wu Ding's main queen was Lady Jing, whose looted burial was the only tomb of a woman in the burial ground of the Shang kings. I infer that she was one of the royal Shang herself, perhaps Wu Ding's patrilineal cousin, and his first queen.

I was intrigued with Lady Hao. Although she was not King Wu Ding's first queen, she seemed to have wielded considerable influence. What palace intrigues did she have to master? Who could have become her allies?

Lady Hao's burial included mirrors and weapons from the "Northern Zone" of China, suggesting that that region may have been her homeland. Did she marry Wu Ding from a matrilineal society? Could that account for her accomplishments? I suggested Lady Hao's northern origins in the first paper I wrote about the Hongshan culture (see Chapter 5). Kathy Linduff (2002) came to the same conclusion. Besides the northern artifacts, the appearance of horses and chariots suggests the north as well. Military success in the Late Shang may have been dependent on the advent of horses and chariots in warfare in central China, and in assuming that Lady Hao grew up with horses, it would have been appropriate for her to lead troops that included horses and chariots.

I had to consider how to create a story from the artifacts, oracle bones, and excavations. I explored Anyang, the central place of Late Shang where the story takes place, on three different occasions. I first visited Anyang in 1982, when I had organized an archaeological tour to China. Much later, I visited Anyang again with the bus tour following the Society for East Asian Archaeology conference, which took place in Beijing in 2008. I took notes at that time, but I still hadn't decided how to organize the story.

One of the threesome who managed the foreign side of the Niuheliang project was Hungjen Niu, a Harvard graduate student originally from Taiwan. The other corner of our leadership triangle was Yangjin Pak, a Harvard graduate from Korea, who was already on his way to high academic success at Chongnam Univeristy in Daejong, Korea. As related previously (Part VII), although Hungjen had worked for years to obtain a national permit for us to survey between Niuheliang and Dongshanzui, when we finally had it in hand, our funding from the Wenner-Gren Foundation and National Geographic was not renewed, to our great disappointment. For our final survey at Niuheliang, I brought one of our University of Denver graduate students, Sara Gale, and we met Yangjin in Jianping, as well as Gwen Bennett and Josh Wright, still hoping to pull off a miracle.

Before we went to Niuheliang, Sara and I visited Hungjen's husband, Jing Zhicheng, at Anyang. Jing provided maps, transportation, and access to artifacts in the museum and was very invested in the novel project. Some of the action at Anyang in *The Jade Phoenix* is similar to our experiences with Jing and his field school students. It was inspirational to walk the paths Lady Hao must have walked.

I was grateful to Jing for arranging a chat with Zheng Zhenxiang, the woman who excavated Lady Hao's burial just as Japanese troops were about to invade. She excavated quickly under extremely difficult conditions, and left with the artifacts on the last train to the south. It was a great privilege to hear her story. I've included it in the novel.

To set up the novel, I've imagined a queendom in Inner Mongolia, which Lady Hao, known to her family as Joy, was first in line to inherit. But when Wu Ding, selected as the future king of Shang, arrives in northern China to learn about horses and chariots, he falls in love with Joy. Persuading her to marry him, they return to Shang with horses and chariots. Joy is unaware that Wu Ding is expected to marry his cousin Lady Jing, but soon after they arrive in Shang, that wedding takes place. Although Joy threatens to leave, she is persuaded to stay.

Among other adventures, she saves the king's mother, Lady Shang, using her northern shaman rites, and is finally accepted as one of the queens. Lady Jing remains jealous of Joy. Lady Hao was buried with a unique bronze stove, in northern style. Lady Jing had in her grave the largest bronze *ding* (a square bronze vessel on legs, used to serve dishes to the ancestors) ever found—not even a king had a bigger one. I created scenes in which Wu Ding has the northern-style stove made for Lady Hao, but Lady Jing is jealous and demands an even bigger bronze.

The current story for this novel is based on selecting artifacts for an exhibit about Lady Hao. Clara's Vietnamese-born sister, Chama, has grown up to be an art historian, and she is tasked with a trip to China to plan the exhibit. Chama invites Clara to come with her as her archaeological consultant. Because Clara is convinced that Lady Hao came from the north, they begin their journey in Chifeng. A mysterious Mr. Na is assigned to escort them through sites in the north and then to behold the real artifacts at museums in Beijing. In Beijing, Clara and Chama are accused of stealing the real jade phoenix, because the jade that the museum showed them is revealed to be only a copy.

Ashley and Kidok are old friends who have been tracing stolen artifacts, so they set forth to locate the jade phoenix from the tomb, expecting that it was taken to a dealer in Hong Kong. Lars appears in this story, too, still trying to curb the looting of China's past, and helps Clara and Chama when they are accused of stealing the jade.

In the beginning of the story, Clara and Chama discuss the archaeological finds. Chama is repelled by the fact that Lady Hao was surrounded in her tomb with the bodies of sixteen other people and three dogs. To make it worse, one of those bodies was dispatched to the other world by severing her spine. I have imagined that she is Peony, Lady Hao's personal maid. Considering how Peony might have been axed in two is the inspiration for the prologue to *The Jade Phoenix* (Chapter 11).

The story of Lady Hao explores the position of royal women in the Shang dynasty, with reference to both documents and archaeology. Although inquiries on oracle bones made by King Wu Ding about Lady Hao's health and well-being imply that he loves her, the Shang culture of royalty made it beyond his power to have a monogamous relationship with her. Archaeology shows that the Shang took human lives promiscuously in the service of their own ancestors. This story imagines the life of a girl brought up to become queen of a matrilineal society embroiled in the sex and violence of the Shang state.

Novels are one way to present archaeology to the public but are more time-consuming than professional papers. However, as time permits, I hope to write more archaeological novels, both for my own entertainment and to think more about life in places in the past. I hope others enjoy them, too.

Chapter 10
Spirit Bird Journey (Excerpts)

THE CYMBALS ABRUPTLY STOPPED CLANGING, leaving a metallic aftertaste in my ear. I watched Elaine end her dance with a graceful turn. She untied the bow that held her costume together and in the same motion slipped out of it and handed it to the shaman's helper, bowing slightly and touching her outstretched right arm with the fingers of her left hand. Later I learned that's the polite Korean way to give people things. At the time I was just absorbing gestures.

As I sat cross-legged on the floor, I had to squint to keep my eyes open at all. Not that I wasn't interested in the ceremonies, but I hadn't slept for a day and a half. In this moment between dances, I looked around at the women here, and felt again the shock of faces like mine that I felt in the airport. At home, the only Asian faces I saw were in my mirror, and on my sister. Ed's blue eyes and sandy hair would be out of place here. It might teach him something about differences! I tried to think about something else. Unhealthy to dwell on him. I came to Korea to forget him.

To quash thoughts of Ed, I deliberately looked around the room, taking in the "orchestra" of drums and gongs, and the way the pale colors of the musicians' dresses set off the bright red of a large hourglass drum. The three musicians were women, who sat on a mat chatting idly. Along the side of the room, a table covered with plates of neatly stacked fruits and bowls of flowers stood in front of a wall of poster-like paintings. Elaine told me this was the altar. I was working on the concept.

Sarah M. Nelson (1999). From *Spirit Bird Journey*, by Sarah Milledge Nelson, pp. 1–6, 38–40. RKLOG Press, Littleton, CO. Republished in *Shamans, Queens, and Figurines: The Development of Gender Archaeology*, by Sarah Nelson, pp. 219–227 (Taylor & Francis, 2015).

The ceremony seemed to be over. I didn't understand it, but it was colorful and like nothing I'd ever seen. Three robed shamans danced themselves into trances, one at a time, like acts in a play. One did something with rolled-up flags, another gathered up what I supposed were blessings from the air, and put them into the skin of the woman who was the center of activity. The third drank something from a brass bowl, and spat out the door. The *mudang* in charge of the ceremony was called Yol-i's Mother in her everyday life, but here she was addressed as *manshin*, meaning ten-thousand spirits.

After the *kut* each of the village women danced, one at a time. Several of them leapt about with abandon when Yol-i's Mother put robes on them. Their dances were laughingly critiqued by the other women. In my semi-stuporous state, I saw the *kut* as both serious and fun, a spiritual occasion, but social, too. The women were enjoying the whole affair, including the patient. She must have believed in it. Maybe they all believed to some extent.

Yol-i's Mother gestured toward me.

"It's your turn now," Elaine nudged my bottom with her socked foot. "The *manshin* wants you to dance next. "

"I only came to watch." I closed my eyes and tried to be invisible. "Leave me alone, Elaine. I'm still groggy from jet lag. I can barely keep my eyes open just sitting here. Next time? Don't you think there's been enough audience participation?"

The toe prodded again.

"You can't refuse, Clara, it isn't polite. Where's your anthropological spirit? I didn't bring you here to decorate the floor. You know we can't offend the *manshin. . . .*"

I'll look a fool, I thought, grudgingly getting up. Give the locals a laugh at the awkward foreigner's expense. As I pushed myself to a stand, the *manshin* gave me a sharp look through narrowed eyes, tossed the blue robe to a helper, and rummaged through an old wooden chest that folded down from the front. With the robe over her arm, she bowed to the altar and rubbed her palms back and forth.

"This one suits you better," Elaine translated for her, as the *manshin* beckoned to me.

I was held hack by a premonition of myself forever changed, but the shaman invitingly held out a robe of shimmering yellow-gold. I slipped into the sleeves, and she tied the ribbon with an expert hand. Unlike the crisp synthetic texture of the blue robe Elaine wore, this one was soft. It was an old robe, made of fine silk, but worn where the bow had been tied many times. Tiny triangles in various colors were embroidered on the edge of the collar and sleeves, and a pattern of flying cranes was woven into the fabric itself, like a brocade.

I sensed that the *manshin* had honored me by choosing this robe, although I didn't know why. A flash of recollection, as if I had been in a place like this before, came and quickly vanished. The room again looked as unfamiliar as it had when I first stepped up to the wooden floor. But I was suddenly wide awake. The dance became a homecoming to a Korea I never knew, or couldn't remember. I caught my upside-down reflection in the brass cymbals, and saw that the yellow-gold costume was becoming to my dark hair. Ed always called me "Jade Princess," which I took for irony, but now I felt like a princess. While I admired myself, the *manshin* placed a light headdress over my hair—a peaked yellow cap that matched the robe.

The drums began a slow rhythm. TONK, tonk, tonk, ta KUNK. I raised my arms tentatively and tried to copy the movements of the other dancers. At least I could begin with the slow and stately movements, even if I couldn't manage the jumping frenzy when the cymbals get fast at the end. Holding my arms shoulder high with elbows slightly bent, I shuffled my feet and made a turn.

****

The percussion beat continued, TONK, tonk, tonk, ta KUNK, but the room changed, and so did I. My feet became bird claws, gripping a wide wooden beam. I looked down on a dimly lit scene, which came into focus as my eyes adjusted. The room had an oval floor, dug down a foot or two into the sandy soil. It was well swept, bare except for a pile of dark brown furs. Two pottery jars covered with gourd bowls stood in a corner beside a bundle of twigs. In the center of the room, river cobbles outlined a square hearth where a small fire sent up red sparks.

At each end of the hut a crotched stick held the roof beam where I perched. Thick braided ropes with pendant tassels swagged from the beam, and a similar rope hung across the doorway. The other roof and wall supports leaned on the central beam, leaving high spaces at each end of the ridgepole for light and ventilation. A bundle wrapped in bark cloth lay next to me on the roof beam.

I noticed movement below, and peered at four women in black and white robes, lit by the flickering fire. Then I saw that these four surrounded another woman in a plain brown wrap-around, who gripped a large pole planted in the floor behind the hearth. A gray-haired granny thumped a small drum with her hand and chanted, while the others joined in after each line with a vigorous shout of "Ho!"

When the central figure of the tableau released a long drawn-out "H-o-o-o-o," mingling with the cry of a newborn infant, the chanting stopped. The drummer picked up the baby while another woman cut the umbilical cord with a shiny black knife. She washed the infant in briny water from a large pottery jar, wrapped her in a rabbit-skin blanket, and held her up to the mother.

"Congratulations, Sunflower, it's a girl! *A girl!*" said the older woman.

"Praise to the Hearth Spirit, a girl at last!" the other birth helpers whispered. Sunflower smiled.

The women attended to Sunflower. One washed Sunflower with water from the large jar, and others untied a bright yellow sash from the new mother's waist, and rewrapped it to hold moss and crumpled elm bark. After helping Sunflower into a fresh black and white robe, they settled her into a thick pile of furs.

A woman picked up the afterbirth with a pair of sticks and dropped it into a small jar, scooped up and added the bloody sand, and replaced the gourd on top. Another woman sprinkled new sand near the hearth, and evened out the floor with a twig broom. The birth hut was tidy again.

The old woman looked up at me, and pointed with her chin.

"A powerful omen! The golden bird on the roof beam beside our family spirit is the baby's spirit guide, who came exactly at her birth. It's a wondrous sign, never seen before. It promises her a bright future but suggests there may be trouble in her life. We should name her for this event—Flyingbird of the Golden clan. The bird will help her become strong and swift and wise and beautiful."

I was flattered to have a namesake, and would have smiled if my beak had let me. The women's faces, turned toward me, showed wide blue tattoos around their mouths, making their lips look huge. Their white ankle-length robes were appliqued with wide black curving designs. The young ones wore sunflowers in their brown wavy hair, but the oldest had fastened her hair at the nape of her neck with a carved bone in the shape of a bird.

After a slight bow to me rubbing their palms back and forth, they went back to the hearth, where each birth helper planted a stick in front of the fire. The sticks had curly shavings cut down from the top but still attached to the stick, each with a different design. They reminded me of stylized poodles. The women again rubbed their palms.

The older woman spoke.

"Hear us, Hearth Spirit, as we present to you Golden Flyingbird, first born daughter of Golden Sunflower, granddaughter of Golden Birdwing, whose other ancestors in this village were Golden Sunlight, Golden Birdnest, Golden Sunrise, and Golden Sunbird. Her mother's sisters, Golden Magpie, Golden Pebble, and Golden Birchleaf, are here to present the child to you. Flyingbird was born in the presence of her familiar spirit, a golden crested bird, and you, guardian of the Golden Clan, must also know her and help her. "

Birdwing stood on her tiptoes and reached for the bundle beside me on the ridgepole. I felt her warm breath. She untied the cord, and unwrapped several layers of cloth, until at last a carved bone figure gleamed in the firelight. Each woman in turn took the figure in both hands, bowed toward the row of sticks, and asked for blessings for the child, while Sunflower held the solemn infant toward the fire. When Birdwing lifted the bone figure toward me, I stretched down to get a better look. To my archaeological eye it seemed to be made from a long bone of a mammal, probably from a deer, maybe *Cervus nippon*. It was decorated only on one end, the other end whittled to a point. The carved end resembled a head, with daisy-petal-like bumps surrounding a crude face, with only circles for eyes and a mouth, and below that circles representing breasts.

One by one the sisters spoke to me.

"Golden Bird of Wisdom, keep this child safe. Help her to become wise in the ways of our people. Let her learn our stories easily and remember them well. Give her the courage to seek, and the persistence to find. "

"Give her all those blessings and more," I added. "Let her have both love and independence, both adventure and security. " My voice sounded only like a chirp to me, but to my surprise the women seemed to understand.

Rustling noises drew my attention outside through an opening in the eaves, where I saw other people gathered, waiting for the news. Birdwing took the bone figure to the door and announced the birth of Golden Flyingbird. The villagers repeated to each other in soft voices, "A girl! A daughter! To carry on the lineage! The village is saved! Give praise to the Hearth Spirit and Grandmother Moon."

A young man with a wavy brown beard and long thick hair stepped forward from the group, and Birdwing beckoned him into the birth hut. "Greet your daughter, Blue Squirrel!" said Birdwing formally but with a big smile, exaggerated by her blue tattoo. "What a beautiful child." Squirrel hugged Sunflower and pressed his cheek by hers. "You did well. The whole village is pleased."

Squirrel held out a translucent stone, almost gold. "I've brought you a crystal of topaz," he said to his newborn daughter. "It was lying near the path to the forest. It's golden, like your clan, so I knew the spirits left it there for you this morning. I don't understand the meaning of its location, but that will become clear in good time. In the meantime its powers will protect you. From this day, my little daughter, you will begin learning to be a wise leader."

Flyingbird's eyes followed the crystal, and her small fists waved in the air. Birdwing knotted a cord around the topaz crystal and fastened the cord around the baby's neck, to keep its crystal power near her heart.

The bone figure, pointed end down, was added to the row of shaved sticks. The group in the birth hut began to sing, while Birdwing picked up the drum again and beat out the irregular rhythm.

****

The sharp sound of the cymbals crashed into my attention and then stopped. I was back in the *mudang's* house beside the colorful altar, so different from the muted tones of the birth hut. My senses were heightened, making the altar seem to shimmer. In front of me brass bowls on pedestals held neatly arrayed cakes and candies, dyed with pinks and greens. Wine, rice, dried fish, and a cooked pig's head lay on the altar, surrounded by large paper flowers in primary colors. Pasted above the altar, bright paintings of various spirits blinded me with an avalanche of color. "Back to 'reality,'" I thought.

Out of breath, I let the shaman's helper take the costume, and tried to dismiss from my mind the small thatched cottage with its new baby. It was only a vision, conjured by my jet lag. The *mudang* looked at me closely, but asked no questions. The village women clapped and laughed —"a wonderful performance!" — "not a bit like a foreigner" — "the girl is really Korean after all!"

After Elaine jotted her final notes, we said good-bye to Yol-i's Mother.

"Come to my next *kut*," she said to Elaine. "I'll call to tell you the time and place—and be sure to bring your new friend. She doesn't know who she is yet, but I will help her get to know her bones. She has a gift. . . ."

****

During the first week at the dig my main task was to make a contour map of the surface of the second area, where I was planning my random sample. First I established a reference point on high ground outside the artifact scatter. Everything would be measured from that point. My crew and I mapped the contours of the ground surface at one-meter intervals. I labored over the map, trying to be very precise.

Next the entire site was gridded with strings two meters apart, set to the points of the compass. Each two-meter square was surface-collected, and the artifacts put into cloth bags labeled with the designation of the square. Dong-su had little to say to me, except for correcting my Korean, and went back to Seoul after one day of this tedious work.

Evenings we washed the artifacts collected during the day and wrote permanent numbers on each one, mulling over similarities to pottery at other sites. It was easy to see that most of the sherds on my hill were different from the first test pit on the other hill—there were more pinched designs and many fewer pieces with impressed designs.

When Saturday came, so did Kim Dong-su. He had his usual big smile, but kept a respectful distance, except for calling me Clara.

"Time for your language lesson, mixed with a little sightseeing. Have you heard of Soraksan, Clara?"

"Everyone here has told me about it. I've heard that it's very beautiful, especially in the fall. Is it far away?" I asked eagerly. I'm a born sight-seer. My dad says I like sights, sites, and cites.

"Not too far. I drove my car, so I could have the pleasure of taking you there. We can't see all of it—the park is huge—but we'll have time to hike around enough to get the flavor of it. It's a national park, so you'll see real Korean wilderness."

Sorak Mountain was indeed a lovely place. Hotels, restaurants, and souvenir shops clustered together where cars were left at the edge of the park, but inside the grounds nature reigned. Only ancient temples, on crags or hillsides, represented human works, and even they blended in or were disguised by the forest, where deep red and orange maple leaves seemed to shine against the dark pines.

We wandered around without a particular plan, up one path and down another. Dong-su was companionable, but walked with a space between us. I relaxed.

A large map showed the way to a Buddhist temple, and we set off toward it through an ancient forest.

"The forests have been protected here," Dong-su told me. "Even during the Korean War, when firewood was so scarce, people wouldn't cut the trees on the temple grounds. That's why such big trees grow here. Around any temple it's like a nature preserve—they're the numinous places in Korea, full of nature spirits. Can you feel them?"

"No, but I can appreciate the beauty."

"You're resisting the spirits, but they'll get to you."

I shrugged. Highly unlikely, but I wasn't going to say so.

At the entrance to the temple, I was surprised to see mats and large red drums for rent—the same kind of double-ended hourglass-shaped drum I'd seen at the *mudang*'s *kut*. They were obviously hot items, with a mob clustered around to rent them. The temple grounds were full of revelers. Family groups had brought picnics, and crowds of school children followed their teachers. People danced in circles, flinging their arms high. Some groups were giddy from drinking *makkolli*—homemade rice wine, Dong-su said. Some sang, accompanied by musical instruments, especially flutes and drums.

"Isn't this a sacred place?" I asked. "Isn't all this merriment sacrilegious?"

"Temples are sacred but not solemn. Restrained and formal behavior in church is a Western idea. Here we know that dancing, singing and drinking are ways to honor the gods. It says so in the oldest Korean writings. Even the ancient Chinese historians wrote that Koreans loved to sing and dance. If it has been going on for millennia, can it be wrong?"

"Women have been suppressed for millennia, but that's wrong," I snapped. "Antiquity is no guarantee of justice or beauty."

Dong-su only smiled and nodded.

The temple was composed of a bunch of wooden buildings, seemingly helter-skelter up the hillside. A drum tower and a bell tower framed the entrance, although neither the bell nor the drum had survived the centuries. The buildings were rectangular, with wooden columns holding up the roof. Each roof was elaborately constructed, and painted on every beam and post in now-faded colors of aqua and coral. Here and there, carved wooden dragons peered down over the roof beams, looking more playful than fearsome. Some rooms contained altars displaying Buddhas of various sizes and materials, sitting in rows, a sensory whirl.

"I want you to see something special," Dong-su told me, leading me into a small room. He pointed to a painting of an old man with a long white beard, riding a tiger.

"Isn't that wonderful? I always look for the Old Man of the Mountain."

The painting was done naively in poster paints, but the lines were so full of tension that the old man seemed alive. The tiger wore a silly smile, and the man's thin white beard jutted out in comical wisps. Even the pine tree was painted with vitality, as if the bark might flake off in your hand.

"I can see why you like it. I wouldn't be surprised if he spoke to us."

Dong-su explained that the painting represented the Mountain Spirit with his tiger helper, and was pre-Buddhist. I thought the painting must be out of place in a Buddhist temple, but Dong-su said that Buddhism didn't try to obliterate prior gods, incorporating them into the belief system instead. A row of painted plaster Buddhas on the altar in front of the Mountain Spirit emphasized his point.

"Sometimes I'd like to believe in the Mountain Spirit," said Dong-su softly, almost to himself. "I wonder what he would think of modern Korea—of all the dams and factories that have reduced his territory. Of polluted rivers and dirty air. Of ancient customs put aside. He must be very sad."

"Do you wish you had lived in Korea in ancient times?" I asked him, thinking of Flyingbird. "Based on nothing but stones and sherds, it's hard to imagine how it might have been. Difficult and dangerous, don't you suppose?"

"I think it was simple, without competing cultures. Everybody knew who they were, and knew their place in society."

"Surely it's better to have a chance to be anything you can be than to have a 'place,'" I objected.

"That's another way to look at it," said Dong-su.

I felt ashamed, not for my values, but for blurting them out judgmentally. But Dong-su hadn't taken offense. I was touched that Dong-su showed me the Mountain Spirit and his tiger, even though I didn't entirely comprehend it.

We wandered back by a group of people wearing their traditional clothing. The women were especially appealing in their pastel *hanbok*—they were a flock of butterflies dancing a round dance.

"Come join us!" someone called from the group, and we went closer.

A man with a white towel wrapped around his head poured some *makkolli* from a pottery jar into a brass bowl, and offered it to us, laughing and making it a challenge. The stuff tasted sour and harsh, but I swallowed it, and wiped the dribbles off my chin with my sleeve.

The red drum beat out a rhythm, and people made a circle. I stood back bashfully. It seemed wrong to intrude. But Dong-su pulled me into the group, and I copied the dancing style as well as I could. Soon we were laughing and shouting along with our hosts, hopping and flinging our arms around. The *makkolli*, or the drum, sent me back to Flyingbird.

Chapter 11

Jade Dragon (Excerpts)

INTRODUCTIONS ALL AROUND the archaeology department at Beida took time, but with far less ceremony than I had experienced in South Korea. The famous Professor Wu spoke excellent English, having spent a couple of years as visiting faculty at Harvard. His black hair was slicked straight back from his forehead, and a small mole on his cheek almost seemed like a beauty mark on his handsome face.

Mr. Gao was balding and stoop-shouldered, with an eager and friendly personality. When he spoke, his words sounded like Chinese, but if I listened carefully I could sort out English words.

The other archaeologists at Beida spoke no English, but they all spoke *putonghua*, regardless of the dialect they grew up with. Luckily I didn't have to translate. Ma Yumei was assigned as our interpreter, and we also had Xiao Li, so I was spared the embarrassment of asking the Chinese professors to repeat their words until I understood.

Miss Ma is slender and tall, with wide Manchurian cheek bones. She wore a red print dress that draped from her shoulders, no make-up, and hair gathered back at the nape of her neck. I was jealous that she looked elegant, while I would look dumpy and frumpy dressed the same. Life isn't fair.

Joe and Dr. Wu discussed ways to get to Daling. If we went by train the radar might cause a problem. It was too thick to go under the bottom berth. Where could it be stored in a small sleeping compartment, unless someone wanted it in bed with them? Even Ashley isn't skinny enough for that to be

Sarah M. Nelson (2004a). In *Jade Dragon*, pp. 47–52, 103–106. RKLOG Press, Littleton, CO. Republished in *Shamans, Queens, and Figurines: The Development of Gender Archaeology*, by Sarah Nelson, pp. 229–236 (Taylor & Francis, 2015).

comfortable. Besides, the stop nearest the Daling archaeological station is a small town, which meant that we couldn't take an express train. A local train stops at every station, and takes many hours. Those of us listening were divided as to whether or not it would be fun to take the overnight train. Dr. Wu suggested that we take his car from Beida, and he would come up later with Mr. Gao. But when we explained about the size of the radar unit, and the addition of Evan, he withdrew the offer. Clearly we'd need two cars, and large ones at that. But he still recommended that we drive.

"If you go by road, you'll have a chance to visit the city of Cheng De, a much older summer palace of the Manchu emperors than the recent one just outside Beijing. Although there are other contenders, it might be the place Marco Polo called Shangdu, or upper capital. The poet Coleridge poeticized the name to Xanadu.

"Even if the city doesn't date back to Marco Polo, it's ancient and interesting, and is being restored. The Lamaist temple there is called the Potala, like the famous one in Tibet. There's a lot to see. Besides, I know a good place for lunch."

That sounded promising. Joe decided to drive to Daling, whatever it might cost.

Next we were rounded up for a tour through the new Sackler museum. I let my thoughts drift when we were shown a mock-up of the Paleolithic site of Zhoukoutian. It's the famous site of "Peking Man" with evidence interpreted as early fire. I learned that the site is near Beijing, across Marco Polo Bridge, of all things, but we don't have time to go there on this trip. The stratigraphy was explained in more detail than I wanted to know, so I stood watching people rather than listening. I saw Ashley give Joe a sly poke in his ribs, which he brushed off like a fly. Laura moved away from them. Something had to be going on there.

I perked up when we arrived at the exhibit with the painted pottery of the Hongshan culture, and listened attentively to Miss Ma's spiel in case I had missed something in my reading, or in case there were new unpublished discoveries.

Laura asked about the Hongshan villages, addressing our interpreter as "Miss Ma."

"Please call me Yumei. Most Americans do."

"What does your name mean?" Laura asked.

"Beautiful Jade," she said with a smile. "But I wasn't named for the Hongshan culture."

She turned back to the exhibits. "The Hongshan culture," Yumei explained, "is mostly represented by ordinary Neolithic villages. The people raised pigs and grew millets. They made brown pottery for everyday use, and fired red pots with black painted horizontal designs for ceremonial occasions.

They knew how to choose the right kind of stone for different purposes. Sharp tools were chipped from the local flint-like stone, and hard granites were ground down to make plows and axes. Softer sandstone slabs were used for querns, with granite handstones for grinding the millet into flour.

"Each village had about a hundred houses in rows, but unlike the earlier cultures, most villages were not surrounded by ditches. Only a few Hongshan villages have been excavated, but hundreds have been located on surveys. The Hongshan culture would not attract so much attention except for the two ceremonial centers and the beautiful carved jades."

We came to a mock-up of a site on a hillside above the curve of a large river. Although I was familiar with the site report, and had even digitized a map of it onto my computer, it wasn't exactly as I expected. Everything looked neater, for one thing.

"The first ceremonial center excavated is called Dongshanzui, high on a hillside overlooking the Daling River. It's known for many enigmatic rock features, including stone-edged platforms and lines of rocks. Two small broken figurines were found here—one very pregnant, and the other possibly nursing an infant. Other female figures were about half life-sized. They sat cross-legged, wearing thick rope belts tied with a double loop."

I was fascinated to see a waist fragment with a rope knotted around it. In a North Korean archaeological encyclopedia there's a photograph of a rope belt of the same thickness and with the same knot, accidentally preserved by arid conditions. It piqued my curiosity, but I couldn't find a ready explanation for the same thickness of rope and identical knots being used several hundred miles apart, with probably a thousand years difference in time. Could there have been a connection through space and time? Did the knotted rope belt, so precisely tied, have a special meaning? But we were whisked on.

"The other ritual center is Daling. Sometimes," continued Yumei, "Chinese archaeologists refer to this locality as *Nushen Miao*, the Goddess Temple. On the slope of another hill about forty kilometers away, archaeologists discovered the floor of a long, low building, with life-sized statues of a woman, a pig, and a bird, along with painted pottery and fragments of a pedestal vessel with a slotted lid."

She stopped to point out a copy of the "goddess" face, with its inset green jade eyes, high cheek bones, and wide smiling lips. I didn't consider her beautiful, but definitely compelling. I found myself wishing she could talk—but then I wouldn't have a dissertation project, unless she spoke only to me.

The map of the Goddess Temple excavation showed a building with a rounded protrusion in the north, two lobes like stubby arms out to the sides, and a rectangular area at the lower end that I couldn't help thinking of as a foot. Fragments of statues were found in the center as well as in the two rounded side lobes. A photograph showed the face when it was first uncovered, without a nose. The nose turned out to be not far away, and had been replaced on the face in the second picture. The photo of the discovery showed three men in Mao caps. It definitely dated the event. No one wears them any more.

The next display case showed a map and some photos of stone piles, tumbled down so that the original arrangement of the stones was difficult to assess. Based on what I've seen elsewhere, the stones could have been parts of walls or towers. But Yumei had a different explanation.

"Above the Goddess Temple is a raised area edged with stones. We call it a platform. It is about ninety meters wide and a hundred meters long. We don't know what it was used for."

"That's about the size of two football fields side by side," Joe pontificated to us students, as if we didn't use the metric system in all our excavations. Laura rolled her eyes, but Ashley cooed, "That's really big," as if she didn't know already. On second thought, she hasn't attended a field school, so maybe she didn't know.

"The rest of the site is a necropolis, a big cemetery, with clusters of graves on hilltops, except for the biggest group of graves, which are in a valley, with a plain round mound that may be an altar." We gathered around the photos and plan drawing.

"Several graves have been excavated. They're unusual in having no tools or pottery deposited in the graves—the only objects buried with the individuals are jade ornaments, up to sixteen jades in a single grave. Pottery was found in the tombs, although it is not utilitarian and it is rarely placed in individual graves. Instead, bottomless painted pots encircle the edge of the tomb. Square tombs have a square of pottery around them. A mounded tomb may have only one or many people buried in it, but a mound of stones and dirt is piled on top of each tomb."

We stopped at the final display in this section. A photograph showed a hill with a lot of square pits sunk deeply into it. "The only other type of structure found so far is an artificial mound, as tall as a pyramid, with circles of dressed white stone embedded within it. Nobody knows what it was used for, but crucibles with traces of copper were found near the top. The copper may be later than the Hongshan era, because only one copper artifact has been excavated. It's a very simple copper wire earring, with an unworked lump of jade attached," Yumei finished her spiel.

Now it was our turn to talk. We filed into a small conference room. Joe fiddled with his computer so we could all show the PowerPoint presentations we had prepared.

Joe showed examples of other archaeological sites where he had used radar, and the Chinese archaeologists were impressed. Then Laura discussed what could be learned from both human and animal bones. Her talk had a lot of graphs and charts in it, and in the end she showed how knowing about the nutrition of both the animals and people had allowed a better interpretation of particular sites.

With some trepidation I talked about leadership. I explained that I thought the Hongshan leaders were *wu,* ancient Chinese shamans, and that by means of asserting connections with spirits, they ran a peaceful society. The evidence consists of the jades themselves, some of which are masklike. Besides, there is no evidence of warfare. None of the bodies represent human sacrifices, nor are there wounds that might have been received in battle. There are no walled sites. The *wu* would have been leaders, I suggested, because of their knowledge, not because they were strong or had armies.

I went on to point out that the two ceremonial sites are very different from each other. One focuses on birth, and life, and the other on death and the world beyond. Both events would have required rituals to smooth the transitions.

Then I went farther out on a limb and discussed the possible effects of climate change. Perhaps decreasing precipitation made it harder to raise pigs, and that's why they are so important in the iconography. Maybe the elite owned the best places to raise pigs.

The Chinese archaeologists asked several questions of Joe, Laura and me, but the topic they really got into was Ashley's. She pointed out that, although jade-working was not new, it became much more elaborate in the Hongshan culture, and many more colors of jade were used. More jade ornaments were produced.

Ashley had also looked into the iconography of the 'goddess' face. She found jade plaques in a couple of museum collections that were similar to the face from the Goddess Temple. They had in common a headband, upturned hair ends, and an enigmatic smile. They were thought to be from the Shang Dynasty. She ended by suggesting that memory of the goddess lasted into Shang times.

Ashley clearly enjoyed the attention her paper had brought her, as she stood in the midst of an admiring crowd.

***

BREAKFAST CONSISTED OF MILLET gruel with some side dishes to flavor it: in this case flat white seeds, peanuts, small pickles, and tiny red peppers. I gave the peppers a miss after Ashley's lesson, but the rest of the additions were delicious. The porridge is eaten with a thick china spoon shaped like a small ladle. Buns were also served, rather tasteless, but filling. I felt as stuffed as a bean bun while we were briefed on the localities of Daling.

I thought I knew Daling by heart after reading and translating all the publications, and mapping of the sites overlaid on a satellite image. Not to mention having seen the museum exhibits at Beida. But reading and studying aren't the same as being able to walk around and experience a site.

We were shown into a one-room museum, with almost the same exhibits we had seen at Beida. The wow factor was still at work, though. I thought what a thrill it must have been to actually unearth the face with green jade eyes.

"Today," said Xiao Li, who turned out to be the son of the local archaeologist in charge of the site, Mr. Li, "we'll go to the Goddess Temple and the localities near it before lunch. After lunch we'll go to Locality Two, which is the area of the big burials in the valley." He pointed to places on the map.

We looked like tourists, with multiple cameras slung around our necks, and knives, GPS units and compasses attached to belts or in pockets. Mr. Li wore an amazing vest with two dozen pockets, each containing some tool or other. I watched to see how many he actually used. All that hardware must have weighed a ton, and he is a slender man.

We jounced up the road in two jeeps and a truck, over the ruts and around the pot holes. A farmer came by with a herd of goats, and Ashley demanded to stop and snap pictures. A goat picture frenzy ensued. The farmer must have thought we were crazy. Hadn't we ever seen goats before? But I admit I took a picture, too—a cute kid nibbling on one of Ashley's cameras.

It felt quite eerie standing by the outline of the Goddess Temple, as if the spirits were still hovering nearby. The floor had been covered up as soon as the Chinese archaeologists unearthed the unbaked clay statue fragments. Some day, when the time and funding and expertise are right, they'll reopen the dig. Until then, we can study their detailed report and published map from the original excavation.

The building probably collapsed soon after the area was abandoned. All that's left is the long, irregular outline of the building. There's a brick guard shed at each locality of Daling, and a roof protecting the Goddess Temple excavation, but otherwise there is little to see above ground.

Mr. Li pointed out Pig Mountain, a large looming presence at the Goddess Temple. It doesn't show up well in photographs, but when you're there it does look like a giant pig head, with small peaks forming erect ears on either side of a rounded summit. You can even imagine two dark boulders down the slope as eyes, and a flat area in front at the snout. Whether the prehistoric people also saw it as a pig is impossible to know, but given the prevalence of pig imagery it seems likely.

We did our usual picture-taking in front of Pig Mountain, including the Korean and Chinese archaeologists in some of the shots. Our Korean colleagues were as eager and curious as we, and hard to line up, so the photos are somewhat haphazard. Evan was trying to get a picture of everyone, and correlate each picture with a name card. I wasn't so ambitious, and asked Evan to send me copies.

Adjacent to the Goddess Temple, and up the slope from it, is the area described as a platform. It took a while to walk around the area, as the places where various pits were dug were pointed out to us. One pit had contained a whole painted jar with a lid, another contained sheep bones, and a third had three layers of broken pottery.

Describing an area as a platform conjures up a flat terrace, but in fact it's uneven, with piles of stones in various places. Dr. Wu pointed out where they thought there was an entrance from the Goddess Temple to the platform area. Archaeologists are a curious lot, and we spent at least an hour asking questions about the finds.

Meanwhile, Joe galloped around, putting samples of the soil into little bottles and estimating the depths in various places, using Laura as his assistant.

"At least there aren't any electric wires here," he told Laura, "and only our three vehicles are parked here. It's a long way down to the road and railroad, with metal stuff passing by all the time. I think this would be okay for the radar. I hope the Ox River site is far from a big road, too."

Laura ascertained that no human bones had been found in this vicinity. The sheep bones found in a pit had been thrown away. Laura gave a mini lecture to Mr. Li about how much can be learned from animal bones, but it was too late to retrieve those sheep bones.

Evan roamed around making notes on the landscape, and sketching a map of the site, including noting what other sites were visible from the temple and the platform. He had his GPS turned on constantly, and noted the readings in his notebook, in case the electronic storage should fail. I heard him asking questions like how long it would take to walk to the nearest habitation site, and whether any shrines had been found on Pig Mountain.

I sat on the edge of the Goddess Temple, and wondered about the builders. A car engine broke my reverie. I turned and saw a big white van without markings stop on the road. The back and side windows were painted white, so it was impossible to see into it. Three big men got out, gathering up shovels and buckets from the sliding door.

I went to find Dr. Wu, and pointed at the men. "Who are they? What are they doing?"

After Dr. Wu went to speak to them, they put away their equipment, got back in their vehicle, and drove away.

"What was that about?" I was curious, of course, on behalf of Sandra Wold and my duties here.

"They said they were digging dirt to put into flowerpots," explained Dr. Wu. "There's no way I could prove they were intending to loot. But I got the number of their license plate, in case they turn up around here again."

Chapter 12
The Jade Phoenix (Excerpt)

To set the scene: one of the attendants found in Lady Hao's tomb had been killed by being chopped through at the waist with an axe. The narrator, a young archaeologist, is disturbed by this and recounts her dream.

Prologue, The Jade Phoenix
(A story about Lady Hao of the Shang Dynasty)

Before I even knew I was going to China, I dreamed about the Shang. My mind played a trick as it does when I'm thinking about the archaeological past—in my dreams I'm a bird, able to observe and be seen, but not interfere.

I had been half watching a *kung fu* movie on TV with actors in period Chinese costumes. I must have fallen asleep about the time the characters with swords were bouncing through beautiful bamboo groves because the sword wielders vanished and I was in a bamboo tree myself as it swayed up and down. I hung on with my claws and thought about how, as a human, I always hated carnival rides. As a yellow bird, it wasn't so bad because I could always take flight if I began to get tree-sick.

The bamboo tree grew in a courtyard encircled by large wooden pillars painted red. Below the tree a woman lay propped on silken cushions. She was so bony her shoulder blades poked up under her embroidered yellow robe. She shivered in the last warmth of a fading day. Two figures knelt in front of the woman. One was a girl wearing only a plain hempen shift, her face awash in tears but her shoulder blades stiff with defiance. Beside her a muscular man with a shaved head carried an axe in one hand. His other hand encircled the girl's thin arm.

"You must accompany me to the Spirit World, Peony," the woman on the cushions spoke with steel in her soft voice. "You know that I cannot leave you here to seduce my husband the king and bear a son to supplant Prince Zu Ji."

She nodded at the bald man. "And you, Axeman, why haven't you already obeyed my order to chop off Peony's head? I will begin my travel to the Spirit World before sun-up and everything must be ready. My other companions will soon be lying in the tomb niches in all their finery, and my favorite lion dog Dozo will be curled in the pit under my coffin, guarding me from noxious Earth Spirits. I will expect to see Peony in the Spirit World when I awake because she is the only one I trust to dress my hair."

Peony answered without raising her head. "My Lady, My Lord the king has forbidden the act that you require. The Most High King said," she paused and sniffed while more tears continued to wet her cheeks, "the King said that my head was too beautiful to chop off. He has forbidden it. Isn't that so, Axeman?"

"Yes, My Lady, the Most High King has spoken so. Although he grieves for you, My Lady, and will miss you acutely when you have gone to the Spirit World."

"What were the King's exact words?"

"You will not cut off Peony's beautiful head."

"Then you will not cut off her head. The King has spoken."

Peony raised her head and smiled.

"Instead," said the yellow-robed woman to the axeman, "You will cut her in two where she is narrowest."

Peony screamed. "No! No! I will appeal again."

The woman ignored her and spoke to the axeman again.

"Cutting her through the waist may be even easier than severing her neck. Her neck seems to be very stiff and willful. Use the axe with the tiger designs on it, perhaps the tiger blade will teach her to be more obedient in the Spirit World. Although the time is short, let her blood finish flowing before the handmaidens who are staying in this life dress her for our journey. Take her away. And hurry. You see that my Spirit Bird has arrived in the bamboo tree. My journey in the Spirit World is soon to begin."

I woke with a shiver. I rather hoped not to return to be the spirit guide of this woman.

Afterword

Many archaeologists who study gender in archaeology have shown that feminist theory refines and challenges archaeological processes and interpretations. Great strides have been made by feminist perspectives, and I have tried to follow as well as lead, incorporating new topics into my own work. This final reprinted paper (Chapter 13) represents a rethinking of several issues in East Asian archaeology.

I wrote the paper in response to an invitation to a symposium at a social science conference, with the theme "Temporalities." All the speakers in the session were archaeologists, with perspectives about improving the way time periods have been constructed in the past. For my talk, I used examples from East Asia, a region that for more than thirty years had challenged my thinking about how to fit the discoveries into standard archaeological categories. Knowing that the Yellow River basin of China, out of all the cultures in East Asia, was the only one included in cross-cultural analyses of times and stages, I found that a wider East Asian perspective was more useful for thinking about categories of dividing time, the standard for which is based primarily on European sites.

One major change, but not the only one, is simply to include women as actors in the past (no stirring is necessary). Another is to rethink our paradigms, especially with an awareness of all categories of people who have been omitted from the story of the past. One reviewer was offended, which may sound familiar to others who have had to learn the field and break taboos, or at least twist the rules to make them fit their own data. With enough twisting and some judicious breaking, the discipline gradually changes.

Some feminist writers who have influenced my thinking about archaeology include Carole Crumley, who brought the notion of heterarchy to our attention; Janet Levy, who developed the concept further; and Anne Pyburn, who challenged her students to reconsider what is missing from theories of state-level organization and produced an edited volume of their papers that discussed a variety of difficulties with the way the topic of state formation has been approached. Susan Kus brings landscape and poetry to an understanding of cultures. Julia Hendon calls attention to the importance of households. Tom Patterson and Alice Kehoe, in their different ways, call archaeology to account for supporting the status quo. Rosemary Joyce demonstrates the importance of analyzing bodies. Suzanne Spencer-Wood continues to insist on the importance of feminist theory. Diane Gifford-Gonzales, perceptive in many ways, also coined the phrase "the drudge on the hide" to epitomize the ways women in ancient societies have been depicted. Many others whose work I regularly cite were influences as well.

The reprint that follows addresses several problems in archaeology, made clearer by a stereoscopic vision that includes both a gendered perspective and data that were not used to create the common schemes. I consider the functions of the earliest pottery containers now known, surprisingly, from all over East Asia, not just Japan, but from far north in the Russian Far East to southeastern China. A focus on pottery has an effect on gendered interpretations, as well as rearranging our sense of the times and places of this important invention for human culture.

I further suggest that archaeology's familiar divisions into technological ages and stages do not fit East Asia well, perhaps because the wrong technologies were selected to make time divisions. Technologies for cooking, carrying, and clothing may have made more difference to the survival of our Paleolithic ancestors than the manufacturing methods for stone tools. Finally, in this paper I return to the question of whether women were disadvantaged by the origin of the state. My answer, familiar to the reader of the previous chapters, is that in some East Asian cultures, women were rulers, perhaps believed to be able to protect the state from capricious spirits and approach benevolent ancestors for aid. Not only has feminist theory provided new possibilities for interpreting the past, but also an East Asian perspective is valuable for suggesting alternative ways to think about the very rich past of humanity.

Chapter 13

A Perspective from East Asia on Periodizations in Archaeology

The divisions of time and cultures that archaeologists make may present particular difficulties when divisions created to understand one region are stretched to include regions other than those for which they were devised. This may be most problematic for prehistoric archaeology (and anthropological archaeology in general), because the divisions (whether temporal or stage-related) are used for the precise purpose of comparing regions and attempting to understand the development of cultures in a systematic way. While this is a worthwhile goal, the periodization schemes themselves may prevent each region from being described in the most appropriate way. I will begin to make this point by posing three problems for East Asia caused by the application of "world-wide" archaeological periodizations.

Examples of Problems Created by Standard Archaeological Periodizations in East Asian Archaeology

Problem I. Some of the groups of people who lived in East Asia toward the end of the Ice Ages, and before or at the beginning of a global rise in sea level, created and used pottery containers—the earliest clay pots known (so far) in the world. These baked clay containers appear to have been created and used in the absence of plant or animal domestication. Colleagues from the rest of the world scold East Asianists for using the label "Neolithic" for

Sarah M. Nelson (2012). In *Labrys*, Online Journal, July/December 2012 (*http://www.tanianavarroswain.com.br/labrys/labrys22/archeo/sarah%20nelson.htm*). Republished in *Shamans, Queens, and Figurines: The Development of Gender Archaeology*, by Sarah Nelson, pp. 241–250 (Taylor & Francis, 2015).

such sites.[1] But what term should be used? What characteristics should the term Neolithic highlight? What does it obscure?

Problem II. A large number of "Neolithic" and "Bronze Age" sites in East Asia are described as burials of shamans. Shamans are an active force in many East Asian societies today, and Siberia, the region believed to be the home of "original" shamanism is not too far away to consider diffusion to China, Korea and Japan. Thus it is not unreasonable to posit shaman leaders in ancient East Asia. However, the terminology of leadership—chiefs, kings, emperors—leaves no room to discuss shamanism as part of the equation of leadership, or indeed of any of the ways that ideology/religion may have played a part in expanding leadership to larger and larger polities, while the evidence in East Asia points to religious beliefs as driving the political realm as well as social structure. Does an emphasis on chiefs and kings mask other important processes? Could state formation be better understood using other terminology?

Problem III. Enormous tomb mounds commonly mark elite burials in ancient East Asia. Some of those containing royal paraphernalia are burials of women. Yet leadership continues to be described in masculine terms. Does the terminology of "chiefdoms" and "kingdoms" prevent the recognition of women leaders? Is it important to know if women were leaders always, sometimes, or never? What are the consequences for society in each case?

A Feminist Critique

All of the ways of dividing up the human past arise from androcentric and Eurocentric perspectives. The questions the profession asks about *how* societies developed are unconsciously infused with gender and ethnic biases, based as they are on the interests of males in western societies—technology (especially weapons), predation, and leadership, all of which are assumed to define the male. Archaeology has been written as if men invented everything, all leadership was male, and civilization was built by males. Therefore, presumed male activities are weighted more heavily in assessing culture change than presumed female activities. Cultural anthropology has changed, with more attention paid to women's activities, rituals, and beliefs as well as to their contributions to society. But archaeologists cannot query informants about what was important to them. So how can we deal with the fact that the assumption that all culture was created by males is built into the discourse about human development?[2]

The usual division of labor by gender in prehistory and early history is shown in Table 3.

TABLE 3 Gendered Activities

Men's Activities	Women's Activities
Warfare	Having babies
Long distance trade	Staying home
Hunting	Gathering
Tool making (especially pointed ones)	Asking hubby to make them a tool
Leadership	Other boring stuff*

*Other boring stuff includes: Gardening, gathering (shellfish, nuts, and other staples), diving for food, technology such as basketry, pottery, weaving, hide working, cooking, and making tools to create the above.

In 1983 I tried to establish a "Womankind Museum" based on the collections in the University of Denver Museum of Anthropology. The first (and, it turned out, only) exhibit was called "Working Within Walls." This exhibit highlighted women's work by including both ethnographic and archaeological collections. Somewhat to our surprise, almost everything in the collection, with the possible exception of projectile points, was available for inclusion. Preparing that exhibit opened my eyes to the fact that women's technologies have been largely unacknowledged in the scope of cultural evolution.

For prehistoric and early historic periods, the selected technological innovations are based on hunting tools and weaponry. Ignoring other technologies that are usually attributable to women in ethnographic settings (e.g. potting, cordage, the preparation of skin and fur, weaving) affects the way both professional archaeologists and the general public conceive of life in the distant past. For example, for a very long time, bone tools suggesting tailoring in Upper Paleolithic sites were overlooked and often unreported (Kehoe 1990). Other technological changes may have profoundly affected the lives of prehistoric peoples, but they have been ignored. The result is that archaeological divisions exclude technological innovations which are likely to be attributable to women. Understanding of pivotal changes in the ancient past would be improved by including creative activities that have traditionally been women's work, whatever gender actually made the pots, baskets, fabric, etc.

For example, grinding of stone is considered more elegant than chipping, but with the mindset that men make tools, women are not given credit for creating grinding technologies, in spite of the fact that grinding is considered to be drudge work (see Gifford-Gonzalez [1993] for her analysis of depictions of women as the "drudge-on-the-hide"). Women were the chief grain-grinders in societies that use grain, as well as the ones who rubbed hides to rid them of fat and hairs, and to soften them. Awls, tools to make baskets (more "women's work"), are made of bone, too, by grinding.

I am not arguing that stone tool technology was not important, and the increasing elegance of tools may demonstrate increasing small muscle control as well as sharpened cognitive skills. But it is unlikely that even very early bipedal humans would have managed without slings and baskets for carrying (Zihlman and Tanner 1978). Bone tools such as needles for clothing, awls for basketry, and hooks for fishing were certainly important for human survival, but bone artifacts are rarely central in the story of cultural evolution. Making bone tools is a complex process (Dobres 1995), and the objects are often adorned with incised designs or realistic depictions of plants or animals. Intentional marks on some bone objects have been studied as possible evidence of purposeful timekeeping (Marshack 1972). Yet the emergence of bone tools does not call for a new stage in archaeological time divisions. Fiber technologies are dependent on bone and sometimes wooden implements. The resulting objects are complex, and often important to human survival, including traps and snares, fishnets, and carrying devices such as slings and baskets. Fiber technology includes mats to sit on and sleep on, and often clothing to wear.

The invention of pottery likewise does not rate a stage of its own, in spite of the complexity of the technology involved—to make a pot requires far more steps than the flaking of stone tools. Making pottery required cooperative work, from finding the clay, processing the clay and shaping the pots, to firing the pots and perhaps decorating them, before or after firing. In making pottery, decoration became much more varied with many different techniques, including incising, painting, and impressing. Pottery necessarily changed food habits, because items not digestible by humans became not only tastier but fundamentally edible by cooking. Perhaps the clay vessels provided a solution to food scarcity as the climate warmed, and in the northern hemisphere animals such as reindeer moved north with the boreal forest. In different places, pottery containers seem to have performed different functions. Pottery is seen as a part of the "Neolithic Revolution" but not as stage divider, although in East Asia it is used as the marker for the Neolithic, as is discussed below.

Turning to stages of cultural evolution—bands, chiefdoms and states—it is evident from the terminology that leadership is presumed to be the defining characteristic of various sizes and types of polity. Whether this is the case has never been questioned in anthropological archaeology. Religious leadership, in the form of priests, or ideology that upholds the leader is sometimes acknowledged, but they are seen as secondary. The politics of small and large polities has reigned supreme.

Furthermore, the maleness of these leaders is never questioned, even when the de facto leader is female. A recent burgeoning literature demonstrating women leaders is still ignored in most theoretical archaeology. Ruling queens existed widely through time and space, if they are looked for (Nelson 2003b). New scholarship shows that women chiefs or queens are known from many areas of the world, especially Egypt (Troy 2003), Mesoamerica (Bell 2003), North America (Troccoli 2002), and even China (Linduff 2003). These queens may not have been absolute monarchs, but neither were most of the men designated as "chiefs" or "kings." Turning these terms into categories and chiefdoms and kingdoms into stages may obscure the very characteristics we are trying to discover in the formation of the state.

East Asian Archaeology

Most of my archaeological fieldwork in the last several decades has been in East Asia, where the basic assumptions about both periodization and the purposes of archaeology diverge from those of the western world. Especially in China and Korea, archaeology is considered to be a technique for verifying history. The textual Chinese dynasties are used as temporal divisions beyond the boundaries of the dynasty itself. In other words, ancient texts drive archaeology, including the choice of sites to excavate, the context provided for excavations, and interpretations of the discoveries. Chinese texts tell a story of unilineal history, especially the development of "civilization," and Korean and Japanese early texts follow Chinese examples, although they also raise additional complications. Western terminology has been borrowed, but it is squeezed to fit the story told by ancient documents of East Asia. To explore this perspective and how it meshes with or opposes Western temporalities, the examples set out in the beginning will be explored further.

Problem I: Origins of Pottery

In East Asia, the invention of pottery containers, rather than either ground stone tools or plant and animal domestication, marks the most definitive change in human behavior at the end of the Pleistocene. The first known pottery occurs late in the Pleistocene, before sea level began its precipitous Holocene rise. In Japan, the first pottery was produced even before the dramatic rise in sea level (Ikawa-Smith 2000). The most recent C14 dates for these sites—and there are several of them—are calibrated to about 16,000 years ago. Other early pottery found in Asia is found in association with Mesolithic tools, although the assemblages include more microliths than ground stone tools (Kononenko and Cassidy 2007). Such sites include Gasya on the Amur River, quite far north in the Russian Far East (Zhuschchikovskaya 2006), and several sites in both northern and southern China (MacNeish and Libby 1995, Yan 1992). Possible sites in Korea, perhaps as early as 10,000 BP, are not as firmly established (Im and Kwon 1984, Jeju 1998), but it is clear that pottery began in East Asia, and probably spread by water transport along East Asian coasts.

Possible functions of early pottery vessels in East Asia are for boiling, brewing, storage, and food processing. Even if the technology of potting spread, in each region the function of the pots may have been quite different. Each invention of pottery may have been a separate event. Some of the possibilities, largely untested, follow.

Boiling. Boiling requires a fire-safe material for exposure to an open hearth. Very little plant food can be eaten raw—mostly fruit and nuts, but not all of them. Cooking renders edible many parts of plants, such as roots, stems, and leaves. But these plant parts can't be roasted on a stick or placed directly in the fire; they have to be boiled in water. Gourds cut in half are adequate for serving vessels, but they would burn if placed directly in the fire. Stone bowls take a long time to make, as well as to heat, and may crack in a fire. Of all the materials available in nature, clay vessels work best. This is a possible explanation for the appearance of pottery in inland sites, especially those in the northern edges of East Asia, where large game might have moved north.

Brewing. Liquids require pottery containers. Traces of brewing alcoholic beverages have been found in a Chinese clay pot dated around 7000 BCE (Henry 2005). There is no reason to suppose that this pot represents the earliest fermentation in East Asia. Until more residues are tested, we will not know when and where brewing first occurred. But it is interesting to think of brewing as preceding the "Neolithic Revolution."

Storage. Pottery could have been created to store a wild grain crop for the winter, safe from small rodents who would have been happy to deplete the stores. Pits might also work, if lined with clay as in southwest Asia, or granaries built on raised platforms, which are known to have been used later in Japan and Korea. However, wet storage of vegetable crops would surely require pottery containers. This is likely where vegetables were preserved for the winter, which would have been necessary in northern communities (Nelson 1975).

Food Processing. It has been suggested that in the case of pottery in coastal Japan, bivalve shellfish could be opened up more easily by dropping them in boiling water (Kidder 1965). Especially in sites where rising sea levels created a new and indented coastline with shallow waters newly inhabited by shellfish, this seems to be a likely explanation for the invention of pottery containers. Another possibility is leaching nuts such as acorns, which need to have tannin removed.

The above discussion makes obvious that most of the uses for pottery are related to food getting. The food may have been gathered from the wild rather than cultivated or domesticated. So far there is no evidence of intensive agriculture, although wild plants have been found in abundance wherever they have been retrieved by flotation (Crawford et al 2005, Crawford and Lee 2000). Pottery represents both a certain amount of sedentism and intensified use of plant food. In East Asia the presence of pottery is a marker for a division we call "Neolithic," whether or not there is agriculture, even though ground stone tools (the original definition of Neolithic!) are often present as a further indication of food processing. We are told by our colleagues from elsewhere that the sites cannot be designated as Neolithic if there is no evidence of agriculture. But this complaint demonstrates the power of periodizations. The creation of pottery is an important dividing line in East Asia, which seems to occur earlier than plant and animal domestication. Perhaps we should call it the "Pottery Age." We don't need the term Neolithic, but we do need a term that highlights the differences among areas of the world in peri-Holocene archaeology. Perhaps the change in terminology would allow a broader understanding of this time period.

PROBLEM II: SHAMANS AS LEADERS

The eminent archaeologist K. C. Chang (1983) devoted an entire book and several papers in order to demonstrate that the Shang dynasty (1600–1100 BCE) was ruled by shaman-kings. Several archaeologists in China have described many Neolithic sites in China with elements that could be interpreted as shamanistic (Chang and Xu 2005). A number of indications, ranging from depictions on bronzes to writings on oracle bones, cause these archaeologists to suggest that the kings of the first well-attested dynasty (by contemporaneous texts as well as archaeology) were shamans (Chang 2005). This group of archaeologists therefore argues that shamans were important in the origin of the state in East Asia.

If one takes shamanism to be a historical process rather than a universal trait emanating from the human mind, it is reasonable that Siberian shamanism could occur in China, especially taking the borders of the current Chinese state as "China." This territory includes Inner Mongolia, the western provinces of Xinjiang and Gansu, the northeast region where Manchu ancestors lived, once called Manchuria, and a strip of land along the East Coast from Shanghai to Liaoning Province where the earliest jade-using cultures were found. For example, bones with holes drilled for divination have been found in Inner Mongolia, some 2,000 years before the inscribed oracle bones of the Shang dynasty (Guo 1995a), and they have been found in several places in northern China around this time (Li Min 2008). We do not know for sure what languages were spoken in these regions in Neolithic times, but there are reasons to suppose they may have been neither Chinese nor languages related to Chinese. Inscribed oracle bones, however, appear only in the Late Shang, and are definitely inscribed in early Chinese characters. How the concept of drilling holes and putting the bones in a fire to question the spirits became a Chinese rather than a non-Chinese trait is unknown.

Much that is known about the way oracle bones were used is due to the fact that inscriptions are numerous from the Late Shang period. The written words make clear the divinatory nature of scapula prepared with holes to be cracked in the fire, and the additional use of turtle plastrons in the same way. A newly discovered inscribed oracle bone from Shandong from the Middle Shang period can be partly read, and shows that even outside of the center of the Shang polity, oracle bones and writing were important (Li Min 2008). These bones were carefully prepared by people called *wu* (often translated as "shaman"), were inscribed by specialists, and were interpreted as the will of the spirits. Sacrifices took place as a result of the interpretations of the will of the spirits. Later in Chinese history written references to shamans appear, including a book thought to be a manual for shamans. Thus it seems that Chang and his cohorts in mainland China are on solid ground.

However, a problem arises with the fierce declaration by these same archaeologists that the Shang dynasty shamans were men only (Chang 2005). This is problematic in several ways. First, shamans still thrive in most of present East Asia, and they are predominantly women (Nelson 2008b), as they are in Central Asia (Tedlock 2005). Second, the Shang textual evidence describes the kings' wives as shamans, including Lady Hao, the favored wife of King Wu Ding of the Shang dynasty (ca 1200 BCE), whose tomb is the only intact tomb found in the Shang (Linduff 2002, 2003). Lady Hao was buried with a number of objects that are often associated with shamanism in East Asia, notably mirrors, musical instruments, and jade figurines (Linduff 2002, Nelson 2008b). Inscriptions on some of Lady Hao's burial bronzes give her a posthumous temple name, indicating that she became an ancestor to be worshipped, although she was not a member of the Shang royal lineage or even a local lineage (Keightley 1999a). Third, the word *wu* is used both for shamans in general and for women shamans. If men must be specified, the word used is *xi*. Women are in this case the unmarked gender, suggesting that the expected gender of shamans was female.

Attention to shamanism has changed the discussion about the origin of the state in China, but it has obscured the gender of the shamans. Maybe it would help to designate an "Age of Shaman Leaders," and to admit the possibility of women shamans—and even women leaders. Although not a ruler, writing on oracle bones and the contents of her tomb show that Lady Hao was an influential person in the Late Shang polity (Keightley 1999a).

Problem III: Recognizing a Reigning Queen

Although Korean texts discussing the Korean Three Kingdoms were written much later than the events they describe, they were created on the basis of annals of the kingdoms that are now lost. The *Samguk Sagi* asserts that the state of Old Silla (traditional dates 58 BCE–668 CE), arose in the southeastern part of the Korean peninsula, during the (Chinese) Han dynasty. It is known that Old Silla was a society that was divided into endogamous bone ranks (Grayson 1976, Kim, C.S. 1977). The highest rank, from which kings and queens were selected, was known as Holy Bone, and lower nobles came from the True Bone rank. It has been inferred that to be Holy Bone, and therefore eligible to rule, Holy Bone individuals had to be born from two Holy Bone parents. The founding kings *and* queens are mythologized in the earliest legends. Kings were born from magic eggs, found in a golden box, or related to white horses. Queens are described as daughters of goddesses, especially mountain goddesses. The list of kings includes the parentage of both kings and queens. It is quite clear that both the kings and queens were important.

Some ten large tomb mounds have been excavated from the 3rd–5th centuries, with very rich grave goods interpreted as trappings of royalty, including pure gold crowns and belts, covered with curved jewels and gold dangling ornaments. The largest and highest mound of all is called Hwangnam Taechong, or Tomb 98. This monument is a double tomb overlapping in the middle, each side having been constructed at a different time. The earlier mound was that of the king—identified by a single tooth as a male. It contained a great quantity of weapons, but neither a gold crown nor a gold belt. The northern mound did have the expected high gold crown covered with curved jewels and sheet gold belt inscribed "Belt for milady." It would seem that the lady outranked the warrior, and also outlived him. By all the usual critieria, the grave of the ruler is that of the queen.

Yet Korean archaeologists are reluctant to interpret this female tomb as a ruling queen, even though she was exclusively buried with the trappings of royalty. Three later women do appear in the king list as queens, or literally "female kings." Two were the final members of the Holy Bone, and following them, True Bone persons could be selected as rulers—and one of those selected was a woman. This is less a periodization problem than blindness to the possibility that gender was not the salient factor in choosing a Silla ruler. The blindness is partly linguistic. Maybe it would help to call this an "Age of Queens."

CONCLUSION

Periodizations are tools to think about changes in human societies. But they can also put thinking in strait jackets, which prevent us from seeing in new and more productive ways, ways that respond to the evidence rather than preconceived ideas about human nature and the importance of various technologies. These examples from East Asia contrast with the usual ways of dividing time and explaining cultural evolution in archaeology, and therefore are useful to highlight a general problem with labels, whether of periods or stages.

NOTES

[1] Vigorous discussions about the use of the term "Neolithic" took place at the World Archaeological Congress 6 in Dublin, Ireland, June 6–10, 2008, and at the Indo-Pacific Prehistory Association in Hanoi, Vietnam, December 1–6, 2009.

[2] A longer discussion of leadership in archaeology can be found in Nelson (1997a: 121–149). The question of the Big Man is deconstructed, and the inherent masculinity of the terminology is further discussed.

References Cited

Abramova, Z. A.

1967 Paleolithic Art in the USSR. *Arctic Anthropology* 4(2):1–179

Absolon, K.

1949 The Diluvial Anthropomorphic Statuettes and Drawings, Especially the So-called Venus Statuettes Discovered in Moravia. *Artibus Asiae* 12: 201–220.

Aldhouse-Green, Miranda, and Stephen Aldhouse-Green

2005 *The Quest for the Shaman.* London: Thames & Hudson.

Allan, Sarah

1991 *Shape of the Turtle: Myth, Art, and Cosmos in Early China.* Albany: State University of New York Press.

1993 Art and Meaning; and Epilogue. In *The Problem of Meaning in Early Chinese Ritual Bronzes,* edited by R. Whitfield, pp. 9–33 and 161–176. London: School of Oriental and African Studies.

1997 *The Way of Water and Sprouts of Virtue.* Albany: SUNY Press.

Ames, Kenneth M.

1995 Chiefly Power and Household Production on the Northwest Coast. In *Foundations of Social Inequality,* edited by T. Douglas Price and Gary M. Feinman, pp. 155–188. New York: Plenum Press.

Anderson, E.

1988 *The Food of China.* New Haven: Yale University Press.

Arwill-Nordbladh, E.

2003 A Reigning Queen, or the Wife of a King—Only? Gender Politics in the Scandinavian Viking Age. In *Ancient Queens, Archaeological Explorations,* edited by S. M. Nelson. Walnut Creek, CA: AltaMira Press.

Atkinson, Jane Monig

1992 Shamanisms Today. *Annual Review of Anthropology* 21:307–330.

Bagley, Robert

1993 Meaning and Explanation. In *The Problem of Meaning in Early Chinese Ritual Bronzes,* edited by R. Whitfield, pp. 34–55. London: School of Oriental and African Studies.

1999 The Archaeology of the Shang Dynasty. In *The Cambridge History of Ancient China*, edited by Michael Loewe and Edward L. Shaughnessy, pp. 124–231. Cambridge: Cambridge University Press.

Bahn, P. G.

1986 No Sex Please, We're Aurignacians. *Rock Art Research* 3(2):99–105.

Balzer, Marjorie Mandelstam, ed.

1990 *Shamanism: Soviet Studies of Traditional Religion in Siberia and Central Asia*. London: M.E. Sharpe.

1997 *Shamanic Worlds, Ritual and Lore of Siberia and Central Asia*. London: North Castle Books.

Barnes, Gina

2007 *Women in the Nihon Shoki: Mates, Mothers, Mystics, Militarists, Maids, Manufacturers, Monarchs, Messengers and Managers*. Durham East Asian Papers 20. Durham, UK: Department of East Asian Studies, Durham University.

Barnouw, V.

1978 *Physical Anthropology and Archaeology*. 3rd ed. Homewood, IL: The Dorsey Press.

Basilov, Vladimir N.

1997 Chosen by the Spirits. In *Shamanic Worlds, Ritual and Lore of Siberia and Central Asia*, edited by M. Balzer, pp. 3–48. London: North Castle Books.

Behar, Ruth, and Deborah A. Gordon, eds.

1995 *Women Writing Culture*. Berkeley: University of California Press.

Bell, Karen

2003 Ancient Queens of the Valley of Mexico. In *Ancient Queens: Archaeological Explorations*, edited by S. M. Nelson, pp. 137–50. Walnut Creek, CA: AltaMira Press.

Beller, A. S.

1977 *Fat and Thin*. New York: Farrar, Strauss and Giroux.

Berenguer, Magín.

1973 *Prehistoric Man and His Art: The Caves of Ribadesella*. Translated by M. Heron. London: Souvenir Press.

Binford, Lewis

1962 Archaeology as Anthropology. *American Antiquity* 28:217–225.

Binford, Sally, and Lewis Binford, eds.

1968 *New Perspectives in Archeology*. Chicago: Aldine.

Blacker, Carmen

1975 *The Catalpa Bow: A Study of Shamanistic Practices in Japan*. London: George Allen & Unwin Ltd.

Bolger, Diane, ed.

2013 *Companion to Gender Prehistory*. Wiley/Blackwell.

Boulding, Elise
1976 *The Underside of History*. Boulder, CO: Westview Press.
Boule, M., and H. Vallois
1957 *Fossil Man*. New York: Dryden Press.
Boyer, Ernest L.
1990 *Scholarship Reconsidered, Priorities of the Professoriate*. Princeton: The Carnegie Foundation for the Advancement of Teaching.
Brumfiel, Elizabeth M.
2006 Methods in Feminist and Gender Archaeology: A Feeling for Difference—and Likeness. In *Handbook of Gender in Archaeology*, edited by S. M. Nelson, pp. 31–58. Walnut Creek, CA: AltaMira Press.
Cahill, S. M.
1993 *Transcendence and Divine Passion: The Queen Mother of the West in Medieval China*. Stanford: Stanford University Press.
Campbell, B. G.
1982 *Humankind Emerging*. 3rd ed. Boston: Little, Brown and Company.
1988 *Humankind Emerging*. 5th ed. Glenview, IL: Scott, Foresman and Company.
Chang, Chen-hsiang
1986 A Study of the Bronzes with the "Ssu T'u Mu" Inscriptions Excavated from the Fu Hao Tomb. In *Studies in Shang Archaeology: Selected Papers from the International Conference on Shang Civilization*, edited by Kwang-Chih Chang, pp. 81–103. New Haven: Yale University Press.
Chang, C. L.
1986 A Brief Discussion of Fu Tzu. In *Studies of Shang Archaeology: Selected Papers from the International Conference on Shang Civilization*, edited by Kwang-Chih Chang, pp. 103–119. New Haven: Yale University Press.
Chang, Kwang-Chih
1976 *Early Chinese Civilization*. Cambridge: Harvard University Press.
1977 Introduction; and Ancient China. In *Food in Chinese Culture: Anthropological and Historical Perspectives*, edited by K.-C. Chang, pp. 1–21, 24–52. New Haven: Yale University Press.
1980a The Chinese Bronze Age: A Modern Synthesis. *In The Great Bronze Age of China*, edited by Wen Fong, pp. 35–50. New York: Metropolitan Museum of Art.
1980b *Shang Civilization*. New Haven: Yale University Press.
1983 *Art, Myth, and Ritual: The Path to Political Authority in Ancient China*. Cambridge, MA: Harvard University Press.
1986 *The Archaeology of Ancient China*. 4th ed. New Haven: Yale University Press.
1994a Ritual and Power. In *Cradles of Civilization: China*, edited by Robert E. Murowchick, pp. 61–69. Norman: University of Oklahoma Press.

1994b Shang Shamans. In *The Power of Culture*, edited by W. J. Peterson, A. H. Plaks, and Y. Yu, pp. 10–36. Hong Kong: Chinese University Press.

1999 China on the Eve of the Historical Period. In *The Cambridge History of Ancient China*, edited by M. Loewe and E. L. Shaughnessy, pp. 37–73. Cambridge: Cambridge University Press.

2005 The Rise of Kings and the Formation of City-States. In *The Formation of Chinese Civilization: An Archaeological Perspective*, edited by K.-C. Chang and P. Xu, pp. 125–140. New Haven: Yale University Press.

Chang, Kwang-Chih, ed.

1986 *Studies in Shang Archaeology: Selected Papers from the International Conference on Shang Civilization*. New Haven: Yale University Press.

Chang, K.-C., and P. Xu, eds.

2005 *The Formation of Chinese Civilization: An Archaeological Perspective*. New Haven: Yale University Press.

Chang Pin-chuan

1986 A Brief Description of the Fu Hao Oracle Bone Inscriptions. In *Studies in Shang Archaeology: Selected Papers from the International Conference on Shang Civilization*, edited by Kwang-Chih Chang, pp. 121–140. New Haven: Yale University Press.

Chard, Chester

1975 *Man in Prehistory*. 2nd ed. New York: McGraw-Hill.

Chen Lie

1996 The Ancestor Cult in Ancient China. In *Mysteries of Ancient China: New Discoveries from the Early Dynasties*, edited by Jessica Rawson, pp. 269–272. New York: George Braziller, Inc.

Cheng Cheng-lang

1986 A Brief Discussion of Fu Tzu. In *Studies in Shang Archaeology: Selected Papers from the International Conference on Shang Civilization*, edited by Kwang-Chih Chang, pp. 103–120. New Haven: Yale University Press.

Childe, V. G.

1951 *Man Makes Himself*. New York: The New American Library.

Childs-Johnson, Elizabeth

1995 Ghost Head Mask and Metamorphic Shang Imagery. *Early China* 20:79–92.

Ching, Julia

1997 *Mysticism and Kingship in China: The Heart of Chinese Wisdom*. Cambridge: Cambridge University Press.

Ch'oe, Pyong-hon

1981 The Evolution and Chronology of the Wooden Chamber Tomb of the Old Shilla Period. *Han'guk kogo hakpo* (Journal of the Korean Archaeological Society) 10–11:137–228. (In Korean)

Claessen, Henri J. M., and Peter Skalnik, eds.
1978 *The Early State.* The Hague: Mouton Publishers.

Claessen, H. J. M., and Pieter van de Velde
1985 Social Evolution in General. In *Development and Decline. The Evolution of Sociopolitical Organization,* edited by H. J. M. Claessen, P. van de Velde, and M. E. Smith, pp. 1–12. South Hadley, MA: Bergin & Garvey.

Clark, G.
1977 *World Prehistory in New Perspective.* 3rd ed. Cambridge: Cambridge University Press.

Cohen, David
2001 The Yueshi Culture, the Dong Yi, and the Archaeology of Ethnicity in Early Bronze Age China. PhD dissertation, Harvard University.

Conkey, Margaret, and Joan Gero
1991 Tensions, Pluralities, and Engendering Archaeology: An Introduction to Women and Prehistory. In *Engendering Archaeology: Women and Prehistory,* edited by J. Gero and M. Conkey, pp. 1–30. London: Basil Blackwell Ltd.

Conkey, Margaret, and Janet Spector
1984 Archaeology and the Study of Gender. In *Advances in Archaeological Method and Theory* 7, edited by M. Schiffer, pp. 1–38. New York: Academic Press.

Conkey, Margaret, and Ruth Tringham
1995 Archaeology and the Goddess: Exploring the Contours of Feminist Archaeology. In *Feminism and the Academy,* edited by D. C. Stanton and A. J. Stewart, pp. 199–247. Ann Arbor: University of Michigan Press.

Connelly, Joan B.
2007 *Portrait of a Princess: Women and Ritual in Ancient Greece.* Princeton: Princeton University Press.

Cook, Constance A., and John S. Major, eds.
1999 *Defining Chu, Image and Reality in Ancient China.* Honolulu: University of Hawaii Press.

Coward, Rosalind
1983 *Patriarchal Precedents.* London: Routledge.

Cowgill, George
1993 Distinguished Lecture in Archeology: Beyond Criticizing New Archeology. *American Anthropologist* 95(3):551–573.

Crawford, Gary, Anne Underhill, Zhijun Zhao, Gyoung-Ah Lee, Gary Feinman, Linda Nicholas, Fengshi Luan, Haiguang Yu, Hui Fang, and Fengshu Cai
2005 Late Neolithic Plant Remains from North China: Preliminary Results from Liangchenzhen, China. *Current Anthropology* 46(2):1–14.

Crawford, Gary W., and Gyoung-Ah Lee
2000 Agricultural Origins in the Korean Peninsula. *Antiquity* 77:87–95.

Creel, H. G.
1970 *The Origins of Statecraft in China*. Chicago: University of Chicago Press.
Cutter, Robert Joe, and William G. Cromwell
1999 *Empress and Consorts*. Honolulu: University of Hawaii Press.
Davis-Kimball, Jeannine
2003 *Katuns*: The Mongolian Queens of the Genghis Khanite. In *Ancient Queens*, edited by S. M. Nelson, pp. 151–173. Walnut Creek, CA: AltaMira Press.
DeGroot, J. J. M.
1910 *Religious System of China*, Vol. 6. Leiden: E. J. Brill.
Delporte, H.
1979 *L'image de la femme dans l'art préhistorique*. Paris: Picard.
Deuchler, Martina
1992 *The Confucian Transformation of Korea*. Cambridge, MA: Council on East Asian Studies, Harvard University.
Devlet, Ekaterina
2001 Rock Art and the Material Culture of Siberia and Central Asia. In *The Archaeology of Shamanism*, edited by N. Price, pp. 43–55. London: Routledge.
Dobres, Marcia Anne
1995 Gender and Prehistoric Technology: On the Social Agency of Technical Strategies. *World Archaeology* 27(1):25–49.
Earle, Timothy K.
1987 Chiefdoms in Archaeological and Ethnographic Perspective. *Annual Review of Anthropology* 16:279–308.
1997 *How Chiefs Come to Power: The Political Economy in Prehistory*. Stanford: Stanford University Press.
Eddy, F. W.
1984 *Archaeology, A Cultural-Evolutionary Approach*. Englewood Cliffs, NJ: Prentice Hall.
Eliade, Mircea
1964 *Shamanism, Archaic Techniques of Ecstasy*. Translated by W. R. Trask. Princeton: Princeton University Press.
Elster, Ernestine S.
2007 Marija Gimbutas: Setting the Agenda. In *Archaeology and Women: Ancient and Modern Issues*, edited by Sue Hamilton, Ruth D. Whitehouse, and Katherine I. Wright, pp. 83–120. Walnut Creek, CA: Left Coast Press.
Engels, Friedrich
1972 [1884] *The Origin of the Family, Private Property, and the State*. New York: Pathfinder Press.
Fagan, B.
1986 *People of the Earth, An Introduction to World History*. 5th ed. Boston: Little, Brown.
2007 *Ancient Lives*. Upper Saddle River, NJ: Pearson Prentice Hall.

Falkenhausen, Lothar von

1995 Reflections on the Political Role of Spirit Mediums in Early China: The Wu Officials in the Shou Li. *Early China* 20:279–300.

2006 *Chinese Society in the Age of Confucius: The Archaeological Evidence.* Los Angeles: Cotsen Institute of Archaeology, UCLA.

Fang, Dianchun, and Wei Fan

1986a Brief Report on the Excavation of Goddess Temple and Stone Graves of Hongshan Culture at Niuheliang in Liaoning Province. *Liao Hai Wen Wu Xue Gan* 1986(8):1–17.

1986b Excavating a Lost Culture. *China Reconstructs* (December): 33–39.

Feinman, Gary M.

1995 The Emergence of Inequality: A Focus on Strategies and Processes. In *Foundations of Social Inequality*, edited by T. Douglas Price and Gary M. Feinman, pp. 255–279. New York: Plenum Press.

Fitzgerald-Huber, Louisa F.

1995 Qijia and Erlitou: The Question of Contacts with Distant Cultures. *Early China* 20:17–68.

1999 Tombs of the Lower Xiajiadian Culture at Dadianzi, Aohanqi, Inner Mongolia. In *The Golden Age of Chinese Archaeology*, edited by Xiaoneng Yang, pp. 150–161. New Haven: Yale University Press.

Fitzhugh, William W., J. Bayarsaikan, and P. K. Marsh, eds.

2005 *The Deer Stone Project: Anthropological Studies in Mongolia, 2002–2004.* Washington, DC, and Ulaanbaatar: Arctic Studies Center, Smithsonian Institute.

Flannery, Kent V.

1972 The Cultural Evolution of Civilizations. *Annual Review of Ecology and Systematics* 3:339–426.

Fleury, C.

1926 Quelques considerations sur la pseudo-steatopygie des Venus Aurignaciennes. *Archives Suisses d'anthropologie generale* 11(1):137–141.

Fraser, Antonia

1989 *The Warrior Queens.* New York: Alfred A. Knopf.

Fung, Christopher

2000 The Drinks Are on Us: Ritual, Social Status, and Practice in Dawenkou Burials, North China. *Journal of East Asian Archaeology* 2(1):67–92.

Gamble, C.

1986 *The Paleolithic Settlement of Europe.* Cambridge: Cambridge University Press.

1987 Interaction and Alliance in Palaeolithic Society. *Man* (N.S.) 17:92–107.

Gero, Joan M.

1985 Socio-Politics and the Woman-at-Home Ideology. *American Antiquity,* 50(2):342–350.

Gifford-Gonzalez, Diane
1993 You Can Hide, but You Can't Run: Representations of Women's Work in Illustrations of the Paleolithic. *Visual Anthropology Reviews* 9(1):21–41.
Gilman, Antonio
1995 Prehistoric European Chiefdoms: Rethinking "Germanic" Societies. In *Foundations of Social Inequality*, edited by T. Douglas Price and Gary M. Feinman, pp. 235–254. New York: Plenum Press.
Gimbutas, Marija
1982 *The Goddesses and Gods of Old Europe.* Berkeley: University of California Press.
Glavatzkaya, Elena
2001 The Russian State and Shamanhood: The Brief History of Confrontation. In *Shamanhood: Symbol and Epic*, edited by J. Pentikainen, H. Saressalo, C. M. Taksami, and Ch. M. Taksami, pp. 237–248. Budapest: Acadêmiai Kiadó.
Goodale, Jane
1971 *Tiwi Wives.* Seattle: University of Washington Press.
Gorman, Michael S. F.
1999 *The Quest for Kibi and the True Origins of Japan.* Bangkok: Orchid Press.
Grayson, James H.
1976 Some Structural Patterns of the Royal Families of Ancient Korea. *Korea Journal* 16(6):27–32.
Gryaznov, Mikhail P.
1969 *The Ancient Civilization of Southern Siberia.* Translated by James Hogarth. New York: Cowles Book Company, Inc.
Guo Dashun
1995a Hongshan and Related Cultures. In *The Archaeology of Northeast China: Beyond the Great Wall*, edited by Sarah M. Nelson, pp. 21–64. London: Routledge.
1995b Lower Xiajiadian Culture. In *The Archaeology of Northeast China: Beyond the Great Wall*, edited by Sarah M. Nelson, pp. 147–181. London: Routledge.
Guo Dashun and Zhang Keju
1984 Brief Report on the Excavation of Construction Sites of Hongshan Culture at Dongshanzui in Kezuo County, Liaoning Province. *Wenwu* 11:1–11.
Hamada Kosaku
1938 *Hung-shan-hou, Chihfeng, Prehistoric Sites at Hung-shan, Chihfeng, in the Province of Jehol, Manchukuo.* Archaeologia Orientalis, Series A, Vol. VI. Tokyo.
Hamblin, D. J.
1973 *The First Cities.* New York: Time-Life Books.

Han, Rubin

1993 Recent Archeological Metallurgical Achievements at the University of Science and Technology, Beijing. Paper presented at the International Conference: Chinese Archaeology Enters the 21st Century, May 29, 1993.

Hancar, F.

1940 Zum Problem der Venusstatuetten im eurasiatischen Jungpaläolithikum. *Prähistorische Zeitschrift* 30–31:85–156.

Harris, M.

1974 *Cows, Pigs, Wars and Witches: The Riddles of Culture.* New York: Random House.

Hawkes, J.

1964 The Achievements of Paleolithic Man. In *Man Before History,* edited by C. Gabel, pp. 21–35. Englewood Cliffs, NJ: Prentice Hall.

Hayden, Brian

1995 Pathways to Power: Principles for Creating Socioeconomic Inequalities. In *Foundations of Social Inequality*, edited by T. Douglas Price and Gary M. Feinman, pp. 15–86. New York: Plenum Press.

Hays-Gilpin, Kelley A.

2004 *Ambiguous Images: Gender and Rock Art.* Walnut Creek, CA: AltaMira Press.

Henry, Celia M.

2005 Chinese Beverage Is Ancient History. *Chemical and Engineering News* (January 3):32–33.

Hester, J. J., and J. Grady

1982 *Introduction to Archaeology.* 2nd ed. New York: Holt, Rinehart and Winston.

Hill, James N.

1968 Broken K Pueblo: Patterns of Form and Function. In *New Perspectives in Archaeology*, edited by Sally Binford and Lewis Binford. Chicago: Aldine.

Hodder, Ian

1982 *Symbols in Action*. Cambridge: Cambridge University Press.

1991 Gender Representation and Social Reality. In *The Archaeology of Gender, Proceedings of the 22nd Annual Chacmool Conference, Calgary,* edited by Dale Walde and Noreen Willows, pp. 11–17. Calgary: Department of Archaeology, University of Calgary.

Hogarth, Hyun-key Kim

1998 'Trance' and 'Possession Trance' in the Perspective of Korean Shamanism. In *Korean Shamanism: Revivals, Survivals, and Change*, edited by K. Howard, pp. 45–54. Seoul: Seoul Press.

Howard, Keith

1998 Korean Shamanism Today. In *Korean Shamanism: Revivals, Survivals, and Change*, edited by K. Howard, pp. 1–14. Seoul: Seoul Press.

Howells, William W., and Patricia J. Tsuchitani
1977 *Paleoanthropology in the People's Republic of China.* Report No. 4, Committee on Scholarly Communiction with the People's Republic of China. Washington, DC: National Academy of Sciences.
Hsu, Cho-yun
1986 Historical Conditions of the Emergence and Crystallization of the Confucian System. In *The Origin and Diversity of Axial Age Civilizations,* edited by S. N. Eisenstadt, pp. 306–324. Albany: State University of New York.
Humphrey, Caroline
1996 Shamanic Practices and the State in Northern Asia: Views from the Center and Periphery. In *Shamanism, History, and the State,* edited by Nicholas Thomas and Caroline Humphrey, pp. 191–228. Ann Arbor: University of Michigan Press.
Humphrey, Caroline, and Urunge Onon
1996 *Shamans and Elders: Experience, Knowledge and Power among Daur Mongols.* Oxford: Clarendon Press.
IACASS (Institute of Archaeology, Chinese Academy of Social Sciences)
1996 *Dadianzi: Excavations on the Residence and Cemetery of the Xiajiadian Lower Culture.* Beijing: Science Press.
Ikawa-Smith, Fumiko
1992 Kanjodori. In *Pacific Northeast Asia in Prehistory,* edited by M. Aikens and S. N. Rhee, pp. 83–90. Pullman: Washington State University Press.
2000 Younger Dryas Radiocarbon Calibration and the Beginning of Pottery Use in Eastern Asia. Paper delivered at the Society for American Archaeology, Montreal, Canada.
Ilyon
1972 *Samguk Yusa.* Translated by T. Ha and G. Mintz. Seoul: Yonsei University Press.
Im Hyojai and Kwon Haksu
1984 *Osanni Site: A Neolithic Village Site on the East Coast.* Archaeological and Anthropological Papers, Vol. 9, Seoul National University.
Insoll, Timothy
2004 *Archaeology, Ritual, Religion.* London: Routledge.
Ito, Akio
1971 *Zur Chronologie der fruhsillazeitlichen Graber in Sudkorea.* Bayerische Akademie der Wissenschaften, New Series, Vol. 71 (in German). Munich.
Janelli, Roger A., and Dawnhee Yim Janelli
1982 *Ancestor Worship and Korean Society.* Stanford: Stanford University Press.
Janeway, Elizabeth
1981 *Powers of the Weak.* New York: Morrow Quill.
Jeju National University Museum
1998 *Jeju Gosanni Yujok.* Jeju: Jeju National Museum.

Juliano, Annette
1985 Possible Origins of the Chinese Mirror. *Source Notes in the History of Art* 4(2/3):36–50.

Jurmain, R., H. Nelson, H. Kurashina, and W. Turnbaugh
1981 *Understanding Physical Anthropology and Archaeology.* St. Paul: West Publishing Co.

Kehoe, Alice B.
1990 Points and Lines. In *Powers of Observation: Alternative Views in Archeology*, edited by S. M. Nelson and A. B. Kehoe, pp. 23–38. Archeological Papers of the American Anthropological Association, No. 2. Washington, DC.
2000 *Shamans and Religion.* Prospect Heights, IL: Waveland Press.

Keightley, David N.
1978a The Religious Commitment: Shang Theology and the Genesis of Chinese Political Culture. *History of Religions* 17:211–225.
1978b *Sources of Shang History: The Oracle-Bone Inscriptions of Bronze Age China.* Berkeley: University of California Press.
1982 Akatsuka Kiyoshi and the Culture of Early China. *Harvard Journal of Asiatic Studies* 42:299–301.
1983 The Late Shang State: When, Where, and What? In *The Origins of Chinese Civilization*, edited by David N. Keightley, pp. 523–564. Berkeley: University of California Press.
1986 The Eastern Yi: Archaeological and Textual Evidence. Paper presented at Association for Asian Studies Annual Meeting, Chicago.
1994 Sacred Characters. In *Cradles of Civilization: China*, edited by Robert E. Murowchick, pp. 71–79. Norman: University of Oklahoma Press.
1997 Shang Oracle Bone Inscriptions. In *New Sources of Early Chinese History*, edited by Edward L. Shaughnessy, pp. 15–55. Berkeley: Institute of East Asian Studies, University of California.
1999a At the Beginning: The Status of Women in Neolithic and Shang China. *Nan Nu* 1(1):1–63.
1999b Theology and the Writing of History: Truth and the Ancestors in the Wu Ding Divination Records. *Journal of East Asian Archaeology* 1(1–4):207–230.
1999c The Shang: China's First Historical Dynasty. In *The Cambridge History of Ancient China*, edited by Michael Loewe and Edward L. Shaughnessy, pp. 232–291. Cambridge: Cambridge University Press.
2000 *The Ancestral Landscape: Time, Space, and Community in Late Shang China.* Berkeley: Institute of East Asian Studies, University of California.

Kendall, Laurel
1985 *Shamans, Housewives, and Other Restless Spirits.* Honolulu: University of Hawaii Press.
1996 Korean Shamans and the Spirits of Capitalism. *American Anthropologist* 98(3):512–527.

1998 The Shaman's Journey: Real and Ideal in a Living Folk Tradition. In *Korean Shamanism: Revivals, Survivals, and Change*, edited by K. Howard, pp. 91–112. Seoul: Seoul Press.

Kidder, J. Edward, Jr.

1965 *The Birth of Japanese Art.* London: George Allen & Unwin, Ltd.

Kim, Chae-Kuei, and Eunchang Yi

1975 *A Report on the Excavation of the Tombs at Hwangnam-dong, Kyongju.* Taegu: Yeungnam University Museum Monograph 1 (in Korean).

Kim, Chong-Sun

1965 The Emergence of Multi-centered Despotism in the Silla Kingdom: A Study of the Origin of Factional Struggles in Korea. PhD dissertation, University of Washington.

1977 The Kolp'um System: Basis for Sillan Social Stratification. *Journal of Korean Studies* 1(2):43–69.

Kim Seong-Nae

1994 Burials, Pigs, and Political Prestige in Neolithic China. *Current Anthropology* 35:179–241.

1998 Problems in Defining Shaman Types and Local Variations. In *Korean Shamanism: Revivals, Survivals, and Change,* edited by K. Howard, pp. 33–44. Seoul: Seoul Press.

Kim Tae-gon

1998 What Is Korean Shamanism? In *Korean Shamanism: Revivals, Survivals, and Change,* edited by K. Howard, pp. 15–32. Seoul: Seoul Press.

Kim, Won-yong

1983 *Recent Archaeological Discoveries in the Republic of Korea.* Tokyo: UNESCO.

1986 *Art and Archaeology of Ancient Korea.* Seoul: The Taekwang Publishing Co.

Kim, Won-yong, and Richard Pearson

1977 Three Royal Tombs: New Discoveries in Korean Archaeology. *Archaeology* 30(5):302–313.

Kim Yung-Chung, ed.

1977 *Women in Korea: A History from Ancient Times to 1945.* Seoul: Ewha Woman's University Press.

Klima, B.

1962 The First Ground-Plan of an Upper Paleolithic Loess Settlement in Middle Europe and Its Meaning. In *Courses toward Urban Life*, edited by R. Braidwood and G. Willey, pp. 193–210. Chicago: Aldine.

Knecht, Peter

2003 Aspects of Shamanism: An Introduction. In *Shamans in Asia,* edited by C. Chilson and P. Knecht, pp. 1–30. London: Routledge.

Koenigswald, G. H. R. von

1972 Early *Homo sapiens* as an Artist: The Meaning of Paleolithic Art. In *The Origin of Homo sapiens, Ecology and Conservation,* Vol. 3, edited by F. Bordes, pp. 133–139. Proceedings of the Paris Symposium 1969.

Kononenko, Nina, and Jim Cassidy

2007 The Prehistory of Eastern Asia. *North Pacific Prehistory* 2:15–36.

Lattimore, Owen

1951 *Manchuria, Cradle of Conflict.* New York: The Macmillan Company.

Leacock, Eleanor

1972 Introduction to F. Engels, *The Origin of the Family, Private Property and the State,* pp. 7–67. New York: Pathfinder Press.

1978 Women's Status in Egalitarian Society: Implications for Social Evolution. *Current Anthropology* 19: 247–275.

1981 *Myths of Male Dominance.* New York: Monthly Review Press.

Lebra, William P.

1964 The Okinawan Shaman. In *Ryukuan Culture and Society,* edited by A. H. Smith, pp. 93–98. Honolulu: University of Hawaii Press.

Lee, Gyoung-Ah

2011 The Transition from Foraging to Farming in Prehistoric Korea. *Current Anthropology* 52:307–329.

Lee, R. B., and I. De Vore, eds.

1968 *Man the Hunter.* Chicago: Aldine.

Lerner, Gerda

1986 *The Creation of Patriarchy.* New York: Oxford University Press and Liaoning Province Cultural Relics and Archaeology Institute.

Leroi-Gourhan, Andre

1967 *Treasures of Prehistoric Art.* Translated by N. Guterman. New York: Henry N. Abrams.

Liaoning Province Cultural Relics and Archaeology Institute

1986 Brief Report on the Excavation of the 'Goddess Temple' and the Stone Graves of the Hongshan Culture at Niuheliang in Liaoning Province. *Wenwu* 8:1–17.

Li Chi

1977 *An yang.* Seattle: University of Washington Press.

Li Min

2008 Conquest, Concord, and Consumption: Becoming Shang in Eastern China. PhD disseration, University of Michigan, Ann Arbor.

Linduff, Katheryn M.

1996 Art and Identity: The Chinese and Their "Significant Others" in the Shang. In *Cultural Contact, History, and Ethnicity in Inner Asia,* edited by Michael

Gervers and Wayne Schlepp, pp. 12–48. Toronto: Toronto Studies in Central and Inner Asia.

1997 An Archaeological Overview. In *Ancient Bronzes of the Eastern Eurasian Steppes*, edited by E. Bunker, pp. 18–112. New York: Arthur M. Sackler Foundation.

2002 Women's Lives Memorialized in Burial in Ancient China at Anyang. In *In Pursuit of Gender: Worldwide Archaeological Perspectives*, edited by S. M. Nelson and M. Rosen-Ayalon, pp. 257–287. Walnut Creek, CA: AltaMira Press.

2003 Many Wives, One Queen in Shang China. In *Ancient Queens: Archaeological Explorations*, edited by S. M. Nelson, pp. 59–75. Walnut Creek, CA: AltaMira Press.

Linduff, Katheryn, and Karen Rubinson, eds.

2008 *Are All Warriors Male?* Walnut Creek, CA: AltaMira Press.

Linduff, Katheryn, and Yan Sun, eds.

2004 *Gender and Chinese Archaeology.* Walnut Creek, CA: AltaMira Press.

Lin Yun

1986 A Reexamination of the Relationship between Bronzes of the Shang Culture and the Northern Zone. In *Studies in Shang Archaeology: Selected Papers from the International Conference on Shang Civilization*, edited by Kwang-Chih Chang, pp. 237–274. New Haven: Yale University Press.

Liu, Li

2000 Ancestor Worship: An Archaeological Investigation of Ritual Activities in Neolithic North China. *Journal of East Asian Archaeology* 2(1–2):129–164.

2003 "The Products of Minds as well as Hands": Production of Prestige Goods in the Neolithic and Early State Periods of China. *Asian Perspectives* 42(1):1–40.

Loehr, Max

1975 *Ancient Chinese Jades.* Cambridge, MA: Fogg Art Museum, Harvard University.

Longacre, William A.

1968 Some Aspects of Prehistoric Society. In *New Perspectives in Archaeology*, edited by Sally Binford and Lewis Binford. Chicago: Aldine.

Luquet, G. H.

1926 *L'art et la religion des hommes fossiles.* Paris: Masson et Cie.

Ma Cheng yuan

1980 The Splendor of Ancient Chinese Bronzes. In *The Great Bronze Age of China*, edited by Wen Fong, pp. 1–19. New York: Metropolitan Museum of Art.

MacNeish, Richard S., and Jane G. Libby, eds.

1995 *Origins of Rice Agriculture.* Publications in Anthropology, No. 13. El Paso: University of Texas at El Paso.

Major, John
1999 Characteristics of Late Chu Religion. In *Defining Chu, Image and Reality in Ancient China*, edited by C. A. Cook and J. S. Major, pp. 121–144; Conclusion pp. 167–169. Honolulu: University of Hawaii Press.
Marshack, A.
1972 *The Roots of Civilization.* New York: McGraw-Hill.
McCafferty, G. G., and S. D. McCafferty
2003 Questioning a Queen? A Gender-Informed Evaluation of Monte Alban's Tomb 7. In *Ancient Queens: Archaeological Explorations*, edited by S. M. Nelson, pp. 41–58. Walnut Creek, CA: AltaMira Press.
McCune, Evelyn
1962 *The Arts of Korea.* Rutland, VT: Charles E. Tuttle Co.
Merrifield, Ralph
1987 *The Archaeology of Ritual and Magic.* London: B.T. Bedsford, Ltd.
Miller, Barbara, ed.
1991 *Sex and Gender Hierarchies.* Cambridge: Cambridge University Press.
Miller, D., and A. Tilley
1984 Ideology, Power and Prehistory: An Introduction. In *Ideology, Power and Prehistory*, edited by Daniel Miller and Christopher Tilley, pp. 1–15. Cambridge: Cambridge University Press.
Miller, Roy Andrew
1971 *Japanese and the Other Altaic Languages.* Chicago: University of Chicago Press.
1980 *Origins of the Japanese Language.* Seattle: University of Washington Press.
Moore, J. A., and A. S. Keene
1983 Archaeology and the Law of the Hammer. In *Archaeological Hammers and Theories*, edited by J. A. Moore and A. S. Keene, pp. 3–13. New York: Academic Press.
Muller, Viana
1987 Kin Reproduction and Elite Accumulation in the Archaic States of Northwest Europe. In *Power Relations and State Formation*, edited by T. C. Patterson and C. W. Gailey, pp. 81–97. Washington, DC: American Anthropological Association.
Myers, Carol
2001 *Women in Scripture.* Grand Rapids, MI: Eerdmans.
Nelson, Sarah Milledge
n.d. "Venus" Figurines as Evidence of Sedentism in the Upper Paleolithic. Manuscript on file, Department of Anthropology, University of Denver.
1975 The Subsistence Base of Middle Han Sites of the Chulmun Period. *Asian Perspectives* 18(1):5–14.
1976 The Fallen Tree Site. Report for the Bureau of Land Management, Moab, Utah.

1978 Investigations at Cholla Knoll. Bureau of Land Management, Moab, Utah.

1990a Diversity of the Upper Paleolithic "Venus" Figurines and Archeological Mythology. In *Powers of Observation: Alternative Views in Archeology*, edited by S. M. Nelson and A. B. Kehoe, pp. 11–22. Archeological Papers of the American Anthropological Association, No. 2. Arlington, VA: American Anthropological Association.

1990b The Social Structure of Korean Neolithic Sites. *IPPA Bulletin* 9:15–21.

1991a The Goddess Temple and the Status of Women at Niuheliang, China. In *The Archaeology of Gender: Proceedings of the 22nd Annual Chacmool Conference, Calgary*, edited by Dale Walde and Noreen Willows, pp. 302–308. Calgary: Department of Archaeology, University of Calgary.

1991b The Statuses of Women in Ko-Shilla: Evidence from Archaeology and Historic Documents. *Korea Journal* 31(2):101–107.

1993a *The Archaeology of Korea*. Cambridge: Cambridge University Press.

1993b Gender Hierarchies and the Queens of Silla. In *Sex and Gender Hierarchies*, edited by B. D. Miller, pp. 297–315. Cambridge: Cambridge University Press.

1993c Hongshan, An Early Complex Society in Northeast China. Paper delivered at the Annual Meeting of the Society for American Archaeology, St. Louis.

1995a Introduction. In *The Archaeology of Northeast China: Beyond the Great Wall*, edited by Sarah M. Nelson. London: Routledge.

1995b Roots of Animism in Korea. In *Korean Cultural Roots*, edited by H. Kwon, pp. 19–30. Chicago: North Park College and Seminary.

1996 Ideology and the Formation of an Early State in Northeast China. In *Ideology and the Formation of Early States*, edited by Henri J. M. Claessen and Jarich G. Oosten, pp. 153–169. Leiden: E. J. Brill.

1997a *Gender in Archaeology: Analyzing Power and Prestige*. Walnut Creek, CA: AltaMira Press. (2nd ed., 2004.)

1997b Mound Burials and Deep Burials in China. Lecture presented at the Denver Museum of Natural History to University of Denver alumni on the opening of the exhibit "Imperial Tombs of China," 1997.

1998a Pigs in Hongshan Culture. In *Ancestors for the Pigs: Pigs in Prehistory*, edited by Sarah M. Nelson, pp. 99–107. Philadelphia: University of Pennsylvania Museum of Archaeology and Anthropology.

1998b Reflections on Gender Studies in African and Asian Archaeology. In *Gender in African Prehistory*, edited by Susan Kent. Walnut Creek, CA: AltaMira Press.

1999 *Spirit Bird Journey*. Littleton, CO: RKLOG Press.

2002a Introduction. In *The Quest for Queens in Archaeology*, edited by Sarah Milledge Nelson. Walnut Creek, CA: AltaMira Press.

2002b Performing Power in Early China: Examples from the Shang Dynasty and the Hongshan Culture. In *The Dynamics of Power*, edited by M. O'Donovan, pp. 151–67. Carbondale: Center for Archaeological Investigations, Southern Illinois University.

2003a Feasting the Ancestors in Early China. In *The Archaeology and Politics of Food and Feasting in Early States and Empires*, edited by T. L. Bray. New York: Kluwer Academic/Plenum Publishers.

2003b The Queens of Silla: Power and Connections to the Spirit World. In *Ancient Queens, Archaeological Explorations*, edited by S. M. Nelson, pp. 77–92. Walnut Creek, CA: AltaMira Press.

2004a *Jade Dragon*. Littleton, CO: RKLOG Press.

2004b *Korean Social Archaeology: Early Villages*. Seoul: Jimoon Press.

2006 Archaeology in the Two Koreas. In *An Archaeology of Asia*, edited by M. Stark, pp. 37–54. Malden, MA: Blackwell.

2008a *Shamanism and the Origin of the State: Spirit, Power and Gender in East Asia*. Walnut Creek, CA: Left Coast Press.

2008b Horses and Gender in Korea: The Legacy of the Steppe on the Edge of East Asia. In *Are All Warriors Male?* edited by K. Linduff and K. Rubinson, pp. 111–127. Walnut Creek, CA: AltaMira Press.

2011 Feminist Theory, Leadership, and the Spirits of States in East Asia. *Archaeologies, Journal of World Archaeological Congress* 7(1):34–55.

2012 A Perspective from East Asia on Periodizations in Archaeology. In *Labrys*, Online Journal, July/December 2012.

Nelson, Sarah M., ed.

1995 *The Archaeology of Northeast China: Beyond the Great Wall*. London: Routledge.

1998 *Ancestors for the Pigs: Pigs in Prehistory*. Philadelphia: Museum Applied Science Center for Archaeology, University of Pennsylvania Museum of Archaeology and Anthropology.

2003 *Ancient Queens, Archaeological Explorations*. Walnut Creek, CA: AltaMira Press.

2006 *Handbook of Gender in Archaeology*. Walnut Creek, CA: AltaMira Press.

Nelson, Sarah M., and Margaret C. Nelson

1994 Conclusion. In *Equity Issues for Women in Archeology*, edited by S. M. Nelson, M. C. Nelson, and A. W. Wylie, pp. 229–235. Archeological Papers of the American Anthropological Association, No. 5. Washington, DC: American Anthropological Association.

Nelson, Sarah M., Margaret C. Nelson, and Alison Wylie, eds.

1994 *Equity Issues for Women in Archeology*. Archeological Papers of the American Anthropological Association, No. 5. Washington, DC: American Anthropological Association.

Nelson, Sarah M., and M. Rosen-Ayalon, eds.
2002 *In Pursuit of Gender: Worldwide Archaeological Perspectives.* Walnut Creek, CA: AltaMira Press.

Nelson, Sarah M., R. Matson, R. Roberts, C. Rock, and R. Stencel
2014 Archaeoastronomy at Niuheliang. In *The Hongshan Papers: Studies on the Archaeology of Northern China,* edited by Sarah Nelson, pp. 97–105. BAR International Series 2618. Oxford: Archaeopress.

Nowak, M., and S. Durrant
1977 *The Tale of the Nissan Shamaness.* Seattle: University of Washington.

O'Hara, Albert, S.J.
1971 *The Position of Women in Early China, Including a Translation of the Lieh Nu Chuan.* Taipei, Taiwan: Mei Ya Publications.

Okladnikov, Alexei
1981 *Art of the Amur: Ancient Art of the Russian Far East.* Leningrad: Aurora Art Publishers.

Ortner, S. B., and H. Whitehead, eds.
1981 *Sexual Meanings: The Cultural Construction of Gender and Sexuality.* Cambridge: Cambridge University Press.

Overmeyer, Daniel L., David N. Keightley, Edward L. Shaughnessy, Constance A. Cook, and Donald Harper
1995 Chinese Religions: The State of the Field Period (Part I). Early Religious Traditions: The Neolithic through the Han Dynasty. *Journal of Asian Studies* 54:124–161.

Pai, Hung Il
2012 *Heritage Management in Korea and Japan.* Seattle: University of Washington Press.

Pankenier, David W.
1995 Cosmo-Political Background of Heaven's Mandate. *Early China* 20: 121–176.

Paper, Jordan H.
1995 *The Spirits Are Drunk: Comparative Approaches to Chinese Religion.* Albany: State University of New York Press.

Parker, E.H.
1890 On Race Struggles in Korea. *Transactions of the Asiatic Society of Japan* 18(20):157–228.

Passemard, L.
1938 *Les statuettes féminines paléolithiques dites Vénus stéatopyges.* Nîmes: Librairie Teissier.

Patterson, Thomas
1992 *Archaeology, The Historical Development of Civilizations.* Englewood Cliffs, NJ: Prentice Hall.

Patterson, Thomas C., and Christine W. Gailey
1987 Power Relations and State Formation. In *Power Relations and State Formation,* edited by T. C. Patterson and C. W. Gailey, pp. 1–26. Washington, DC: American Anthropological Association.

Pearson, Richard
1981 Social Complexity in Chinese Coastal Neolithic Sites. *Science* 213:1078–1086.
1985 Some Recent Studies in the Chronology and Social Development of Old Silla. *Essays in Honour of Prof. Dr. Tsugio Mikami on His 77th Birthday—Archaeology,* pp. 181–201. Tokyo: Heibonsha.
1988 Chinese Neolithic Burial Patterns. *Early China* 13:1–45.
2007 Debating Jomon Social Complexity. *Asian Perspectives* 46(2):361–388.

Pearson, Richard, Jong-wook Lee, Wonyoung Koh, and Anne Underhill
1989 Social Ranking on the Kingdom of Old Silla, Korea: Analysis of Burials. *Journal of Anthropological Archaeology* 8(1):1–50.

Pfeiffer, J.
1985 *The Emergence of Humankind.* 4th ed. New York: Harper and Row.

Piggott, Joan
1997 *The Emergence of Japanese Kingship.* Palo Alto: Stanford University Press.
1999 Chieftain Pairs and Co-Rulers: Female Sovereignty in Early Japan. In *Women and Class in Japanese Society,* edited by H. Tonamura, A. Walthall, and Wakita Haruko, 17–62. Ann Arbor: Center for Japanese Studies, University of Michigan.

Poirier, F. E.
1987 *Understanding Human Evolution.* Englewood Cliffs, NJ: Prentice Hall.

Pokara, Timoteus
1978 China. In *The Early State,* edited by H. J. M.Claessen and P. Skalnik, pp. 191–212. The Hague: Mouton.

Pomeroy, Sarah
1974 *Goddesses, Whores, Wives and Slaves in Classical Antiquity.* New York: Schocken.

Price, Barbara J.
1977 Shifts in Production and Organization: A Cluster Interaction Model. *Current Anthropology* 18:209–233.

Price, Neil, ed.
2001 *The Archaeology of Shamanism.* London: Routledge.

Pyburn, K. A.
2000 *Ungendering Civilization.* London: Routledge.

Qian, Hao
1981 The Yin Ruins and the Tomb of Fu Hao. In *Out of China's Earth,* edited by Qian Hao, Chen Heyi, and Ru Suichi, pp. 9–28. New York: Harry N. Abrams.

Rapp, Rayna R.
1977 The Search for Origins: Unraveling the Threads of Gender Hierarchy. *Critique of Anthropology* 3(9–10):5–24.

Rappaport, Roy
1967 *Pigs for the Ancestors: Ritual in the Ecology of a New Guinea People.* New Haven: Yale University Press.

Ratnagar, Shereen
1996 Ideology and the Nature of Political Consolidation and Expansion: An Archaeological Case. In *Ideology and the Formation of Early States,* edited by H. J. M. Claessen and J. G. Oosten. Leiden: E.J. Brill.

Rawson, Jessica
1996a The Great Dynasties. In *Mysteries of Ancient China: New Discoveries from the Early Dynasties,* edited by Jessica Rawson, pp. 85–162. New York: George Braziller, Inc.
1996b The Ritual Bronze Vessels of the Shang and the Zhou. In *Mysteries of Ancient China: New Discoveries from the Early Dynasties,* edited by Jessica Rawson, pp. 248–265. New York: George Braziller, Inc.

Reid, Anna
2002 *The Shaman's Coat: A Native History of Siberia.* New York: Walker and Co.

Renfrew, Colin
1982 Socio-economic Change in Ranked Societies. In *Ranking, Resource and Exchange: Aspects of the Archaeology of Early European Society,* edited by C. Renfrew and S. Shennan, pp. 1–8. Cambridge: Cambridge University Press.

Rice, P. C.
1981 Prehistoric Venuses: Symbols of Motherhood or Womanhood? *Journal of Anthropological Research* 37(4):402–416.

Rohrlich, Ruby
1980 State Formation in Sumer and the Subjugation of Women. *Feminist Studies* 6(1):76–102.

Rokkum, Arne
1998 *Goddesses, Priestesses, and Sisters: Mind, Gender and Power in the Monarchic Tradition of the Ryukyus.* Oslo: Scandinavian University Press.

Rosaldo, Michelle, and Louise Lamphere, eds.
1974 *Women, Culture and Society.* Stanford: Stanford University Press.

Rubinson, Karen S.
2002 Through the Looking Glass: Reflections on Mirrors, Gender, and Use among Nomads. In *In Pursuit of Gender,* edited by S. Nelson and M. Rosen-Ayalon, pp. 67–72. Walnut Creek, CA: AltaMira Press.

Saccasyn Della Santa, E.
1947 *Les figures humaines du Paléolithique Superior eurasiatique.* Paris: Amberes.

Sacks, Karen
1979 *Sisters and Wives: The Past and Future of Sexual Equality.* Westport, CT: Greenwood Press. (Reprint ed. 1982, Illini Books.)

Saitta, D. J.
1983 The Poverty of Philosophy in Archaeology. In *Archaeological Hammers and Theories,* edited by James A. Moore and Arthur S. Keene, pp. 299–304. New York: Academic Press.

Sample, L. L.
1967 Culture History and Chronology in South Korea's Neolithic. PhD dissertation, University of Wisconsin.

Sanday, Peggy R.
1981 *Female Power and Male Dominance: On the Origins of Sexual Inequality.* New York: Cambridge University Press.
2003 The Divine Queens of Minangkabau Lore. In *Ancient Queens: Archaeological Explorations*, edited by Sarah M. Nelson, pp. 175–192. Walnut Creek, CA: AltaMira Press.

Sanders, William, and Barbara Price
1968 *Mesoamerica: The Evolution of a Civilization.* New York: Random House.

Sandberg, Sheryl
2013 *Lean In: Women, Work, and the Will to Lead.* New York: Knopf.

Sauer, Carl
1952 *Agricultural Origins and Dispersals.* Bowman Memorial Lectures, Series 2. New York: Geographical Society.

Schafer, Edward H.
1973 *The Divine Woman: Dragon Ladies and Rain Maidens in T'ang Literature.* Berkeley: University of California Press.

Sered, Susan
1999 *Women of the Sacred Groves.* Oxford: Oxford University Press.

Service, Elman
1962 *Primitive Social Organization: An Evolutionary Perspective.* New York: Random House.
1975 *Origins of the State and Civilization: The Process of Cultural Evolution.* New York: Norton.

Seyock, Barbara
2004 *Auf den Spuren der Ostbarbaren.* Bunka, Vol. 8. Tübingen: Lit Verlag.

Shao Wangping
2005 The Formation of Civilization: The Interaction Sphere of the Longshan Period. In *The Formation of Chinese Civilization: An Archaeological Perspective,* edited by K.-C. Chang and Pingfang Xu, pp. 85–120. New Haven: Yale University Press.

Silverblatt, Irene
1987 *Moon, Sun, and Witches. Gender Ideologies and Class in Inca and Colonial Peru.* Princeton: Princeton University Press.

Silverman, Sydel
2002 *The Beast at the Table: Conferencing with Anthropologists.* Walnut Creek, CA: AltaMira Press.

Smith, J. W.
1976 *Foundations of Archaeology.* Beverly Hills: Glencoe Press.

So, Jenny
1993 *Neolithic Jades.* Freer Gallery Guide.

Soffer, O.
1988 Upper Paleolithic Connubia, Refugia and the Archaeological Record for Eastern Europe. In *Pleistocene Old World: Regional Perspectives,* edited by O. Soffer, pp. 333- 348. New York: Plenum Publishing Co.

Stutley, Margaret
2002 *Shamanism, an Introduction.* London: Routledge.

Sun Shoudao and Guo Dashun
1984 On the Primitive Civilization of the Liao River Basin and the Origin of Dragons. *Wenwu* 6:11–20.
1986 Discovery and Study of the 'Goddess Head Sculpture' of the Hongshan Culture at Niuheliang. *Wenwu* 8:18–24.

Sun, Xiaochun
2000 Crossing the Boundaries between Heaven and Man: Astronomy in Ancient China. In *Astronomy across Cultures: The History of Non-Western Astronomy,* edited by H. Selin, pp. 423–454. London: Kluwer.

Takiguchi Naoko
2003 Miyako Theology: Shamans' Interpretation of Traditional Beliefs. In *Shamans in Asia,* edited by C. Chilson and P. Knecht, pp. 120–152. London: Routledge.

Tang Jigen
1999 The Burial Ritual of the Shang Dynasty: A Reconstruction. In *Exploring China's Past: New Discoveries and Studies in Archaeology and Art,* translated and edited by Roderick Whitfield and Wang Tao, pp. 173–188. London: Saffron.

Tedlock, Barbara
2005 *The Woman in the Shaman's Body.* New York: Bantam Books.

Thomas, Nicholas, and Caroline Humphrey
1994 Introduction. In *Shamanism, History, and the State,* edited by Nicholas Thomas and Caroline Humphrey, pp. 1–12. Ann Arbor: University of Michigan Press.
1996 *Shamanism, History and the State.* Ann Arbor: University of Michigan Press.

Thorp, Robert L.
1980 Burial Practices of Bronze Age China. In *The Great Bronze Age of China*, edited by Wen Pong, pp. 51–64. New York: Metropolitan Museum of Art.

Tong, Enzheng
2002 Magicians, Magic, and Shamanism in Ancient China. *Journal of East Asian Archaeology* 4(1–4):27–74.

Triestman, J.
1972 *The Prehistory of China: An Archaeological Exploration*. Garden City, NY: Natural History Press.

Troccoli, Ruth
2002 Mississippi Chiefs: Women and Men of Power. In *The Dynamics of Power*, edited by M. O'Donovan, pp. 168–187. Carbondale: Center for Archaeological Investigations, Southern Illinois University.

Troy, Lana
2003 She for Whom All That Is Said and Done: The Egyptian Queen. In *Ancient Queens, Archaeological Explorations*, edited by S. M. Nelson, pp. 91–176. Walnut Creek, CA: AltaMira Press.

Tylor, E. B.
1865 *Researches into the Early History of Mankind and the Development of Civilization*. London: J. Murray.

Ucko P J., and A. Rosenfeld
1973 *Palaeolithic Cave Art*. New York: McGraw-Hill.

Underhill, Anne P.
2000 An Analysis of Mortuary Ritual at the Dawenkou Site, Shandong, China. *Journal of East Asian Archaeology* 2(1–2):93–127.
2002 *Craft Production and Social Change in Northern China*. New York: Kluwer Academic/Plenum Publishers.

Van Deusen, Kira
2001 *The Flying Tiger, Women Shamans and Story Tellers of the Amur*. Montreal: McGill-Queens University Press.
2004 *Singing Story, Healing Drum: Shamans and Storytellers of Turkic Siberia*. Montreal: McGill-Queens University Press.

Vogel, M. A.
2003 Sacred Women in Ancient Peru. In *Ancient Queens: Archaeological Explorations*, edited by S. M. Nelson, pp. 117–136. Walnut Creek, CA: AltaMira Press.

Wagner, Mayke
1993 Traces of Prehistoric Population and Desertification Processes in Horqin Grassland. In *Proceedings of the Japan-China International Symposium on the Study of Desertification*, edited by M. Ichikuni, pp. 54–66. Tsukuba, Japan.
2006 *Neolithikum und frühe Bronzezeit in Nordchina vor 8000 bis 3500 Jahren*. Mainz: Verlag Philipp von Zabern.

Waley, Arthur
1955 *The Nine Songs: A Study of Shamanism in Ancient China.* London: Allen and Unwin.

Waltham, Clae
1971 *Shu Ching: Book of History.* Chicago: Henry Regnery Company.

Wang Ningsheng
1984 Yangshao Burial Custom and Social Organization: A Comment on the Theory of Yangshao Matrilineal Society and Its Methodology. *Early China* 11–12:6–32.

Weiner, Annette
1976 *Women of Value, Men of Renown: New Perspectives in Trobriand Exchange.* Austin: University of Texas Press.

Wen Fong
1980 *The Great Bronze Age of China.* New York: Metropolitan Museum of Art and Alfred A. Knopf.

Wenke, Robert
1984 *Patterns in Prehistory, Humankind's First Three Million Years.* 2nd ed. New York: Oxford University Press.
1990 *Patterns in Prehistory.* 3rd ed. New York: Oxford University Press.

Whallon, R. E.
1968 Investigations of Late Prehistoric Social Organization in New York State. In *New Perspectives in Archaeology*, edited by Sally Binford and Lewis Binford, pp. 223–244. Chicago: Aldine.

Woolf, Virginia
1992 *A Room of One's Own. Three Guineas.* New York: Quality Paperback Book Club.

Woodall, J. N., and P. J. Perricone
1981 The Archaeologist as Cowboy: The Consequence of Professional Stereotype. *Journal of Field Archaeology* 8:506–509.

Wu, K. C.
1982 *The Chinese Heritage: A New and Provocative View of the Origins of Chinese Society.* New York: Crown Publishers, Inc.

Wu, Xiaolong
2004 Exotica in the Funerary Debris in the State of Zhongshan: Migration, Trade, and Cultural Contact. In *Silk Road Exchange in China,* edited by K. Linduff. *Sino-Platonic Papers* 142:6–16.

Wylie, Alison
1991 Gender Theory and the Archaeological Record: Why Is There No Archaeology of Gender? In *Engendering Archaeology: Women and Prehistory*, edited by J. M. Gero and M. W. Conkey, pp. 31–54. Malden, MA: Blackwell.
1992 Interplay of Evidential Constraints and Political Interests. *American Antiquity* 57:15–35.

2002 *Thinking through Things: Essays in the Philosophy of Archaeology.* Berkeley: University of California Press.

Yan Wenmin

1992 Origins of Agriculture and Animal Husbandry in China. In *Pacific Northeast Asia in Prehistory: The Emergence of Hunter-Fisher-Gatherers, Farmers, and Socio-Political Elites,* edited by M. Aikens and S. N. Rhee, pp. 113–123. Pullman: Washington State University Press.

Yellen, John

1991 Women, Archaeology, and the National Science Foundation. In *The Archaeology of Gender: Proceedings of the 22nd Annual Chacmool Conference, Calgary,* edited by D. Walde and N. Willows, pp. 201–210. Calgary: The Archaeological Association of the University of Calgary.

Zhang, J., G. Harbottle, C. Wang, and Z. Kong

1999 Neolithic Flutes. *Nature* 401:366–368.

Zhang Yachu and Liu Yu

1981–1982 Some Observations about Milfoil Divination Based on Shang and Zhou *bagua* Numerical Symbols. Translated by Edward Shaughnessy. *Early China* 7:46–54.

Zhang Zhongpei

2005 The Yangshao Period: Prosperity and the Transformation of Prehistoric Society. In *The Formation of Chinese Civilization: An Archaeological Perspective,* edited by K.-C. Chang and P. Xu, pp. 43–84. New Haven: Yale University Press.

Zheng Zhenxiang

1996 The Royal Consort Fu Hao and Her Tomb. *Mysteries of Ancient China: New Discoveries from the Early Dynasties,* edited by Jessica Rawson, pp. 240–247. New York: George Braziller, Inc.

Zhuschchikovskaya, Irina

2006 Neolithic of the Primorye. In *Archaeology of the Russian Far East: Essays in Stone Age Prehistory,* edited by S. M. Nelson, A. P. Derivianko, Y. V. Kuzmin, and R. Bland. London: British Archaeological Reports International Series, No. 1540. Archaeopress.

Zihlman, Adrienne L.

1978 Women in Evolution. Part II. Subsistence and Social Organization among Early Hominids. *Signs: Journal of Women in Culture and Society* 4(1):4–20.

Zihlman, A., and N. Tanner

1978 Gathering and the Hominid Adaptation. In *Female Hierarchies,* edited by L. Tiger and H. T. Fowler, pp. 163–194. Chicago: Beresford Books. (Reprint ed. 2007, New Brunswick, NJ: Transaction Publishers.)

Znamenski, Andrei A.

2003 *Shamanism in Siberia. Russian Records of Indigenous Spirituality.* Dordrecht: Kluwer.

Subject Index

Author Index

About the Author

Sarah Milledge Nelson is John Evans Professor of Archaeology at the University of Denver. She is a specialist in cultural development, the origins of agriculture, and archaeology of East Asia. She has been one of the leaders of bringing gender research into the field of archaeology. Her books include *The Archaeology of Korea* (1993), *The Archaeology of Northeast China* (1995), *Handbook of Gender and Archaeology* (2005), and two editions of the textbook *Gender in Archaeology* (1997/2004), which won a Choice Outstanding Academic Book Award. She is also author of three novels set in ancient East Asia.